NEW PERSPECTIVES ON THE SOUTH

Charles P. Roland, General Editor

THE SOUTH
AND THE
NEW DEAL

ROGER BILES

THE UNIVERSITY PRESS OF KENTUCKY

Publication of this work has been assisted by a grant from
Oklahoma State University.

Editorial and Sales Offices: Lexington, Kentucky 40508-4008

Library of Congress Cataloging-in-Publication Data

Biles, Roger.
The South and the New Deal / Roger Biles.
    p.   cm. — (New perspectives on the South)
Includes bibliographical references and index.
ISBN 0-8131-1836-0 (acid-free) :
    1. New Deal, 1933–1939—Southern States.   2. Southern States—
History—1865–1951.   3. Southern States—Economic conditions—1918-
4. Southern States—Social conditions.   I. Title.   II. Series.
F215.B55 1993
975'.042—dc20   93-20816

This book is printed on recycled acid-free paper meeting
the requirements of the American National Standard
for Permanence of Paper for Printed Library Materials.

For my family

CONTENTS

PREFACE

In an earlier monograph on the Great Depression in Memphis, Tennessee, I concluded that much of the New Deal's impact was blunted in that southern city by the powerful weight of custom and tradition. It became evident to me that, for all of the impact of federal programs, Memphis's identity continued to be shaped by its location within one of the nation's most distinctive regions. The city's "southernness" mattered. Writing a subsequent book on the 1930s convinced me that there was no generic New Deal affecting all communities, states, or regions equally; rather, the collision between national laws and local conditions determined the degree of change. I read with great profit Richard Lowitt's model study *The New Deal and the West* and concluded that the South's story is similar to the West's in some ways but very different in others. This book attempts to characterize the interplay between the federal government and the South during the presidency of Franklin D. Roosevelt, a phenomenon of great importance in understanding the manifest changes sweeping Dixie after the Second World War. In this book I define the South as the eleven states of the former Confederacy, plus Kentucky, Maryland, Missouri, and Oklahoma; the addition of these four states reflects an inclusiveness commonly used today by such organizations as the U.S. Census Bureau and the Gallup polling agency.

This study could not have been completed without the able assistance of many people, and I am pleased to acknowledge their contributions. Although much of the book is based upon previously published work, I consulted primary sources in a few collections. For their help, I would like to thank the staffs at the Alabama Department of Archives and History, the Atlanta Historical Society, Atlanta University Center, the University of Alabama in Birmingham Library, the Birmingham Public Library Archives, the Dallas

Public Library, Emory University Library, Georgia State University Library, the Houston Public Library, the Memphis-Shelby County Archives, the Memphis State University Library, the National Archives, the New Orleans Public Library, the University of New Orleans Library, the Franklin D. Roosevelt Presidential Library, Southern Methodist University Library, the Tennessee State Library and Archives, and the Tulane University Library. The College of Arts and Sciences at Oklahoma State University granted me a sabbatical leave for writing and provided financial assistance, as did the provost and the vice-president for research. James A. Hodges and Richard L. Watson, Jr., provided sound suggestions for revision. Whatever flaws remain, the book is much better for my having had the benefit of their ideas. I would also like to thank my family, to whom the book is dedicated, for their continued love and encouragement.

1

ON THE EVE OF DEPRESSION

Fundamentalism, Ku Kluxry, revivals, lynchings, hog wallow politics—these are the things that always occur to a northerner when he thinks of the south.

—H. L. Mencken, 1924

In the decade following the First World War, the South's continuing resistance to change intensified. Long committed to preserving the status quo, many white southerners clung tenaciously to a belief in the Lost Cause and refused to surrender a romanticized ideal of the Old South. Forced to suffer defeat in the Civil War and the humiliation of Reconstruction, they sought to preserve a uniquely southern way of life, judged superior to that existing in the urbanized, industrialized North. White superiority, racial segregation, one-party politics, and fundamentalist religion characterized much of the region. Nevertheless, the 1920s brought challenges of unprecedented force to southern isolation. Although farming still dominated, cities grew, and industries arrived at a rapid rate. Blacks remained second-class citizens in the South, but hundreds of thousands left for more inviting environments elsewhere. The prewar progressive spirit of reform revived, and discontented workers exhibited a new assertiveness in challenging management's control of their lives. The clash between modernism and traditionalism—a struggle ongoing for decades—was vividly illustrated by the dramatic Scopes trial in the mid-1920s. Further aggravating the turmoil, the economy dealt unevenly with southerners: at a time of urban expansionism, farming entered a period of profound crisis. For some southerners the 1920s was truly an era of great prosperity; for others the Great Depression arrived long before the stock market crash of 1929.

In the 1920s the South remained a predominantly rural and agricultural region. At decade's end approximately two-thirds of the region's people lived in rural areas, and 42.8 percent still labored on farms. World War I brought prosperity in the form of extraordinarily high prices: in 1919 a pound of cotton cost 35 cents; a pound of tobacco, 86 cents; and a hundred pounds of rice, $5.46. Lack of foreign competition and the resultant market expansion induced farmers to plant "fence row to fence row." But then came a severe collapse with the end of the war and the return of "normalcy." Cotton prices, as high as 41 cents a bale in April 1920, plummeted to 13.5 cents by December. Throughout the cotton belt, panicked farmers called for an end to harvesting and processing, and night riders torched gins and warehouses that continued to operate. Cotton rotted in the fields as glutted markets kept prices perilously low.[1]

Commodity prices rebounded somewhat after the depression of 1920–21, but the situation for southern farmers remained serious. Cotton prices rallied in 1922–24, then fell for the remainder of the decade. Tobacco prices fell less precipitously but achieved stasis at only about twenty cents per pound, while rice prices halved and remained below five dollars per hundred pounds until after World War II. Also contributing to cotton's collapse was the conquest by the boll weevil, which had appeared in Texas in the 1890s and had worked its way eastward to Alabama by 1913 and to South Carolina by 1917. By 1922 North Carolina and Virginia suffered, and in 1929 University of North Carolina sociologist Rupert Vance concluded sadly: "Today the world's largest consumer of raw cotton is the boll weevil." The development of insecticides and improved planting techniques finally brought the boll weevil plague under control, but increased production simply revived the problem of surpluses. Beleaguered cotton farmers continued to suffer, and many of them came to view their situation as retribution from God.[2]

Distraught southern farmers seeking secular solutions looked in many different directions. The new American Cotton Association launched a cooperative marketing movement, but it enjoyed only limited success owing to corruption and lack of capital. The National Grange, which had been defunct since the 1890s but revived in the late 1920s, and the Farmers' Union attracted limited followings in their crusades to resuscitate populism. While such radical organizations appealed especially to the region's sharecroppers and tenant farmers, the American Farm Bureau Federation represented the concerns of more prosperous commercial farmers. The Farm Bureau enjoyed success initially in the midwestern corn belt—among the southern states, only Tennessee and Alabama maintained viable organizations in the 1920s—and it achieved widespread popularity in the South only in the 1930s. In Congress a coalition of western Republicans and southern Democrats allied to form the Farm Bloc, an ad hoc lobby for agricultural interests that challenged the business-minded conservatism of the decade's Republican presidents. Suspicious of western Progressives, southerners never fully devoted themselves to the Farm Bloc, whose effectiveness as a foil to administrative policies ebbed by 1924.[3]

The preeminent proposal for agricultural recovery in the decade was the McNary-Haugen Bill. The creation of George N. Peek and Hugh S. Johnson, both of the Moline Plow Company, the bill proposed the federal government's dumping of surplus crops abroad in combination with high protective tariffs. Adhering to their traditional opposition to protectionism, southerners saw McNary-Haugenism as designed to benefit perishable crops with large domestic and relatively limited international markets. Southern votes helped defeat the bill in 1924, 1925, and 1926 and forced midwesterners to revise it through reduced emphasis on surplus dumping in favor of more cooperative marketing. With southern support the McNary-Haugen Bill passed Congress in 1927 and 1928, only to be vetoed both times by President Calvin Coolidge. The political alliance of midwestern and southern farmers (the so-called marriage of corn and cotton) achieved little success in the conservative 1920s. Farmers in Dixie—black and white, sharecropper and landowner—continued to struggle as commodity prices stayed depressed.[4]

By contrast, the decade prior to the onset of the Great Depression was for southern cities a time of economic success and optimism, the apparent payoff for years of fealty to the New South ethic. In the late nineteenth century avid southern boosters led by Atlanta *Constitution* editor Henry W. Grady determined to attract northern industry through elaborate public relations campaigns. Referring to Atlanta as a "Yankee city in the South," Grady portrayed his hometown as bustling and prosperous, crackling with energy, nothing like the images northerners harbored of sleepy backwater southern towns mired in antediluvian traditions. By the 1920s Atlanta had firmly established itself as the Gate City of the New South, and in 1926 the local chamber of commerce looked to build on that foundation with its Forward Atlanta campaign. A nonprofit corporation closely tied to the chamber of commerce, the Forward Atlanta

Commission garnered $722,000 in subscriptions to advertise the city's advantages as a business center. Calling the South the nation's fastest growing market, the commission cast Atlanta as the "distribution city" for the region. Local authorities reported that 679 new firms, employing over 17,400 workers and having an annual payroll exceeding $30 million, relocated in the city as a result of the campaign. The fact that the 679 new establishments included 387 sales offices and only 78 manufacturing plants failed to dampen local enthusiasm.[5]

Throughout the South local chambers of commerce and other civic associations took the lead in boosting their cities before a national audience. The promotional din reached a crescendo after the First World War as southerners set out to share in "Coolidge prosperity." To a great extent they did. Construction boomed, impressive skyscrapers sprang up to adorn vibrant downtowns, and new businesses arrived by the hundreds. Nashville welcomed a multi-million-dollar Du Pont rayon plant, several textile firms relocating from the Northeast, factories that manufactured shoes and shoelaces, and a number of radio stations, which made the city a regional broadcasting center. In New Orleans, where trade and tourism formed the foundations of the local economy, a twenty-million-dollar inner-harbor navigation canal opened in 1921 to provide a second water route to the Gulf of Mexico, and the city initiated a drive to preserve the historic Vieux Carre. In 1927 Dallas approved civic planning engineer C. E. Ulrickson's ambitious plan for Trinity River reclamation and a nine-year program of street and parks improvements. Industrial Dallas, Inc., a chamber of commerce creation, claimed to have attracted an average of 761 new businesses annually from 1928 to 1930. Of the South's largest cities, only Birmingham failed to achieve notable economic growth in the 1920s. The giant northern-based iron and steel companies employed thousands of workers in Birmingham, and company fortunes dictated to a great extent the city's economic health. Unfortunately, the iron and steel industry sputtered in the 1920s, and northern financial interests continued to take precedence over southern ones in the far-flung boardrooms where corporate decisions were made. Notwithstanding the case of the region's Iron City, most urban southerners enjoyed good times in the 1920s.[6]

While city boosters avidly pursued northern-based manufacturers, much of the region's prosperity resulted from the success of industries already situated in the South. Leading the industrial boom, hydroelectric power advanced dramatically during the decade. From

1921 to 1930 generating capacity in the southern states increased 156 percent, a remarkable feat owing to the growth of mammoth holding companies headquartered both above and below the Mason-Dixon line. By 1930 seven conglomerates controlled 84 percent of the electric properties in the southern states east of the Mississippi River; three of them (Commonwealth and Southern, Electric Bond and Share, and Duke Power) operated 71 percent. Moreover, the residents of those states used more electric power per worker than did their counterparts in the Northeast.[7]

The expansion of hydroelectric power proved especially vital in the textile mills of the Piedmont states. Building on the momentum of the war years, textile companies constructed new facilities, and southern communities went after northern capital for additional building projects. Many northern plants uprooted and moved southward to take advantage of cheaper power rates, closer proximity to raw materials, and lower labor costs. From 1921 to 1929 over fifty mills, containing more than 1.3 million spindles, left New England for southern sites. The 1920s saw the culmination of a change ongoing for decades, the shift of the nation's textile industry from New England to the Appalachian foothills of the South. By 1933 over two-thirds of textile workers were employed in the Piedmont. Many critics, however, labeled this achievement a mixed blessing, for the industry offered a plethora of jobs but little remuneration for workers. Moreover, at least 80 percent of Piedmont textile workers lived in employer-owned mill villages, where they were easily exploited by the companies.[8]

The boom in textile production gave impetus to the increased manufacture of rayon and other synthetic fibers. Taking the lead in changing the clothing industry, World War I veteran J. Spencer Love established Burlington Mills in 1923, when the Burlington, North Carolina, chamber of commerce underwrote his issuance of common stock. The southern boom in chemical production involved a host of materials, ranging from sulfur in the Texas Gulf Coast to air-nitrogen in Virginia. In many cases, World War I production of nitrates and other compounds for explosives gave way to peacetime applications in a region rich in raw materials. By 1927, according to one source, the makers of twenty different major chemicals produced 25 percent of their output value in southern plants.[9]

In the 1920s the discovery, drilling, and refining of petroleum became a larger part of the Texas, Louisiana, and Oklahoma economies. After the war, inflated prices and new discoveries brought thousands of drillers into the oil fields. As the decade passed, corporate "majors," who controlled drilling, pipelines, refining, and marketing, replaced the "wildcatters," who dominated earlier in the century. Refineries sprang up along the Texas Gulf Coast and in Baton Rouge, Louisiana, as pipelines crisscrossed the southwestern landscape. Although many of the "majors" were headquartered outside the region, companies like Standard Oil, Gulf Oil, and Sun Oil brought jobs, support services, and land development to a sparsely settled land crying for investment capital.[10]

Industrial domination by a few giant corporations also described the tobacco industry during the 1920s. The spectacular rise of cigarette consumption and the corresponding decline of other tobacco products resulted largely from multi-million-dollar advertising campaigns ("Reach for a Lucky Instead of a Sweet"). By 1927 the Big Three (American, R. J. Reynolds, and Liggett and Myers) produced 90 percent of cigarettes made in the United States, and by 1930 almost two-thirds of all cigarettes were manufactured in North Carolina. The dismantling of James B. Duke's monopolistic American Tobacco Company for antitrust violations in 1911 induced more competition, World War I expanded markets, and the phenomenal increase in sales brought record profits to southern concerns.[11]

The rapid sale of real estate brought additional wealth and speculative capital, nowhere more so than in the financial frontier of Florida. The building of railroads along both coasts and the drainage and agricultural development of the interior earlier in the century paved the way for the promotional orgy of the 1920s. The "Dixie Highway" from Michigan to Miami opened in 1925, and the suddenly ubiquitous automobile made Florida's inviting climate accessible as never before. Along with the wintertime vacationing "snowbirds" came aged pensioners seeking a more salubrious climate for their retirement years. With three-time presidential candidate William Jennings Bryan hawking the bargains of Florida real estate, a frantic race for quick riches spawned overnight subdivisions. Before the speculative mania ended with a destructive hurricane in 1926, many out-of-state investors arrived to find their suburban havens located in mangrove swamps. Close investigation uncovered inadequate transportation, poor planning, and innumerable cases of outright fraud. The mid-decade end to the Florida land boom returned some sanity to land purchases. Thereafter, the state's development proceeded steadily, but at a more rational pace.[12]

Despite the undeniable economic expansion, the South remained largely a poor and backward region. Decades of misuse and neglect rendered much of the plantation South's soil depleted; in the Appalachian hills—and, to a lesser degree, in the Ozarks—the unrestrained extraction of mineral wealth and the rapacious lumber industry left a denuded landscape. Residing in company-owned housing, purchasing all their goods at company-operated commissaries, and even receiving medical care from company-employed physicians, coal miners lived as virtual serfs. As a miner from the Cumberland Plateau region of Tennessee ruefully recalled: "Most folks just had scrip all the time. Money, why I didn't see no money till I was 25 years old."[13]

Progress made few inroads in many of the backwaters, where fear and distrust predominated. Moreover, because migration from southern farm to southern city fueled so much of southern cities' growth and so few migrants came from more cosmopolitan sources outside the region, attitudes and customs changed slowly in urban areas. The southern states continued to suffer from unusually high disease rates. Owing to unique climatic and topographic conditions, exacerbated by substandard sanitation and drainage, southerners exhibited high incidences of malaria, hookworm, pellagra, and tuberculosis; poverty and ignorance led to near-epidemic rates of syphilis and other venereal diseases. The burgeoning public health movement, a product of the prewar Progressive movement, made notable progress in combating these diseases, but depressed agriculture meant inadequate diets for millions of rural southerners in the 1920s. The Public Health Service made laudable advances in the South, but the final victory over "poverty diseases" stood decades in the future.[14]

In addition to a high incidence of disease, the South also reported shockingly high crime rates. Long plagued by excessive violence, the region continued to nurture what journalist W. J. Cash called "the savage ideal." Indeed, the uncertainty wrought by the many changes in the southern landscape no doubt heightened the atmosphere in which lawlessness prevailed. Homicide rates compiled by the Prudential Insurance Company consistently ranked southern cities at or near the top nationally, a reflection of the predilection of transplanted rural people to maintain their custom of packing firearms and settling disputes personally. Although some white southerners blamed exorbitant homicide rates on blacks, statistics indicated that more commonly blacks were the victims of white violence. The Memphis *Commercial Appeal* lamented that "this thing of killing negroes without cause" was being "overdone," for "white men who kill negroes as a pastime . . . usually end up by killing white men."[15]

Southerners charged with committing crimes had to deal with a dysfunctional legal system that officially or unofficially condoned a host of evils, including peonage, convict leasing, chain gangs, and lynching. In 1921 a Georgia farmer's murder of eleven blacks whose fines he had paid to the county exposed the survival of peonage in the modern South. Eight years later another sensational exposé revealed the existence of forced labor in Florida lumber and turpentine camps. In 1923 the League of Women Voters publicized the sadistic beatings and occasional homicides in convict mining camps. The publication in 1932 of Robert Elliott Burns's first-person account, *I Am a Fugitive from a Georgia Chain Gang!* brought national attention to bear on southern penology. Such disclosures aided reform-minded criminologists and civic organizations, but the huge profiteering made possible by forced labor and the convict lease system gave their beneficiaries additional incentive to resist change.[16]

Even more than for its nightmarish penal system, the South became infamous for lynching. After the turn of the century the number of lynchings declined, but the frequency of such incidents rebounded after World War I. According to Walter White, executive secretary of the National Association for the Advancement of Colored People during the 1930s, lynching took the lives of 454 persons (416 of them black) from 1918 to 1927. Moreover, the lynchings of the 1920s seemed to be more sadistic than ever before. Seldom did mobs simply hang an offender from a nearby tree; instead, the meting out of "justice" became infinitely more gruesome, frequently including torture, dismemberment, and immolation.[17]

White southerners defended lynching as essential to keeping blacks "in their place." Repeatedly its defenders spoke of protecting southern white womanhood. South Carolina senator James F. Byrnes told the U.S. Congress: "Rape is responsible directly and indirectly for most of the lynching in America." A southern metropolitan newspaper editorialized: "There are other things dearer than life, and the chief among these is female virtue. When this is slain . . . the avenger has the right to go forth in quest of blood-atonement and if he does not do so he is unworthy of the civilization of the day." Although the NAACP reported that only one out of six victims of lynch mobs had been accused of rape, the paeans to chivalry persisted as lynching's primary defense. From 1919 to 1925 Congressman L. C. Dyer of St. Louis introduced several antilynching bills in Congress that proposed holding local authorities accountable for failing to protect prisoners and fining counties in which lynchings occurred. A Dyer bill came closest to becoming law in 1922, when it passed in the House but fell victim to a filibuster by southern senators.[18]

Along with the threat of lynching, blacks in the South had to endure a jim crow system that segregated the races into separate and unequal positions. Having inferior education, blacks monopolized the lowest paying, most undesirable jobs in the cities and, almost everywhere barred from owning land, eked out an existence in rural areas usually as sharecroppers and tenant farmers. The few labor unions operating in the South at that time denied membership to blacks. In the 1920s several municipalities adopted residential segregation statutes to assure the separation of the races, but the 1926 U.S. Supreme Court decision of *Smith* v. *Atlanta* ruled the practice illegal. Segregated housing prevailed, however, by custom if not by legal fiat. A series of devices adopted earlier by southern states, such as the poll tax, the white primary, and the grandfather clause, systematically disfranchised blacks in all but a handful of locations. Essentially powerless in a hostile environment, second-class citizens deprived of human rights by a firmly entrenched system of apartheid, blacks found life in the South in the 1920s as hazardous as their forebears had in the nineteenth century.

While millions of blacks simply endured the harsh conditions, a large and growing number left for the North. The Great Migration began during the First World War, when a number of developments made emigration an attractive alternative. The boll weevil's devastation of the cotton kingdom, coupled with floods in 1915 and 1916, drove many farm workers off the land. More important, the war's curtailment of foreign immigration and the subsequent exodus of the American Expeditionary Force for European battlefields left northern factories starved for labor. Recruiting agents from the industries headed south with inducements of jobs, good wages, and plentiful housing. To southern blacks hesitant to resitutate in the foreboding North, the Chicago *Defender*, which played a major role in spurring the migration, contended: "To die from the bite of frost is far more glorious than at the hands of a mob." The wartime movement continued in the 1920s: during that decade 615,000 blacks vacated the South. By 1930 slightly more than 78 percent of the nation's blacks still lived in Dixie, but the decline from 89 percent in 1910 was striking. Many southern whites reacted angrily to the loss of what they saw as their property. One southern newspaper saw an organized plan "to rifle the entire South of its well-behaved, able-bodied Negro labor." Another daily, expressing resignation, asked: "If you thought you might be lynched by mistake, would you remain in South Carolina?"[19]

The commitment to maintain white supremacy also contributed to the growth of the Ku Klux Klan. Reborn in 1915, the Klan limped along in virtual isolation for several years, until postwar Bolshevik scares, race riots, and rising xenophobia ignited a membership surge in 1920. KKK publicists worked overtime turning out slick propaganda, and a congressional investigation in 1921 brought the organization additional notoriety. Broadening its list of enemies to include Catholics, Jews, Communists, and other "non-Americans," as well as blacks, the Klan steadily gained popularity throughout much of the South that lasted until scandal and bankruptcy sundered the organization in 1925. During that time, despite heroic opposition by courageous newspaper editors and other leading citizens who condemned bigotry and violence, the KKK conducted a reign of terror that forced the governors of Louisiana and Oklahoma to deploy state militia to restore order. Even after the rampant lawlessness subsided, the Invisible Empire dominated the politics and governments of countless southern communities where local officials owed their elections to KKK backing. In Texas, Georgia, and Alabama, Klan influence decided key statewide contests.[20]

The Klan's popularity in the 1920s reflected the fear and mistrust with which so many southerners viewed the rapid changes after the war. As historian Kenneth T. Jackson discovered, the KKK attracted a larger following in the cities, where different groups from varied backgrounds confronted each other, than in the countryside. Jackson concluded: "Fear of change, not vindictiveness or cruelty, was the basic motivation of the urban Klansman. . . . Sensing that the traditional values, religion, and way of life of an older America were in danger, he donated ten dollars to a hypocritical secret society in a vague attempt to halt the forces of time."[21]

Southerners attracted to organizations such as the KKK opposed the diversity of beliefs and behaviors tolerated in the growing cities. Disturbed by the ruthlessness and impersonality that seemed to characterize modern society, they clung to the churches, whose authority they feared modernism was undermining, and the moral standards threatened by new doctrines and scientific findings. As philosophers dared to question the Bible's inerrancy and the theory of evolution crept into public literature and school textbooks, evangelical Protestants rallied around their religious convictions. William Louis Poteat, president of Baptist-affiliated Wake

Forest College, argued the feasibility of reconciling science with Christian faith and led a successful effort to defeat a bill prohibiting the teaching of evolution in North Carolina public schools. For many other southerners, however, opposition to Darwinism became fundamentalist Protestantism's litmus test of devotion. The belief in evolution seemed to symbolize the repudiation of all the foundations supporting the southern Christian community.[22]

With legendary political orator William Jennings Bryan assuming the role of defender of the faith, fundamentalists took evolution to court in the famous Scopes trial in Dayton, Tennessee. Biology teacher John T. Scopes admitted violating a state law by teaching evolution to his high school classes and accepted the services of the American Civil Liberties Union for his defense. The ACLU's decision to employ famed defense attorney Clarence Darrow, an avowed atheist, to oppose Bryan added to the trial's notoriety. In a carnival atmosphere, reporters, soft drink vendors, curiosity seekers, evangelists, and Florida land salesmen joined local townsfolk in one of the decade's most publicized events. The anticlimactic verdict—the jury found Scopes guilty and fined him one hundred dollars—took a back seat to the fiery confrontation between the two principal adversaries in the courtroom. In his skillful, occasionally spiteful cross-examination, Darrow exposed Bryan's inconsistencies and appalling ignorance of biblical scholarship. Bryan's sudden death just days after the trial's conclusion seemed symbolically to seal modernism's triumph over the blind, irrational faith of fundamentalism. The spectacle at Dayton may have discredited fundamentalism in some quarters, but uneasiness about modernism and devotion to traditional religious beliefs persisted in much of the South.[23]

Evangelical Protestants also played a key role in Dixie's support of Prohibition in the 1920s and before. Southerners like Methodist bishop James M. Cannon, Jr., led the successful campaign for temperance, and Texas senator Morris Sheppard introduced the resolution into Congress that would eventually become the Eighteenth Amendment. Events in the decade demonstrated the impossibility of enforcing the Volstead Act, and many Americans expressed their desire to rescind the "noble experiment," but southerners insisted on continuing the crusade against demon rum. Yet just as the South remained an unshakable stronghold of Prohibition, denizens of the region consumed illicit alcohol in substantial quantities. While speakeasies flourished in the North, rural southerners more often operated stills producing moonshine. A South Carolina editor concluded: "If there is, as a product of sincere conviction and honest observance of the law, such a reality as the 'Dry South,' I have yet to see it, and I have lived and journeyed over it for more than 40 years."[24]

Though ultimately unsuccessful, Prohibition was one of the great reforms achieved by pre-World War I Progressives, who continued their crusades in the 1920s. Advocates for "good government" and better public services called for efficiency first and foremost. In the South what historian George B. Tindall termed "business progressivism" meant reform that would aid economic growth. Thus, business progressive governors like Cameron Morrison of North Carolina, Thomas Kilby and Bibb Graves of Alabama, and Austin Peay of Tennessee adopted programs of highway extension, school construction, and public health improvement. Straining at budgetary limitations imposed by limited tax revenues, state governments strove to shore up the inadequate services considered vital if southern manufacturers intended to compete in national and international markets.[25]

Although the reform tradition survived the First World War, southern one-party politics remained predominant. With the Republican party still hopelessly ineffective, the Democrats dominated in every state. In the solid South, planters, industrialists, and county-seat merchants slowly, incrementally surrendered influence to a rising new business elite, but the traditional have-nots—blacks and poor whites—made few inroads. Even with the Nineteenth Amendment's enfranchisement of women, barely 20 percent of southern adults cast ballots in the 1920s. In a one-party region, the winners of Democratic primaries (from which virtually all blacks were barred from voting) invariably won general elections, often unopposed. With a severely limited franchise, one-party dominance, and low voter participation, the South deserved its reputation as the nation's most undemocratic region.[26]

Democrats dominated local as well as state politics and government. In the early years of the twentieth century many southern cities had forsaken the traditional mayor-council form of civic government and, in a search for greater efficiency, had adopted such alternatives as the city commission and city manager. In virtually all cities the leading entrepreneurs (the men whom historian Blaine A. Brownell called the "commercial-civic elite") exerted the most influence in selecting the community's leadership or making crucial policy decisions. In Birmingham, for example, the executives of the giant iron, steel, and coal companies, the so-called Big Mules, played the dominant role in the city's politics. In some cities political bosses and machines thrived. Ed Crump in Memphis, Hillary Howse in Nashville, and Martin Behrman, chief of the Choctaw machine in New Orleans, ruled as autocratically as any big city sachem in a northern metropolis. Whatever the particular variation in local government, decision makers assured Democratic primacy, upheld white supremacy, and adopted policies congenial to growth-minded business interests.[27]

Community and state leaders intent on economic expansion promoted as one of the South's great assets its large, docile labor force accustomed to working for minuscule wages. Accordingly, they feared the incursion of labor unions, whose call for collective bargaining and higher pay would limit profits. Trade unionism also fostered worker independence, a clear threat to management paternalism. Workers exercised the least control of their own lives in textile mill villages, and not surprisingly, the principal confrontations between management and labor occurred in the Piedmont company towns. The situation worsened for mill workers after the war because of the introduction of new equipment that both routinized work and vastly elevated owners' expectations of higher profits. The "stretch-out," whereby workers had to increase productivity with no reductions in the fifty-five-hour work weeks, took a terrible human toll. The collapse of agriculture provided a labor surplus, so if overworked "lintheads" balked at the frenetic pace, displaced farmers willingly stepped forward to take their positions at the looms. Women and children toiled alongside men in the unhealthy environment, which resulted in high illness and mortality rates. Married women suffered especially from the "stretch-out," for only the slower pace of the pre-World War I era allowed them to work in the mills and maintain their households, to serve as both wage earner and homemaker.[28] One female mill worker remembered:

I had been working for the Manville-Jenkes mill in Loray, near Gastonia [North Carolina], for eight years—ever since I was fourteen. We worked thirteen hours a day, and we were so stretched out that lots of times we didn't stop for anything. Sometimes we took sandwiches to work, and ate them as we worked. Sometimes we didn't even get to eat them. If we couldn't keep our work up like they wanted us to, they would curse us and threaten to fire us. Some of us made twelve dollars a week, and some a little more.[29]

As early as 1919 the United Textile Workers (UTW) moved into the Carolinas, originally setting as its goal the reduction of the work week to forty-eight hours. Violence flared repeatedly in 1920–21, as the mill owners successfully quashed union uprisings. Several years of uneasy quietude followed, but in 1927 workers struck for higher wages in Henderson, North Carolina. Although the strike failed, the UTW enrolled five hundred new members and renewed the interest of area workers in labor unionism. In 1929 strikes erupted throughout the Piedmont, with the UTW, the American Federation of Labor, and the communistic National Textile Workers Union vying for control. Considerable violence occurred in Elizabethton, Tennessee; Marion, North Carolina; and, most sensationally, Gastonia, North Carolina, where the list of fatalities included the police chief and a twenty-nine-year-old mother of five who had marched in sympathy with the strikers. The tragic loss of life led to some improvement in the mills, but the owners staunchly refused to recognize the unions or to participate in collective bargaining.[30]

Southern workers stirred in other industries as well, generally with as little success. After achieving encouraging wartime gains, unions in the tobacco factories and oil fields lost membership and surrendered recently won pay raises and benefits in the 1920s. The once formidable United Mine Workers lost a decisive strike in Alabama after the war, and its membership dwindled to token numbers throughout the region. In city after city, chambers of commerce formed open-shop associations to deflect unionism's appeal and enjoyed consistently good results. In Dallas, for example, local officials boasted that 95 percent of laborers in the city worked in open shops and that no factory lost a single day because of a strike during the entire decade. To be sure, a rising level of worker discontent simmered below the surface, but management enjoyed great success in holding the lid on during the 1920s.[31]

The tensions that divided southern society—in the workplace and elsewhere—brought a sense of uneasiness to a historically isolated region. Growing cities and an uprooted landless peasantry caused dissonance among a people with a strong sense of place. Life in growing urban areas provided more opportunities and amenities, and the quality of life improved for many southerners, yet much nostalgia for an idealized past remained. That longing for the old familiar ways showed in the rural music that also made the trip to the cities. Fiddler Alexander ("Eck") Robertson recorded the first country music record in 1923, and the spread of radios took the tunes into more and more homes as the decade advanced. Country music appealed to a largely illiterate work force, many members of which identified with songs about, as historian Pete Daniel noted, "average people and their work, loves and heartbreak, music about dogs, mothers, train wrecks, and death." More than anything else, its sounds served as an audible lifeline to another time and place that seemed to be slipping away.[32]

The same ambivalence about progress and concern for the disappearance of the Old South surfaced in more scholarly circles, as evidenced by the publication of *I'll Take My Stand* in 1930. Written by twelve southern authors based at Vanderbilt University, this collection of essays lionized the agrarian past and condemned the dehumanizing impact of industrialization. The Fugitives, as they called themselves, lambasted the huckstering spirit of Atlanta, the cold empiricism of science, and the nightmarish bureaucracy of modern industrial life. In unvarnished terms, they applauded agrarianism as the only system in which family, gentility, honor, hospitality, and culture could thrive. Intentionally provocative, the "agrarian manifesto," authored by "unreconstructed rebels," pilloried capitalism and communism as two sides of the same devalued coin. Critics took the Fugitives to task for idealizing the rural past beyond recognition. Southern author Lillian Smith charged: "The basic weakness of the Fugitives' stand, as I see it, lay in their failure to recognize the massive dehumanization which had resulted from slavery and its progeny, sharecropping and segregation, and the values that permitted these brutalities of spirit." Less severe critics found much of merit in *I'll Take My Stand* but lamented that nothing could be done to halt industrialism's advance. "It is at least important that this voice has been raised," concluded southern writer Howard Mumford Jones.[33]

The brouhaha sparked by the Fugitives simply brought to a national audience the concerns bandied about by southerners during the preceding decade. Indeed, the idea for *I'll Take My Stand* came several years before the book's 1930 publication. Ironically, however, the book's appearance coincided with the apparent collapse of the economic system the authors held responsible for much of the South's problems. The onset of the Great Depression lent real authority to the jeremiads of the Nashville Agrarians. If, as 1920s boosters insisted, the much heralded New South had finally arrived, did the collapse of the nation's economy signal its abrupt end? For a region already in the throes of wrenching change, the Great Depression raised additional questions and left the people even more uncertain.

2

DEPRESSION AND RESPONSE, 1929–1933

If people do not . . . practice the habits of thrift and conservation or if they gamble away their savings in the stock markets or elsewhere, is our economic system, or government, or industry to blame?

—John Edgerton, president of the
National Association of Manufactures, 1930

The Great Depression exacted a heavy toll in the South. Already reeling from years of substandard prices, farmers saw conditions worsen. In 1930–31 the most severe drought in history exacerbated the situation, and of course, sharecroppers and tenant farmers suffered the most. Southern industry, employing only 15 percent of the nation's factory workers, lost whatever momentum it had gained the previous decade and fell even further behind northern manufacturing. Long reluctant to spend huge sums of money for the care of the indigent, southern communities lacked the institutions—and indeed, the inclination—to provide relief on a large scale. When the stock market crashed in October 1929, very few cities operated municipally funded relief bureaus. Typical of southern communities, Atlanta underwrote some of the expense of indigent care at the city's Grady Hospital and contributed to several of the local Community Chest's thirty-nine charitable agencies. Several cities operated municipal employment offices that dispatched workers to surrounding farms to pick and chop cotton. Generally southern communities left relief to private initiative and depended upon rugged individualism to help people survive the Depression.[1]

In the months following the crash, no widespread panic ensued, nor was there any admission that existing community relief organizations would be inadequate to meet a crisis. Downplaying the severity of economic conditions and quoting the reassurances of business magnates, southern newspapers predicted a short duration for hard times and optimistically referred to the "sunshine syndrome." That is, they told readers that temporary winter layoffs in 1929–30 would melt away with the arrival of warmer weather. The Nashville *Tennessean* boasted, "There's No Depression Here," in a full-page display in September 1930. The Dallas *Morning News* dismissed the significance of the stock market collapse, noting: "Many individuals, undoubtedly, have suffered a loss far heavier than they could afford. Yet economic conditions in general are sound . . . and, after the storm, the sun of prosperity will again shine on thrift, hard work and efficient effort." The Lexington, Kentucky, *Herald* published on its front page a syndicated column by Will Rogers that opined: "What does the sensational collapse of Wall Street mean? Nothin'. Why, if the cows of this country failed to come up and get milked one night it would be more of a panic." The New Orleans *Times-Picayune* was similarly upbeat: "The stock market collapse that shattered so many dreams elsewhere . . . finds our city less affected . . . and in better position perhaps than almost all the rest to carry on through the year without distress."[2]

Local business organizations seconded the newspapers' sanguinity. The Birmingham Chamber of Commerce dismissed the notion of a depression, predicting that the city would be "decidedly on the upward trend from now on." The Atlanta Chamber of Commerce concurred: in its monthly organ, the Atlanta *City Builder*, the author of an editorial entitled "Sure, Business Will Be Good!" concluded: "Certainly no barometer visible to the public presages a doleful future for our city and section." Nor did local governments countenance any negativism. The Birmingham City Commission underlined its faith in the health of the local economy by adopting an operating budget for the 1929–30 fiscal year that exceeded the previous year's by two hundred thousand dollars. In Dallas, when a local lawyer spoke on a radio broadcast about rising unemployment, the city commission enacted a statute requiring that any negative remarks be submitted in advance for approval.[3]

Indeed, a number of positive developments in 1929–30 seemed to verify such optimism. The Atlanta-based Coca Cola Corporation reported record profits in 1930 and continued to thrive in subsequent years. So did the tobacco industry, proving to be as "depression-proof" as its executives claimed. Cigarettes were inexpensive, addictive, and quickly consumed, and tobacco company profits continued to rise in the early 1930s—a fortuitous development for North

Carolina, Kentucky, and Virginia, which produced 40 percent, 20 percent, and 10 percent respectively of the nation's annual tobacco crop. Exactly one month and one day after the stock market debacle, the merger of the Atlanta and Lowry National Bank with the Fourth National Bank made the newly created First National Bank the largest financial institution south of Philadelphia. Similarly, the merger of North Texas Bank with Republic National Bank and Trust Company in Dallas constituted the largest merger of financial institutions in that state's history. Business boomed in the resort community of Miami Beach, Florida, where 47 new hotels, 74 apartment buildings, and 252 homes were built in 1936 alone. Most encouraging, considering the indispensability of the steel industry to Birmingham's economy, was the 1930 expansion of U.S. Steel's operations there. The corporation's decision to invest twenty-five million dollars to overhaul mills owned by its chief subsidiary, the Tennessee Coal and Iron Company (TCI), seemed particularly promising for the region's most industrialized city at a time when reduced production and growing unemployment already plagued communities with parallel economic orientations in the North.[4]

For southern farmers, however, the Great Depression immediately meant more misery and deprivation. Having enjoyed little of the prosperity of the 1920s, farmers also suffered from the great Mississippi flood of 1927 and the drought of 1930–31. From 1929 to 1932 the value of cotton sales dropped from $1.5 billion to $45 million, and income from the cigarette tobacco crop declined by two-thirds. The price of peanuts fell from 5 cents per pound in the 1920s to 1.6 cents in 1932. Many of the South's 8.5 million sharecroppers and tenant farmers lost their jobs, and the depressed cities could offer no substitutes. A former southerner who returned home during the Depression exclaimed: "I could not become accustomed to the sight of children's stomachs bloated from hunger and seeing the ill and aged too weak to walk the fields in search of something to eat." With virtually no system of rural relief, those who remained on the land could only grow their own food, scavenge, beg, or steal. The isolated subsistence farmers of the Appalachians and Ozarks continued to struggle on tiny plots of land with depleted soil. For those mountaineers the collapse of the coal mining and lumber industries removed the means by which they had traditionally supplemented their incomes. Throughout the South, the towns and villages that served the surrounding farm populations saw business decline.[5]

Because overproduction caused many of the farmers' problems, a number of crop reduction plans surfaced in the southern states.

The South Carolina and Mississippi legislatures passed reduction laws, but the failure of other states to do likewise curtailed these laws' effectiveness. Louisiana senator Huey Long advocated a regionwide "cotton holiday" and persuaded his state's legislature to pass a law prohibiting the "planting, gathering, and ginning of cotton" in 1932. Then he led an exhaustive campaign to entice other states to join the movement. Long concentrated much of his efforts on Texas, the leading producer of the crop, and when its state legislature defeated a cotton holiday bill he ceased his efforts. Long's "drop-a-crop" scheme failed, but his work on behalf of desperate cotton farmers added to his growing reputation as a champion of the downtrodden.[6]

By late 1930 conditions in the urban South began to show the strains evident in the countryside, and the situation worsened with each passing year. Mississippi River trade decreased as crippled northern industrial cities dispatched fewer barges toward the Gulf of Mexico. As a result, unemployment figures rose rapidly in river cities, and the volume of foreign trade dropped dramatically. In 1928, for example, New Orleans handled ten million tons of cargo worth more than nine million dollars annually; by 1933 the volume of that trade had declined by half. The number of unemployed stevedores increased quickly, as did the number of visiting sailors whose vessels were dry-docked there.[7]

Unemployment reached alarming levels as employers cut work weeks back to thirty hours or less, then fired larger and larger portions of the work force. Within two years of the stock market crash, unemployment doubled, and by 1933 many communities in the South reported at least 30-percent unemployment. In the largest cities, as many as 150,000 to 200,000 laborers lost their jobs. By 1933, according to social workers' estimates, the rate of joblessness in Atlanta reached 25–30 percent citywide and as much as 70–75 percent in some black neighborhoods. In New Orleans a huge disparity existed between local and federal governments' unemployment estimates: the former's figures were only about one-fourth as large as the latter's. A mayoral commission found many jobless workers reluctant to register, and as a result, all findings seemed tainted. In any event, almost all industries in the Crescent City reduced their labor forces, and most concerns operated only a few days a week. By the end of 1930 unemployment in Nashville had increased to 25 percent.[8]

As government coffers emptied, public employees found their situations imperiled. Especially vulnerable, teachers absorbed wage cuts and in some cases continued to teach without pay for months at a time. Education superintendents employed men and single women rather than married women, so that heads of households received preference. Many school boards adopted policies prohibiting the employment of single women who married; unmarried women had to remain so or resign. Already deficient in many areas, southern education suffered all the more because of funding shortages.[9]

The Depression struck hardest in the South's most industrial city, Birmingham, Alabama. Area coal mines yielded only one-third as much in the mid-1930s as in 1926. From peak production in 1929 of over 1.5 million tons, steel output declined by half from 1929 to 1931 (from 1.5 million tons to .75 million tons) and again by 50 percent in 1932. After operating at over 90-percent capacity in 1929, the U.S. Steel Corporation in 1932 produced at only 17 percent of capacity and lost over seventy million dollars. In 1930 the Tennessee Coal and Iron Company, a U.S. Steel subsidiary, implemented a "share-the-work" plan, dividing hours among employees rather than dismissing them; by 1933 the company cut pay between 50 and 75 percent and threatened termination if workers balked. The other leading companies, Sloss-Sheffield Steel and Iron Company and the Woodward Iron Company, also operated on reduced schedules, initially cutting back to three-day work weeks. Soon, however, workers only managed a full shift's work every two weeks. Conditions seemed so bad that one Birmingham resident ruefully remembered that "the Alabama River wasn't runnin' but three days a week." The sordid situation in one-industry Birmingham led President Franklin D. Roosevelt to label it the worst hit city in the country.[10]

Texas communities seemingly suffered less than other southern cities because of the discovery of oil. In October 1930 wildcatter Columbus Joiner found a veritable lake of oil under two hundred square miles of land about 120 miles southeast of Dallas and slightly farther to the northwest of Houston. By 1933 over 9,900 producing oil wells operated in that field. Dallas businesses quickly installed telephone and telegraph service to Tyler, Gladewater, Kilgore, Longview, and other fledgling outposts in the oil fields. Several Dallas banks introduced new methods of financing, such as production loans made against oil still in the ground. While Dallas supplied and financed the oil field, facilities in Houston stored, refined, and shipped the petroleum. In 1930 the U.S. Congress appropriated over $1.5 million for improvements on the Houston ship channel, assuring its continued service to the burgeoning oil industry and the relative economic health of the city.[11]

Although the fortuitous oil strike no doubt mitigated the economic crisis in these Texas cities, hard times did not bypass them altogether. In Houston the proportion of the jobless reached about 23 percent, and even the oil companies felt the pinch. Houston's Humble Oil Company reduced its work force from 12,500 in 1929 to 9,200 in 1932. Ironically, the federal government reported in 1931 that the most serious unemployment problem in the state existed in the East Texas oil fields, where an estimated 10,000 of the many itinerant laborers who arrived from around the country to get work found none. As the government noted, the responsibility for the care of these new arrivals fell on nearby communities.[12]

An influx of transients further stretched community resources throughout the South. As trade and transportation hubs, southern cities had long served as magnets for the displaced, the homeless, and other indigent groups seeking a new start. In the 1930s landless farmers joined unemployed workers who traveled from city to city in search of better conditions. Arriving in beat-up jalopies and railroad boxcars, they often found a frosty reception. Uncongenial city police discouraged newcomers from disembarking and spoke in sobering tones to those who did about leaving promptly. As a crossroads in the Southeast, Atlanta drowned in new arrivals—particularly after Florida forbade transients from entering in 1934. In Memphis the Southern Railroad posted guards around its trains and refused to admit anyone unable to pay, so the city sometimes transported unwanted drifters to Nashville and other nearby communities. Most cities simply left the transients to fend for themselves.[13]

In addition to high unemployment, a series of bank failures shook the financial foundations of the South. Foolish speculation in the 1920s overextended many banks, which could not withstand the strains when the economy faltered after the 1929 market collapse. The bankruptcy of Caldwell and Company in 1930 was the most spectacular case, because the Nashville conglomerate, with assets of more than a half-billion dollars, affected financial institutions throughout the South. After Caldwell's Bank of Tennessee went into receivership, 120 other banks in seven states followed within two weeks. Arkansas's American Exchange Trust Bank, whose forty-five branches made it the state's largest, failed because of its ties to the Nashville-based empire. In November 1939 the National Bank of Kentucky, the oldest and largest financial institution in Louisville, failed. To lessen the impact at Christmastime, Louisville *Courier-Journal* publisher Robert W. Bingham guaranteed a 50-percent return on all Christmas savings accounts from his own resources. In one month three banks closed in Kinston, North Carolina, leaving that tobacco distribution center without banking services, and the same financial void developed in other North Carolina agricultural trade centers. Two of Houston's largest banks would have failed had it not been for the emergency measures taken by the city's other bankers. Jesse Jones, owner of the National Bank of Commerce and the Houston *Chronicle* as well as head of the federal government's Reconstruction Finance Corporation, organized a consortium that raised the necessary money by assessing each of the other members in proportion to their assets. These measures checked the crisis, but the city's banks survived only through continued retrenchment during the decade.[14]

Many small businesses went bankrupt, as did some of the oldest and most respected establishments in the cities. In Memphis the luxurious Parkview Hotel ceased operation, and the city's two daily newspapers both went into receivership. The sixty-four-year-old Chamberlin-Johnson-Dubose department store in Atlanta filed for bankruptcy in 1930 and closed the next year. Its famed counterpart, Rich's Department Store, saw profits nearly halved from 1930 to 1933 but managed to keep its doors open. Unable to pay its taxes for several years, Atlanta's premier theater, the "fabulous Fox," fell into the hands of a trust company. As empty storefronts increasingly dotted the downtown Atlanta landscape, the alarmed chamber of commerce urged surviving establishments to rent vacant windows for display and thus maintain the facade of a healthy business district.[15]

Clearly, the extent of joblessness and misery was greater in such northern cities as New York, Chicago, and Philadelphia, where the unemployed numbered one million, six hundred thousand, and three hundred thousand respectively, than in communities below the Mason-Dixon line. By the winter of 1932–33, however, southern communities suffered severely from the weight of the Depression. Faced with unprecedented demands, their local governments responded, but not in adequate fashion. Few cities contributed more than a token amount for relief, and burdened by reduced tax collections, many cut other expenditures to keep from going heavily in the red. This resulted in paltry appropriations for vital city services. It became clear that if the ravages of the Great Depression were to be countered, it would not be by crippled municipal governments.[16]

In the Depression's early years, southern communities expanded their relief programs, but they depleted their resources quickly. In Louisville, an emergency relief program initiated in November 1930 ran out of money and ceased to operate the following

April. In Little Rock, Arkansas, a similar program lasted from January to March 1931. By early 1932 many southern cities reported having used all their funds for family relief. New Orleans proved to be the most niggardly in its provision of aid to the unfortunate. By 1932 the city ranked last among the nation's thirty-one largest metropolitan areas in the amount spent on relief; it also had the distinction of being the only city making provision neither for family welfare (except for the blind) nor for aid to needy mothers. As late as 1934 New Orleans was the nation's largest municipality not to provide a single penny for family relief. At the same time, however, the city council gave ten thousand dollars to the chamber of commerce to advertise nationally New Orleans's preferred status as the "home of cheap and docile labor."[17]

Some southerners criticized local and state governments for their limited responses to worsening conditions, arguing that much more needed to be done. The Richmond *Times-Dispatch* editorialized: "Behind all the maneuverings of the Virginia political leaders, the reluctance of those leaders to provide any State funds for the relief of the cities may be clearly discerned. . . . they are determined not to spend any of the State's money for the State's neediest unemployed." Atlanta mayors I.N. Ragsdale and James Key became the targets of public criticism for their scant responses to widespread unemployment, particularly in light of the passage of a city ordinance requiring a license to peddle and the announcement in November 1930 that the city was launching a "war on vagrants." Such insensitivity by public officials made minimal relief all the more unpopular with some people.[18]

Although some despaired at the paucity of local relief, others applauded the continued emphasis on individual initiative and the absence of government involvement. Indeed, voters repeatedly elected mayors and other officials who urged fiscal responsibility, balanced budgets, and laissez-faire economics. In Houston, attorney Walter Monteith defeated incumbent Oscar Holcombe in the 1929 mayoral election largely as a result of the latter's "profligate spending." In 1931 Holcombe lambasted Monteith's penuriousness and promised to do more for the unemployed, but the voters reelected the incumbent. Referring to more government spending to aid the needy, Monteith said that "it simply cannot and will not be done." In response to a 1931 U.S. Senate questionnaire, Monteith proudly proclaimed that Houston did not provide any assistance for the unemployed and would issue no bonds for such work. In his opinion, the federal government should not assist local governments in meeting their relief obligations. The Houston *Post-Dispatch* concurred in a stringent editorial, dismissing the need for government to create jobs just because many people desperately needed employment. In Richmond, Mayor J. Fulmer Bright adamantly refused to seek relief from the federal government, and in Oklahoma City, St. Anthony's Hospital ceased feeding hundreds of unemployed people because Governor William ("Alfalfa Bill") Murray threatened to use the National Guard to halt the practice.[19]

At a time when minimal spending on services constituted a fiscal orthodoxy and deficits were considered anathema, economists and bankers as well as government officials saw a balanced ledger as the only effective means of combating depression. In Georgia a Reconstruction-era amendment to the state constitution outlawed municipal debts "except to repel invasion, suppress insurrections . . . or to pay the existing public debt." In Birmingham the city commission passed a budget-control law limiting expenditures to the amount of annual income. Tight-fisted chief commissioner Jimmy Jones concurred, saying: "I am as much in favor of relief for the unemployables as anyone, but I am unwilling to continue this relief at the expense of bankrupting the City of Birmingham." At the same time, Jones expressed his opposition to federal government involvement in local relief matters, especially in his own bailiwick. He wrote to Senator Robert M. La Follette, Jr.: "We do not favor a Federal appropriation to assist local governments in meeting their emergency relief burdens. We believe that this is a matter to be handled locally and that the Federal Government has troubles sufficient of its own to fully engage its entire attention."[20]

Scrupulous municipal officials like Jones not only avoided shortfalls but often produced hefty surpluses at the end of the fiscal year. Houston ended 1935 with a $386,609 surplus and 1936 with a $75,000 cushion. In 1931 Dallas stood over $2.5 million in arrears. The newly instituted city manager government in its initial year trimmed the overdraft by more than $400,000. In its second year, city hall refunded the balance of the deficit, and the city maintained a cash surplus for the remainder of the decade. Such financial wizardry was possible only by cutting municipal workers' salaries from 5 to 20 percent and releasing hundreds of employees. New city manager John Edy refused to allocate funds for street paving or building a levee sewer along the Trinity River in downtown Dallas, despite repeated protests from the business community. Teachers received their monthly paychecks without interruption, but the sums decreased; in the 1931–32 school year, for example, teacher salaries averaged $1,669, but in the 1932–33 year, only $1,463. The Dallas Board of Education reduced the number of faculty by demanding the automatic resignations of married women teachers.[21]

Elsewhere, cities instituted drastic measures to ensure that they would operate in the black. Birmingham municipal employees fortunate enough to keep their jobs absorbed two salary cuts of 10 percent each by 1932 and periodically received payment in scrip. The city's public health program virtually ceased to function, and public education suffered continuous cuts in funding. The Houston city council adopted 5- and 10-percent reductions for municipal workers within a few weeks in 1932. Many employees, including the city's prosecutor and purchasing agent, lost their jobs, and the city council saved money by turning off half the street lights at night. When the city treasury accumulated a half-million-dollar surplus by the end of that year, the city council voted to turn the street lights back on.[22]

Southern cities frequently found themselves at the mercy of local banking communities, who dictated budget alterations as prerequisites for loans. Powerful bankers not only mandated the amount of budget cuts but also recommended which positions should be eliminated and whose salaries should be trimmed. The Houston *Post-Dispatch* defended the bankers' expanding influence, saying: "In view of the obligations already due them by the city, the bankers are not to blame for demanding rigid economy on the part of the city as a condition precedent to further loans." A nettled Mayor Monteith protested sarcastically: "Of course, we could fire all the policemen and let the people carry arms and try to protect themselves. We could discharge all the firemen and let the insurance rates swallow the city. We could nail up the front door of city hall and go home—but we are not going to." The city did make the necessary cuts to satisfy the bankers, though.[23]

Meanwhile, southern cities limited their efforts on behalf of the unemployed to inexpensive—and ultimately ineffective—schemes to create temporary jobs. In Memphis the Mayor's Commission on Unemployment underwrote the "buy-an-apple" campaign, in which eighty men sold fresh produce on downtown street corners. According to the appreciative *Commercial Appeal,* an enterprising salesman could obtain a box of apples for $2.75, sell three boxes a day for a total of $9.00, and net a tidy profit of 75 cents. In 1930 New Orleans mayor T. Semmes Walmsley introduced his primary measure to relieve the distress of the needy, an orange-selling campaign. The city selected a number of destitute persons and authorized them to buy boxes of oranges for $2.70 apiece. By charging five cents for two oranges, the sellers could turn a 100-percent profit. The city reported that thirty-five licensed vendors sold 512 boxes a day and proclaimed the endeavor a smashing success. In Savannah, Georgia, the mayor urged fishermen to donate part of their catch to the indigent, and in Oklahoma City Alfalfa Bill Murray provided ten unemployed men one-half acre each on the gubernatorial front lawn to grow vegetables. Such modest programs left most southerners unaffected.[24]

Despite the evidence of hardship and suffering around them, city officials continued to express concern that their constituents not think the city did too much for the poor. When Memphis in 1935 became the last major southern city to create a permanent welfare department, the organization's charter clearly prohibited the spending of local revenue: it would, instead, facilitate efforts among federal, state, and private agencies. "It is not," Mayor Watkins Overton assured the citizens of Memphis, "an organization for using tax money to buy groceries." In New Orleans, to guard against "boondoggling" and "extravagant living" by those on the relief rolls, Mayor Walmsley and other high city officials regularly visited the homes of the needy. They questioned members of families receiving aid about their condition and took special note of the applicants' appearance and whether they owned automobiles. As a result of unfavorable interviews, some destitute families, including at least one judged "desperately in need" by a federal investigator, lost their stipends. The city's frugal relief policies extended even to an intense scrutiny of each individual case.[25]

Relief recipients in Birmingham accepted payment in "food checks" for canned tomatoes, dried beans, potatoes, rice, milk, and shortening. Officials felt that cash might be squandered on nonessentials like liquor and tobacco. Such paternalism sparked protests by relief recipients, who marched on city hall several times. On one such occasion an estimated seven thousand demonstrators congregated outside the county courthouse, while a delegation presented their complaints to chief commissioner Jimmy Jones. The meeting broke up amid insults and recriminations, as Jones ordered police to disperse the courthouse assemblage. A struggle ensued, and several suffered injuries. Jones's intransigence and parsimony led to talk of his removal from office, but no recall movement developed. The chief commissioner continued to manage the affairs of Birmingham in a miserly fashion.[26]

Although variations existed among southern cities, a pattern of municipal response to the Depression emerged. Chief executives formed ad hoc mayor's commissions to coordinate relief efforts. Typically these commissions lasted for a short time and, hamstrung by limited resources, achieved little success. When the cities dispensed relief, they did so sparingly and often in a grudging and condescending manner—distributing food rather than cash and carefully assessing the personal life-styles of relief applicants. The refusal to spend more on indigent care stemmed from the obsession with balanced municipal budgets. Local banks exerted pressure on city halls to spend within their means; the most influential bankers determined whether city bonds could be issued and demanded salary cuts as well as layoffs for municipal employees. Detroit mayor Frank Murphy, himself committed to orthodox fiscal policies, nevertheless argued that balancing the budget was "only an objective. It isn't a god, a sacred thing that is to be accomplished at all costs. It is not right to shatter living conditions and bring human beings to want and misery to achieve such an objective. . . . To sacrifice everything to balance the budget is fanaticism." Most southern mayors disagreed, however, establishing a remarkable record of avoiding budget deficits by cutting back on services and even in some instances stockpiling surpluses.[27]

The paucity of relief led to occasional public demonstrations and demands for more aid by worried citizens. On March 6, 1930, over six hundred men and women marched to Houston's city hall to protest unemployment and urge recognition of the Soviet Union. When Atlanta's Emergency Relief Center closed its doors in June 1932, more than one thousand protesters convened at Fulton County Courthouse to demand relief. In New Orleans over twenty thousand persons demonstrated in 1932 for "beer and prosperity." Such gatherings occurred in southern cities throughout the 1930s, but little violence ensued from them. Often municipal governments dealt forcefully with demonstrations: in Birmingham in June 1930 police arrested speakers and dispersed a crowd estimated at two hundred. Birmingham newspapers reported no subsequent mass meetings. The relative lack of protest may well be explained by what one observer noted in Dallas: "What seems to have happened . . . is that the people have not been made angry, they have been made apathetic. They have the feeling that all will be well and that their leaders will take care of them."[28]

In the most noticeable exception to widespread quiescence, miners resorted to violence in Harlan County, Kentucky. Coal production there fell from 14,093,453 tons worth $24 million in 1929 to 9,338,951 tons worth $13.5 million in 1931; the average miner's annual income dropped from $1,235 to $749. During those years, 231 children in the county died of diseases traceable to malnutrition. When the mine companies implemented a 10-percent wage reduction in 1931, fatalistic miners decided that they "might just as well die fighting as die of starvation." The ensuing struggle between the United Mine Workers and the operators resulted in thirteen deaths. Harlan County sheriff John Henry Blair openly admitted, "I did all in my power to aid the coal operators." Kentucky governor Flem Sampson deployed the National Guard to prevent picketing. Not surprisingly, the UMW strike failed, as did one called the following year by the Communist-affiliated National Miners Union. Labor militancy produced no immediate improvements for Harlan County miners.[29]

With municipal governments playing a limited role, it fell to the communities' citizens to expand philanthropic activities in existing agencies or organize whatever temporary organizations they could to meet the crisis. Community chests increased their budgets and intensified their fund-raising campaigns but found the going increasingly difficult. Certainly hard times curtailed giving by those fortunate enough to keep their jobs, but much of the resistance experienced by social workers stemmed from firmly entrenched ideological objections to the "dole." For whatever reasons, contributions frequently proved disappointing. When, for example, New Orleans mayor Walmsley sent out two thousand letters to the city's wealthy launching a charity drive, he collected only six hundred dollars for his efforts. When maverick clergyman William Jacobs of the First Presbyterian Church of Houston suggested that the city's problems could be alleviated if twenty or thirty millionaires donated five thousand dollars each, Dr. E.B. West, pastor of the Second Baptist Church, exclaimed: "I do not believe a more dangerous doctrine has ever been preached in a pulpit in Houston." An American Public Welfare Association survey concluded that "analysis of Community Chest giving in Dallas . . . indicates an unusually small proportion, both in number and amount, of gifts, by individuals as compared with business firms and corporations. . . . This is not to indicate that business firms and corporations in Dallas give too much to the Community Chest. Some should give much more." The Dallas *Morning News* editorialized: "The richest of the rich in Dallas have fallen down on the task. They have shirked in the face of the winter's desperate need."[30]

While the level of individual contributions remained disappointingly low, concerned citizens conceived of money-making schemes and alternative relief sources. At best stopgap measures, they never became more than palliatives characterized by their modest goals and limited scope. For example, Houstonian Will Horowitz, owner of three second-run movie theaters, offered a plea before each feature presentation for potential employers in the audience to aid the jobless. Each Friday he presented a Tin Can Matinee, at which anyone presenting a tin of canned food was admitted free; the two thousand cans of food collected on an average Friday were distributed to the needy. Horowitz erected a mammoth tent near Sam Houston Hall, in which he operated a free employment bureau, and during the winter of 1930–31 he sponsored the Grub Stake, serving meals to as many as nine hundred persons a day. William Jacobs operated a soup kitchen at his rectory, despite protests from city leaders who found Jacobs's open display of charity "disgraceful" and thought relief should be dispensed more discreetly.[31]

In Atlanta a clergyman organized the Cooperative Exchange Club, where work could be exchanged for goods. Georgia governor Eugene Talmadge and the Atlanta Retail Merchants Association endorsed the program, and thirty firms enlisted. The local Rotary Club touted a "two-men-in-one-job" plan that would allow men to share a position, each working three days a week. Wealthy Atlanta socialite Mrs. T.K. Glen started the "penny drive" as a hobby: in all restaurants and soda fountains, patrons gave a penny tip for each meal, and the funds were used to feed transients at various stations throughout the city. Georgia Bell Telephone Company vice-president Kendall Weisiger published a pamphlet, *Feeding Your Family*, which gave instructions on the preparation of cheap, nutritious meals and which the Community Chest distributed. Atlanta theater operators sponsored Sunday Movies for Charity, which earned $1,500 each Sunday, in violation of a city ordinance barring charity work on the Sabbath. Mayor James Key vetoed a city council resolution directing police to arrest theater operators ignoring the ordinance, but pressure by the Atlanta Evangelical Ministers' Association and the Christian Council resulted in arrests, fines, and the discontinuance of Sunday fund-raising efforts.[32]

Many concerned urbanites felt that the cure for the Depression lay in vanquishing the region's agricultural problems. Beginning in the summer of 1932 the Atlanta Chamber of Commerce sponsored a "back-to-the-farm" initiative by moving volunteer white families to rural Georgia. By the following year only forty-five families had been resettled, and the chamber terminated the program because of a lack of money for supplies. A more extensive effort developed in Memphis, where the *Commercial Appeal* suggested that an assault on the one-crop economy, cotton, would compel farmers to raise food and lead to greater self-sufficiency. In 1934 the newspaper and the chamber of commerce launched a contest, called Plant to Prosper, in which the winning farmers in several categories earned cash, emblems, and certificates of merit. In the first year 1,780 farmers, cultivating 469,000 acres of land, entered the contest. By 1940 more than 50,000 had participated, and the project's founders could boast that the overwhelmingly successful program, the subject of several magazine articles, had been copied in other parts of the country and abroad.[33]

Dallas, home of the world's largest spot cotton market, suffered as the market slackened; in 1926–27 the Dallas Cotton Exchange handled 3,141,997 bales, but by 1929–30, only 1,527,489 bales. In June 1931 the city declared a "cotton week," and the major downtown stores exhibited cotton bales to stimulate the purchase of the product. Memphis businessmen's concern with low cotton prices led to another Depression-era innovation, Cotton Carnival. Based on the Mardi Gras celebrations in New Orleans, Mobile, and Pensacola, it could not claim, as the others did, to have any particular religious significance. From the outset Cotton Carnival was solely a business venture designed to stimulate interest in the commodity at a time when market prices had fallen drastically. It failed to elevate the price of cotton, but as a symbolic event Cotton Carnival assumed a significant role. Conceived by wealthy businessmen, it became the best-known and certainly the most generously endowed community response to the Depression. A lavish spectacle closed to all but a few wellborn insiders, the pageant struck many citizens as an insensitive display of wealth at a time of widespread misery. Moreover, its goal of elevating cotton prices defined recovery in terms that only advanced the city's wealthy cotton interests. Although it could be argued that the carnival's "trickle-down" effect could benefit all the people, the widely noted inattention of the elites to philanthropy raised doubts about altruism as a motive.[34]

In Birmingham privately funded relief fell traditionally to the Red Cross Family Service and to the major industrial firms that, by the early 1930s, were forced to lay off workers. In thousands of cases, steel companies aided the unemployed by reducing rent on company housing, extending credit at the company commissary, and providing free fuel: all this was done with the expectation that when workers returned to the job, the cost of the companies' beneficence would be deducted from their paychecks. The Tennessee Coal and

Iron Company's Department of Social Science administered an extensive relief operation so closely connected to the city government that Public Welfare Department head Roberta Morgan designated TCI's relief administrator an official city agent. Moreover, community directors distributed federally provided commodities such as flour and cloth through the commissaries. Unfortunately for TCI's employees, however, its expenditures for relief dwindled sharply as the decade passed.[35]

The inadequacy of individual efforts was manifest in southern communities. With local leaders closely adhering to a policy of low taxes, limited expenditures, and balanced budgets, the urban poor turned hopeful eyes to state capitals. They received little succor. Many states had gotten caught up in the speculative mania of the 1920s and had mortgaged their futures to fund extensive construction projects. When Mississippi governor Theodore Bilbo left office in 1932, the state stood fourteen million dollars in arrears, and its treasury contained a total of one thousand dollars. In the worst case, Arkansas governor John Martineau committed his state's resources to fund an ambitious highway construction program. According to Martineau's plan, anticipated revenue would pay the interest on the bonds, worth a total of $160 million. Projected revenues failed to materialize, and by 1932 Arkansas's per-capita debt, the highest in the nation, undermined all recovery efforts. The state defaulted. In 1934 the Arkansas legislature finally adopted a refunding plan designed to complete payment of principal—but not necessarily interest—to all bondholders by 1977.[36]

Other southern states escaped such catastrophes by applying stringent economy measures. The Texas legislature cut appropriations 21 percent, and North Carolina cut salaries and other expenses to reduce the operating costs of government by seven million dollars. Governors in Alabama, Georgia, Louisiana, Tennessee, and Texas all created emergency welfare commissions but distributed no funds to ailing cities. The commissions studied conditions and compiled data, but economic exigencies forestalled any meaningful action. In 1932 Mississippi adopted a 2-percent general sales tax, becoming the first state to opt for regressive taxation as a funding source. Its great success—Mississippi officials estimated that revenue increased 25 percent—led Kentucky, North Carolina, and Oklahoma to adopt similar levies. Revenue shortfalls and laws requiring balanced budgets left states with no opportunity to aid cities. By late 1932 state governments participated in the distribution of federal funds to communities, but their activity depended upon

President Herbert Hoover's provision of relief. With state resources so limited, the federal government became the last resort.[37]

Herbert Hoover maintained a cautious distance from relief plans for the states, touting the virtues of decentralized government, individual initiative, and fiscal orthodoxy. Southerners generally approved of Hoover's prudent policies—at least during the initial years of the Depression. After Alabama senator Smith W. Brookhart proposed a fifty-million-dollar federal provision for unemployment relief, the Houston *Post-Dispatch* rejoined: "It is not an obligation of government to furnish citizens with employment. Government should not enter upon any enterprise for the purpose of supplying jobs, even though there may be many persons in need of work." The Dallas *Morning News* agreed: "The News has steadfastly set its face against tin-cup-and-blue-goggles trips to Washington for 'relief' for Texans." The Memphis *Commercial Appeal* intoned: "The Commercial Appeal long ago took the position that two objectives were necessary to put business back on its feet in this country: 1. Reduce the cost of government. 2. Get the government out of business. . . . This government cannot exist with one-half of the people paying taxes to keep up the other half."[38]

As the Depression worsened, however, ambivalence surfaced among southerners formerly in accord with Hoover's restrained approach. Alabama congressman William Bankhead observed that the times dictated a revision of the old bias against relief, and Texas congressman Wright Patman proposed early payment of bonuses due World War I veterans in 1945. The Memphis *Commercial Appeal*, calling Hoover's performance "disappointing," remained vague on what steps the federal government should take and continued to urge limited involvement. Nevertheless, it recognized the need for federally funded public works as an emergency measure. Fears of spendthrift policies by government remained, but frustration over Hoover's inability to vanquish the Depression bred disenchantment and criticism.[39]

Recent scholarship has absolved Hoover of much of the opprobrium he bore for supposedly doing nothing while millions of Americans suffered. Historians have shown that he did far more to offset economic difficulties than had any previous president and, within certain constraints imposed by his ideological beliefs, developed a substantial number of innovative new programs to induce recovery. Ultimately, of course, his efforts were decidedly inadequate, better remembered for their limitations than their originality. For example, Hoover created the President's Organization for Unemployment Relief (POUR) to oversee local welfare efforts. POUR advised local charity groups, disseminated information, promoted philanthropy, and exhorted citizens to greater effort—in short, did virtually everything but provide aid for the destitute. POUR chose businessmen like Coca Cola's Robert Woodruff, rather than social work professionals, to direct state and municipal programs. Well-intentioned though it may have been, POUR proved to be ineffectual and contributed to Hoover's deteriorating reputation.[40]

Hoover's primary recovery agency, the Reconstruction Finance Corporation (RFC), lent money to banks, insurance companies, railroads, and other huge corporations. As these industrial giants invested the money, expanded their operations, and thereby created new jobs, workers and smaller businesses supposedly would benefit as well. Theoretically sound, the RFC never provided the spark the economy required—at least in part because embattled corporate executives hoarded the government funds or paid off existing obligations rather than investing the capital. More damaging, the funds made available to the RFC were hardly adequate after several years of steadily worsening economic conditions.

On July 21, 1932, in his boldest departure from past practices, Hoover signed the Emergency Relief and Reconstruction Act, which provided $300 million to the RFC for loans to the states and cities and $322 million for federal public works. Tennessee senator Kenneth D. McKellar, a Democratic stalwart and persistent Hoover critic, called the measure "the greatest pork barrel that was ever established in the history of time." In principle, at least, many southerners agreed with McKellar's statement that "the real remedy and the only remedy is to live within our income," but officials wasted no time in applying for the federal aid. By the spring of 1933 Louisiana received $7,602,506 from the RFC, with Texas ($5,513,089), Kentucky ($5,162,166), and North Carolina ($5,074,000) close behind. Just months before, Birmingham chief city commissioner Jimmy Jones had adduced that "we do not favor a Federal appropriation to assist local governments in meeting emergency burdens," but when Alabama governor B. A. Miller reacted slowly, the Steel City's commission moved on its own. Birmingham obtained RFC loans, quickly followed by New Orleans and Atlanta. For the remainder of 1932 RFC funds enabled southern cities to retain family assistance programs and to initiate small work relief projects. The funds provided by the Emergency Relief and Reconstruction Act remained sparse, however, and the RFC distributed them slowly in small increments. The major Hoover recovery initiatives were justly deemed "too little, too late."[41]

Nor did Hoover's farm policies achieve notable success. The Agricultural Marketing Act created a Federal Farm Board empowered to lend up to five hundred million dollars to farm cooperatives and to purchase agricultural surpluses. When prices remained low, the Farm Board urged farmers to induce scarcity artificially by destroying a portion of their crops—by plowing under every third row of cotton, for example. Reluctant to demand mandatory production controls for fear of undermining American individualism, Hoover stood by as farmers opted not to reduce production and harvested bumper crops. As a consequence, the Agricultural Marketing Act failed. The Hawley-Smoot Tariff signed by Hoover in 1930 raised duties on both manufactured goods and farm commodities to record levels. Three-fourths of the southerners in Congress voted against the measure, concerned that agriculture would not fare as well as manufacturing. As many economists feared, other nations met the Hawley-Smoot Tariff with higher barriers of their own, and within two years American exports declined by 50 percent.[42]

By 1932 southerners detested Herbert Hoover and thought his policies thoroughly discredited. In the solid South, the only question was what lucky Democrat would be supported against the incumbent in that year's presidential election. Candidates like Governor Albert Ritchie of Maryland, Speaker of the U.S. House of Representatives John Nance Garner of Texas, Senator Harry F. Byrd of Virginia, and Oklahoma governor Alfalfa Bill Murray garnered some support as "favorite sons," but New York governor Franklin D. Roosevelt quickly emerged as the candidate with the greatest appeal throughout the region. Unlike fellow New Yorker Al Smith, Roosevelt courted southerners, reminding them that his home in Warm Springs, Georgia, made him a "part-time southerner." Whereas Smith's Lower East Side Irish brogue offended southern listeners and his incessant parochialism about New York City seemed almost designed to rankle outlanders west of the Hudson River, Roosevelt parlayed his rural upbringing in the Hudson Valley into a widespread popularity among a largely agricultural people in the South. Roosevelt's stand on the still important issue of prohibition—he was "damp," favoring state option—made him far more acceptable than Smith, who maintained an unyielding alliance with the party's "wets."[43]

Roosevelt's nomination in 1932 met with widespread approbation in the South, even more so because of his selection of Garner for vice-president. One proud Texan even referred to a "kangaroo ticket," because it was "stronger in the hind quarter than in the front." Even though he could surely count on the electoral support of the southern states, Roosevelt campaigned widely there. Mostly he spoke in vague generalities and affirmed his commitment to "Jeffersonian democracy." The campaign orations lacked specifics, but as historian Frank Freidel noted: "Most Southern politicians interested in Roosevelt were attracted less by what he had to say than by his personal charm and his strategic position within the party." Roosevelt's election brought hope to southerners. They had been on his bandwagon from the start, voted for him in decisive numbers, and invested considerably in his candidacy. The South, like the rest of the nation, knew little about what the "new deal" held for them. But after twelve years of Republican presidents and four years of Depression, southerners looked to the future with renewed optimism.[44]

3

FROM SHARECROPPING TO AGRIBUSINESS

> With one hand the cotton landlord takes agricultural subsidies and rental benefits from his government, with the other he pushes his tenants on relief.
>
> —Rupert Vance, 1934

In 1930 fewer than half of southern farmers owned the land they tilled. In 1935, 1,831,470 tenant farmers worked in the South, approximately 63 percent of the nation's total. Contrary to widespread belief, not all tenants and sharecroppers were black. True, 77 percent of black farmers worked on other people's land, but so did 45 percent of southern whites. In Mississippi 70 percent of farmers were tenants. By the end of the Depression decade, however, land ownership patterns—and indeed, southern agriculture itself—looked unmistakably different. The economic conditions of the 1930s along with a plethora of New Deal programs accelerated a number of changes begun earlier in the century. Land consolidation, mechanization, the introduction of new crops, and the displacement of a large segment of the rural work force led to an enclosure movement in the South. By the time all these changes were complete in midcentury, the face of southern farming appeared markedly transformed. Historian Pete Daniel observed: "Neither those who left nor their neighbors who stayed behind shared the traditional relations with landlords that had typified southern rural life since the Reconstruction Era."[1]

The farm problem confronting Franklin D. Roosevelt in the spring of 1933 was serious indeed. In that year farmers still made up 30 percent of the nation's work force, and their situation had been deteriorating for more than a decade. By the early 1930s the situation was worsening at a swifter pace, for by the time of Roosevelt's election farmers earned 60 percent less for their products than they had before the stock market crash. In the South the extreme reliance on a few crops and the refusal to diversify contributed to glutted markets and depressed prices. The South's dearth of urban markets, in conjunction with the shortage of transportation and storage facilities for perishable commodities, made the sale of fruit, vegetables, and dairy products problematic and discouraged diversification. Inundated with a host of crop reduction schemes, cotton farmers still planted over 38 million acres in 1932 (compared with 41 million acres in 1931). Although they acknowledged the logic of diversification, commercial farmers continued to rely on the crop that had sustained the South for centuries. After all, was it wise to alter radically their farming practices in such a foreboding economic climate and with other commodity prices uniformly low? As conditions continued to worsen, most southern farmers resolutely planted what they had always grown and hoped for the best.[2]

Meanwhile, southern farmers suffered horribly. According to a 1934 survey in South Carolina, Alabama, Mississippi, and Texas supervised by famed sociologist Charles S. Johnson, few sharecroppers had earned cash income since the First World War. Those who had in 1933 earned an average of $105.43 per family annually. Landlords exploited their labor's cash shortage by operating commissaries as extortionate as the worst Appalachian coal company stores. These emporiums charged usurious interest rates ranging from 10 to 60 percent and, instead of legal tender, issued scrip, metal tokens, or coupon books. A Prince Edward County, Virginia, farmer reported that hundreds of families subsisted wholly on fatback and corn meal and that a good number lived day-to-day on food donated by the county or the Red Cross. "For God's sake give us work to do so we will not live by begging," he quoted the unfortunates as saying. "We've got to do something."[3] In a letter to Department of Agriculture secretary Henry A. Wallace, an observer described the living conditions among South Carolina tobacco farmers: "I have seen mothers go from the curing barns late in the night, worn out and exhausted, their small children sleepy and pitiful, and crying like hungry pigs following the sow. I have seen men, strong men, bow down between the tobacco rows, like an inverted V, cropping in the August sun with not a dry thread on them. I have seen them faint from overheat and dragged from the field on a tobacco drag."[4]

Most farmers accepted their fate with grim resignation, tightening their belts, scrimping to get by, and leaving peacefully if booted off the land for failure to make payments. Mortgage foreclosures and evictions came with alarming frequency; in Meriwether County, Georgia, for example, 80 percent of farms were mortgaged. A writer for the Scripps-Howard newspaper chain reported having seen "thousands" of uprooted sharecroppers throughout the South, "lonely figures without money, without homes, and without hope." A minority resisted, erecting barricades on farm roads to prevent trucks from getting to market, massing to halt evictions and foreclosure auctions, and threatening law enforcement officers attempting to act on behalf of creditors. Especially in midwestern states, farmers banded together in organizations like the Farmers' Holiday Association and the Farmers' Union to challenge—with force, if necessary—the figures of authority who threatened to take land away. Largely because of tenancy's legacy, southern farmers reacted more stoically and shunned activism. Nevertheless, Edward O'Neal of Alabama, president of the American Farm Bureau Federation, warned in January 1933 that "unless something is done for the American farmer, we will have a revolution in the country-side in less than 12 months."[5]

In Washington the president and members of Congress took note of the worsening farm crisis and moved urgently to forestall a growing militancy. On March 16, 1933, Roosevelt sent to Capitol Hill an omnibus agriculture bill based largely on the domestic allotment program advocated by Montana State College professor M. L. Wilson. Unlike the McNary-Haugen bills of the 1920s, which called for high import tariffs on agricultural products and the federal government's sale of surpluses abroad, the domestic allotment plan provided for voluntary production cuts in return for government price subsidies. The Agricultural Adjustment Act included marketing agreements and export subsidies to mollify the McNary-Haugenites but primarily relied on allotment payments to farmers funded by taxes on the processors of farm products. The bill also contained an emergency farm mortgage act and the Thomas Amendment, an inflationary measure authorizing the president to remonetize silver. Unlike earlier New Deal legislation of the Hundred Days, which Congress had rubber-stamped with only perfunctory attention to detail, the farm bill sparked prolonged discussion. Montana senator Burton K. Wheeler predicted that the measure would aid the "commuting farmer" but not the "dirt farmer," while others balked at the amount of government involvement in the independent farmer's enterprise. After several weeks of debate the farm bill passed, by a margin of 315 to 98 in the House and 64 to 20 in the Senate.[6]

Southerners in Congress generally supported the farm bill, although not without reservations. Marvin Jones of Texas, chairman of the House Agriculture Committee, declined to sponsor the bill, but in the Senate John H. Bankhead, Jr., of Alabama did so with alacrity. Many southerners, including Senator Elmer Thomas of Oklahoma and Representative John Rankin of Mississippi, insisted on inflationary measures, and Roosevelt finally agreed to the inclusion of an amendment giving the president such discretionary powers. The Agricultural Adjustment Act signed by the president on May 12 provided for voluntary acreage reduction in seven "basic commodities," including cotton, rice, and tobacco. Participating farmers would receive benefit payments to restore them to "parity," the level of purchasing power enjoyed by cotton and rice farmers in the flush years of 1909–14 and tobacco farmers in 1919–29.[7]

The Agricultural Adjustment Administration (AAA), unlike many other New Deal agencies that operated independently and reported directly to the president, was situated within the Department of Agriculture and answered to the secretary of agriculture, Henry A. Wallace. The son of a former agriculture secretary, Wallace had edited the family newspaper, *Wallace's Farmer*, and had earned a reputation as an expert in crop genetics and soil science. A native of Iowa, he knew most about corn and hog production. The AAA's chief administrator, George N. Peek, had become an agriculturalist as an executive of the John Deere and Moline Plow companies. A longtime advocate of McNary-Haugenism, Peek reluctantly accepted domestic allotment and never completely reconciled himself to crop reduction. Like Wallace, he too had little firsthand knowledge of the problems unique to southern agriculture, but the administration did not lack for highly placed southerners looking out for the region's interests. Cully A. Cobb, editor of *Southern Ruralist*, the Georgia-Alabama version of *Progressive Farmer*, became chief of the AAA's Cotton Production Control Section, and Oscar Johnston, manager of the Delta and Pine Land plantation in Mississippi, reputedly the South's largest, was named AAA finance director. Moreover, southerners chaired the agriculture committees in both houses of Congress—Marvin Jones in the House and Ellison ("Cotton Ed") Smith of South Carolina in the Senate.[8]

The AAA's creation in May, long after spring planting in the South, forced Cully Cobb to call for an emergency plow-up of cotton well into the growing season. The need for immediate action necessitated the cotton division's utilization of the only existing organization capable of overseeing such activity, the Agricultural Extension Service. The AAA's attachment to county extension agents and their allies, the farm bureaus and land grant colleges, unavoidably set the agency on a political course tied to the region's conservative agricultural interests. The administration's reliance on the Extension Service later caused considerable consternation among the South's have-nots, but in the late spring of 1933 the twenty-two thousand workers deployed to the task signed thousands of farmers to production limitation agreements, calculated acreage restrictions, supervised plow-ups, and confirmed compliance reports. Many planters complained about government intrusion, but they readily followed the AAA's lead and overcame their reservations enough to accept benefit payments. Perhaps the greatest obstacle came from mules trained too well to avoid the cotton rows; ingenious farmers hitched two mules together with a plow carried between them, so that the animals walking between the rows as usual dragged the plow over the sprouting plants. In 1933 the AAA paid farmers $161,771,697 to remove 10,487,991 acres of cotton from production, reducing the yield by an estimated 4,489,467 bales.[9]

Despite the remarkable success of the plow-up effort, the summer continued to be an anxious time for cotton planters. Prices shot up in July to 11 cents per pound but fell at harvest time to an average of 9.72 cents. Although AAA efforts removed one-fourth of the cotton crop, favorable weather produced yet another bumper yield. Bureaucratic snafus delayed the subsidy checks expectant farmers eagerly awaited to get them through the summer, and benefits failed to arrive in most locations until mid-November. In the meantime, Roosevelt experimented with various currency inflation methods, purchasing silver and altering the gold content of the dollar. The AAA also quelled criticism by distributing millions of pounds of surplus pork and other foodstuffs to needy farmers through the Federal Surplus Relief Corporation, but by the end of summer the first attempt at agricultural adjustment in cotton appeared to have had relatively little effect on prices.[10]

Relief for cotton farmers came in October with the establishment of the Commodity Credit Corporation (CCC) within the Reconstruction Finance Corporation (RFC). Following the suggestion of Oscar Johnston, the CCC lent farmers ten cents a pound on their yield, with the cotton itself as security against the loan. In 1933 alone the CCC lent $160 million on 4.3 million cotton bales, and the program worked so well that it expanded to include other commodities in subsequent years under the aegis of the Agriculture Department. In April 1934 Congress passed the Bankhead Cotton Control Act in response to an overwhelming endorsement of compulsory marketing controls. The measure provided that, with the consent of at least two-thirds of cotton growers in a referendum, producers would be taxed at the rate of 50 percent of the market price for all crops ginned in excess of their allotment. With the Bankhead controls renewed for the 1935 growing season as well, the New Deal cotton program took shape.[11]

AAA programs for tobacco and rice developed along similar lines, although neither crop required a plow-up in 1933. Like cotton growers, farmers raising tobacco recognized that overproduction and a decline in foreign markets combined to drive prices down, but they could not implement acreage reduction. A marketing agreement signed in October 1933 obligated domestic buyers to purchase as much tobacco as they had during the previous year at an average price of seventeen cents per pound, and 95 percent of producers signed acreage limitation agreements the next year. The Kerr-Smith Tobacco Control Act of 1934, a companion to the Bankhead Act, provided for 25-33-percent taxes on sales of the commodity in excess of production quotas. Repeatedly during the decade, an overwhelming percentage of tobacco growers voted for mandatory quotas, a reflection of the success the program enjoyed in restoring prices to parity levels (approximately eighteen cents per pound). By 1936, for example, Kentucky tobacco growers reduced their harvests 28 percent after passage of the Kerr-Smith Act and increased their incomes by seven million dollars. As historian Anthony J. Badger noted: "In no other major commodity were the benefits of the New Deal in terms of prices and cash receipts for the crop seen so tangibly or quickly."[12]

In a much healthier economic situation than either cotton or tobacco growers, rice farmers required less drastic controls in the 1930s. After the World War I market collapsed, rice growers reduced production and accelerated the pace of mechanization. In 1933–34 the AAA's Rice Section introduced marketing agreements, in 1935 a processing tax. In all instances, prices remained high, and parity proved readily attainable. In 1934 the AAA added sugarcane and peanuts to the list of crops eligible for government benefits and in later years added watermelons, strawberries, citrus fruits, canned foods, and other kinds of nuts.[13]

In its initial months of operation the AAA succeeded in raising prices on commodities produced in the South and elsewhere. The slaughter of hogs elevated the price of pork approximately 15 percent, and less substantial increases appeared in wheat and corn prices. Such encouraging developments did not, however, defuse a festering problem within the AAA's bureaucracy, a conflict revolving to a great extent around southern agricultural practices. At the core of the contretemps stood two groups of administrators who differed violently on the nature of the AAA's mandate. The first group, led by George Peek, contended that "the sole aim" of the agency was "to raise farm prices" and nothing more. Arrayed with Peek, a number of old hands in the Department of Agriculture, trained in the land grant colleges and imbued with the gospel according to the Extension Service, scoffed at the younger New Dealers infesting Washington with their broader reform agendas. The traditionalists' narrowly defined charge contrasted starkly with the goal of sweeping agricultural planning as propounded by Secretary Wallace and Undersecretary Rexford G. Tugwell.[14]

Peek, Johnston, Cobb, and their allies clashed often with Jerome Frank, the liberal head of the AAA's legal division, and the covey of young attorneys working for him that included Alger Hiss, Lee Pressman, Adlai E. Stevenson, Thurman Arnold, Abe Fortas, Gardner Jackson, and Francis Shea. Peek despaired of the sweeping social reform these Young Turks sought, because he failed to see how it could expedite recovery for most farmers. Peek feared, in fact, that it would retard economic progress. Noting these liberals' urban backgrounds and elite university educations, he dismissed their knowledge of agriculture as superficial and shallow. Moreover, like others in the agriculture establishment, Peek feared that attempts at social upheaval would endanger the support of the farming elites, without whose participation AAA programs would surely fail. For their part, the AAA liberals saw the Great Depression as an unprecedented opportunity to root out the evils of entrenched privilege and uplift the lower classes of farmers. Nowhere could a blow better be struck for poor farmers than in the South, where large landowners controlled a disproportionate share of wealth and sharecroppers, tenant farmers, and farm workers struggled to make ends meet.[15]

The AAA's civil war escalated in September 1933, precipitated by a struggle over the flue-cured tobacco contract. The liberals in the legal division demanded access to tobacco producers' financial records and the authority to set commodity prices, while Peek argued that these activities far exceeded the scope of AAA activities. Roosevelt finally interceded in favor of Peek but refused to remove Jerome Frank and his allies. The infighting continued, with Peek clashing with Wallace, Tugwell, and Frank about a number of agency matters. Finally the president asked the AAA chief to resign. Peek's replacement, Chester Davis, proved less irascible than his predecessor but differed just as strongly with the sweeping changes advocated by the reformers in the legal division.[16]

The final resolution of the struggle for power and the agency's direction resulted from a dispute about the AAA's treatment of labor on cotton farms in the South. The liberals were especially interested in improving the circumstances of tenants and share-croppers, able workers whose impoverished condition shocked New Deal reformers. Later in the Roosevelt years the President's Commission on Farm Tenancy charged that 25 percent of the nation's farmers—and a much larger percentage in the South—lived in such squalor that chronic malnutrition, malaria, pellagra, hook-worm, and other "filth diseases" predominated. In 1934, for example, a public health official reported 250,000 cases of hookworm and 80,000-90,000 cases of malaria in Florida. Here seemed a golden opportunity for the AAA to reform agriculture in a way that would benefit millions of powerless laborers.[17]

Because the greatest federal subsidies went to the farmers able to take the most land out of production, large landholders prospered most. "It takes money to make money," lamented one small land-owner. "Now I can never get ahead because my farm is too durn small." With the 1933 AAA cotton contract virtually ignoring sharecroppers and tenants, landowners felt free to pay their workers as they saw fit. Frequently they deducted old debts from the current year's tally, so debtors seldom received any remuneration and remained as hopelessly bound to the landlord as ever. Tenants in Marked Tree, Arkansas, for example, complained that they received only one-third of the government payments due them from their landlords. Cully Cobb expressed regret but added that "the government did not dictate how landlords split the proceeds."[18]

Worse yet, the reduction in cultivated land resulted in less need for labor and a flurry of evictions, many of which came without warning. A sharecropper's wife in Henry County, Tennessee, complained that the landlord "didn't say a word about our crops we was about middle ways of. The move jist came on us before we could plan for it." Throughout the cotton belt, uprooted tenants and day laborers filled the roads in search of work. Eventually they came to rest in towns and cities, where they overwhelmed already saturated relief rolls. In the Southeast, beaten farmers streamed into the tex-tile villages, where their numbers contributed further to the labor surplus that depressed wages and kept hours distended. In its catering to the landed gentry, the liberals charged, the AAA was creating a rootless peasantry. But bypassing the landlords and distributing

benefit checks directly to sharecroppers and tenants, the course proposed by Frank and his acolytes, would challenge the southern social class alignment. Political titans like Cotton Ed Smith, Cully
Cobb, and Oscar Johnston spoke for the southern landlords in Washington, and the Agriculture Department recognized the need for cooperation with the southern farming establishment if the AAA was
to succeed.[19]

Committed to the concept of "grass-roots democracy," the AAA
arranged for grievances to be submitted to committees of county
agents familiar with local conditions. Invariably, cotton planters
dominated these committees, often in tandem with other members
of the local gentry, who sided with the landholders out of common
interest or friendship. The entire AAA bureaucracy, from county
agents to Cully Cobb, reflected a vested interest in landlords' welfare, and no one spoke for the usually inarticulate and frequently
illiterate sharecroppers. As a result, formal channels offered the
landless farmer scant hope for amelioration. An Alabama woman
expressed this frustration in a letter to Congressman William Bankhead: "Will you please answer if the tenant farmers are to[o] small
to get help from the New Deal? The big farmers . . . is the only ones
that have been profited in the last three years."[20]

The privations of the poor farmer came to national attention in
the 1930s because of the publication of a handful of widely read fic-
tional accounts and muckraking exposés. Erskine Caldwell's best-
selling books *Tobacco Road* and *God's Little Acre* luridly described
a sharecropper culture steeped in depravity, ignorance, and filth.
Painting the picture in more muted hues, Herbert Harrison Kroll's
Cabin in the Cotton and *I Was a Sharecropper* and Charlie May
Simon's *The Share-Cropper* contributed to the growing awareness of
southern rural poverty. At the end of the decade, John Steinbeck's
Grapes of Wrath and James Agee's *Let Us Now Praise Famous Men*
appeared, both portraying not only the sharecroppers' dire situation but also their dignity, courage, and honor. Americans sympa-
thized with the sturdy farmers who were suffering through no fault
of their own and cheered their indomitable will to survive. To
the chagrin of the federal government, scholarly examinations of
southern agriculture, like Charles S. Johnson's *The Shadow of the
Plantation* and Johnson, Edwin Embree, and Will Alexander's *The
Collapse of Cotton Tenancy*, detailed the AAA's leading role in up-
rooting poor farmers.[21]

Nothing brought the sharecroppers' sorry condition into the national limelight more than their own attempts at forming labor

unions. In 1932 the Communist party founded the Alabama Share-croppers' Union (ASU), whose membership grew to an estimated 5,500 within a year. Organized by white radicals, the rank and file quickly became overwhelmingly black, with few Communist party members. Because of the very real fear of persecution, union officers used pseudonyms and conducted much of the organization's business in secret. A shoot-out with sheriff's deputies in Tallapoosa County, which resulted in the wounding of one lawman and the incarceration of a black ASU member, brought headlines nationwide. Overall, however, the union enjoyed little success in its attempts to organize and bargain collectively, and it folded in 1945, long after losing much of its membership.[22]

With a large membership in several states, the Southern Tenant Farmers' Union (STFU) attracted much attention in the 1930s. At the urging of socialist Norman Thomas, eleven white men and seven black men in northeastern Arkansas banded together in July 1934 to protest an epidemic of layoffs and the failure of landowners to pass along a fair share of government benefits to workers. Under the leadership of H. L. Mitchell, a former sharecropper and small businessman, and Clay East, a service station owner and Tyronza, Arkansas, constable, the STFU admitted black as well as white workers. Its membership swelled to about thirty thousand in Arkansas, Missouri, Tennessee, Mississippi, and Oklahoma by 1935. In addition to Norman Thomas, the union received economic and moral support from other nationally prominent figures, like clergyman Reinhold Niebuhr and Oklahoma socialist Oscar Ameringer. In Washington wealthy New Deal liberal Gardner Jackson also took up the STFU's cause.[23]

Caught in the glare of national attention, Arkansas landlords and law enforcement officials reacted with violent retribution. Opposed to the union's biracialism as well as its economic radicalism, planters moved on several fronts to crush the movement. Landlords evicted union members, broke up meetings, brutally beat organizers, and hired spies to infiltrate the organization and undermine worker solidarity. Armed bands of landlords and hired guns chased union leaders across the Mississippi River to Memphis, Tennessee, where STFU headquarters relocated. Sheriffs and justices of the peace, many on landlords' payrolls, arrested prominent union leaders on such charges as anarchy and interfering with free labor. Undaunted, the STFU grew in membership, and public opinion turned against the reign of terror conducted by the planters and their supporters. The union affiliated with the United Cannery, Agricultural,

Packing and Allied Workers of America for several stormy years and, later, with the National Agricultural Workers' Union. Although it never succeeded in its negotiations with the landlords, the STFU made the sharecroppers' condition known to the entire country.[24]

AAA legal division liberals expressed an acute interest in the STFU's struggle. Alger Hiss led the battle within the federal agency to give greater protection to sharecroppers and tenant farmers in the 1934–35 cotton contracts, but Chester Davis, Cully Cobb, and Oscar Johnston countered his objections. Secretary Wallace publicly acknowledged the contract's inequities but reluctantly accepted it as the best that could be achieved. Reporting the findings of his study on cotton acreage reductions, Duke University professor Calvin B. Hoover ratified the STFU's charges of unfair treatment and scored the AAA for faulty enforcement; on the whole, however, he gave the cotton program high marks for its contributions to the southern economy. The 1934–35 contract again urged landlords to share proportionately with their hired labor but pointedly avoided specifics and prescribed no penalties for noncompliance.[25]

Although the AAA liberals failed to alter the agency's policy, southerners in Washington found the attempts at reforms intolerable. Wofford B. Camp, Cully Cobb's subordinate in the Cotton Section, convened a meeting of leading southern congressional leaders to discuss what could be done to silence Jerome Frank and his followers. A delegation including South Carolina senator Cotton Ed Smith, Mississippi senator Pat Harrison, Arkansas senator Joe Robinson, and South Carolina congressman H. P. Fulmer took their complaints to President Roosevelt, telling him that "no significant piece of legislation would come out of Congress until matters were resolved in the Department of Agriculture." Because of their seniority and placement in important committee chairmanships, these southerners had to be taken seriously.[26]

In February 1935 the AAA's legal division challenged the new contract's provision that landlords had to maintain a constant number of tenants but not necessarily the same people. This policy, the reformers contended, made possible the eviction of STFU members or others who complained about their treatment. Led by Alger Hiss and Francis Shea, the liberals drafted a thirty-six-page opinion requiring landlords to retain not only the same number of workers but also the same individuals. During Chester Davis's absence from Washington, Jerome Frank tried to impose the new interpretation on the landlords, but without success. Davis rushed back to the office and persuaded Wallace to countermand the opinion. On February 12

Wallace sent a telegram to the Memphis Chamber of Commerce, which the chamber made public, saying: "Section 7 of cotton contract does not bind landowners to keep the *same* tenants. That is the official and final interpretation of the Solicitor of the Department of Agriculture, and no other interpretation will be given." Further, the secretary fired Frank, Shea, Pressman, and Jackson. Hiss resigned as well. The famous purge of the AAA liberals silenced intra-agency criticism and ratified the official position on cotton tenancy: the federal government would communicate with the landowners, who would then deal with their workers.[27]

Lacking any desire to alter substantially the land tenure system in the South, the AAA leadership recognized the political and economic power arrayed against the kind of alterations the legal division liberals proposed. The New Deal granted authority to the cotton interests, thereby assuring that those who administered the programs would also benefit most from them. Nor was that an illogical choice to make for the future of southern agriculture, government officials felt, for to have sided with landless farm workers would have meant fighting against demographics. Progress meant the shrinking of the labor force, a condition surely to be abetted by mechanization. Henry Wallace noted that international markets would no longer support the one-third of American farmers engaged in cotton cultivation. The sudden eviction of so many landless farmers caused severe hardships, but as Wallace pointed out, this "damming up on the farms of millions of people who normally would have been taken care of elsewhere" would happen in any event. The solution, he saw, was not "in making more farms and more farmers, but in making more city employment." The New Deal accelerated a process painful for many in the short run but necessary for the long-term health of southern agriculture.[28]

In a number of auxiliary programs, the New Deal sought to help the rural poor—those uprooted from the land as well as those who remained on the farms in worsening conditions. The Federal Emergency Relief Administration (FERA), which concentrated most of its resources on the urban poor, provided work relief assignments and allocated small amounts of money to such programs as rural rehabilitation, land-use planning, and resettlement. The FERA provided loans and grants for the purchase of seeds, equipment, fertilizer, and livestock but more often sponsored rural communities (about half of which existed in the South) like Pine Mountain Valley, near Roosevelt's Warm Springs, Georgia, residence. In a service later continued by the Department of Agriculture's Surplus Commodity

Distribution Project, the FERA provided the rural poor with potatoes, grapefruit, prunes, butter, cheese, and powdered milk. As a
result of this program, some Appalachian mountaineers tasted
grapefruit for the first time in their lives.[29]

In addition to its focus on industrial recovery, the National Industrial Recovery Act (NIRA) also provided, in obscure section 208,
the sum of twenty-five million dollars for subsistence homesteads.
Professor M. L. Wilson administered the program within the Department of Interior until protracted difficulties with interior secretary
Harold L. Ickes caused Wilson to retire in 1934. During his tenure,
funds were allocated for twenty-seven homesteads, and eventually
thirty-four, including twenty in the South, were completed. Varying
in size from two to five acres, the homesteads usually existed near
large cities so that urban workers could keep "one foot on the soil."
In a few cases, homeless workers obtained homesteads.[30]

At the outset of the New Deal the modest FERA and NIRA programs offered a modicum of support to the rural poor, but these
small, disjointed efforts had little impact. A growing concern for
the dislocations caused by the AAA led undersecretary of agriculture Rexford Tugwell to call for a unified federal government agency
to aid poor farmers and tenants. Facing considerable congressional
hostility to such action, Roosevelt decided to effect a reorganization
by executive order: he created the Resettlement Administration
(RA) on April 30, 1935, and appointed Tugwell its first administrator. Under Tugwell's direction, the RA worked for sweeping land reform. The press became enamored of the agency's ninety-nine
resettlement areas, sixty-one of which were situated in the South,
but Tugwell always aimed for much more than the creation of
government-built suburban communities. He hoped that better
farming practices in the Appalachian hills and the cotton belt could
reclaim land leeched of its wealth by erosion and indifference to
conservation.[31]

From its inception the RA suffered from negative publicity. As
a result of the great degree of central planning utilized in site selection and the experiments in collectivization that seemed comparable to Soviet farming schemes, the RA found itself the center of
controversy. Congressional critics of the New Deal found a conve-
nient target in Tugwell, one of the New Deal's most outspoken liberals, and southern conservatives led the way in their attacks on the
RA. When Virginia senator Harry F. Byrd objected to having a resettlement project in his state, Roosevelt told Tugwell: "I know what's
the matter with Harry Byrd. He's afraid you'll force him to pay more

than 10 cents an hour for his apple pickers." Despite his disdain for the RA's opponents, however, the president never upbraided them publicly. In 1936, with the comprehensive design for rural rehabilitation derailed by stingy appropriations and with his own reputation assailed by congressional red-baiters, Tugwell resigned his government posts. Will Alexander, Tugwell's successor at the RA, continued to labor with severe handicaps and indifferent support from the White House.[32]

In 1937 the President's Commission on Farm Tenancy, chaired by Secretary Wallace, exonerated the RA. Its report, authored by such leading social scientists as Tugwell, M. L. Wilson, Charles S. Johnson, and Howard Odum, went even further, calling for an increase in funding and an extended mandate for the agency. Later that year Congress passed the Bankhead-Jones Farm Tenant Act, which appropriated ten million dollars the first year, twenty-five million the second year, and fifty million thereafter for tenant purchase loans. The new Farm Security Administration (FSA) replaced the RA and, under the continued direction of Will Alexander, administered the loan program. Although the FSA continued to supervise resettlement communities, the need to appease congressional critics dictated de-emphasizing resettlement. The FSA stressed the improvement of existing family farms, not the relocation of farmers to better land. In its principal activity, the agency proffered loans and grants so that otherwise insolvent tenants could buy the land they worked, repay their debts, or pay for improvements.[33]

Although the new emphasis on preserving the family farm dovetailed nicely with hallowed American agricultural myths and the FSA seemingly engendered much less controversy than the putatively radical RA, no increase in appropriations flowed from Congress. The FSA, like its predecessors, had few weapons with which to attack a massive problem. Within two years the FSA received 146,000 applications but could offer only 6,180 loans. By 1940 the law restricted the FSA to 10,000 loans annually, and the Second World War brought further retrenchment. Southerners received more than their share of FSA benefits—more than half of the rehabilitation loans awarded and nearly 70 percent of tenant purchase loans—but the scope of involvement never came close to aiding the number of farmers eligible for support. Again, if Wallace and other agricultural experts were correct, the goal of family farm ownership would be unrealizable for all but a few landholders. The best the FSA or any government agency could offer was temporary relief in a time of inexorable change.[34]

Perhaps one of the greatest contributions of both the RA and the FSA was their dramatic exposure of southern rural poverty. Under the direction of Roy Stryker, a group of photographers traveled the breadth of the nation taking pictures of rural men, women, and children. Walker Evans, Dorothea Lange, Gordon Parks, Margaret Bourke-White, Arthur Rothstein, Ben Shahn, Marion Post Wolcott, Russell Lee, and others created over 270,000 lasting images of America's impoverished farmers. A huge number of these photographs were taken in the South. Another FSA employee, filmmaker Pare Lorentz, produced two documentaries, *The Plow That Broke the Plains* and *The River,* that appeared in hundreds of movie theaters nationwide in the 1930s. The artful presentation of these rural images by the FSA Photographic Section gave millions of Americans an enhanced appreciation of Depression conditions in the southern countryside.[35]

While New Dealers expressed concern about the rural poor and did a splendid job of publicizing the ravages of the Depression in the isolated rural South, federal agencies continued to implement programs that catered to the interests of large landholders. Increasingly during the 1930s, representation of these interests came to be centered in the American Farm Bureau Federation. In 1933 southern participation in the organization, mostly in Tennessee and Alabama, accounted for only 9,473 members: the Midwest had 98,292 members; the Northeast, 36,542; and the West, 18,939. In 1935 Farm Bureau president Edward O'Neal, an Alabama cotton planter, launched a massive membership drive, and as a result the South trailed only the Midwest by 1936. O'Neal continued the organization's historic role as advocate for commercial rather than subsistence farmers and used his considerable influence to support that orientation in Washington.[36]

For much of the 1930s the Farm Bureau and the AAA forged a powerful coalition. Edward O'Neal avidly endorsed domestic allotment and Roosevelt's reciprocal trade policy, which appealed to the South's traditional free trade position. Henry Wallace credited the Farm Bureau with giving the Agriculture Department its greatest backing, both in securing support for New Deal policies among southern farmers and in lobbying Congress for legislation. The mutually beneficial alliance began to unravel after Roosevelt's 1936 reelection, however, when the Department of Agriculture severed its connections with the Extension Service, a close ally of the Farm Bureau. The Agriculture Department increasingly sought to reach farmers through agencies of its own creation, a development the

Farm Bureau correctly saw as an attempt to diminish the power of other groups. As historian Christiana McFadyen Campbell concluded, "When the AFBF showed signs of seeking to become the dominating force in agriculture, the Department of Agriculture sought to restrain and balance its power." Yet even though the Farm Bureau's influence waned in the late 1930s, its devotion to individual land ownership and support of middle-class farmers remained dominant in the New Deal.[37]

For the southern farmers who participated in New Deal programs, conditions improved by the mid-1930s. In May 1935 several thousand farmers, most of them from the South, voiced their approval of the AAA with a "plowman's pilgrimage" to the capital. Overall, agricultural prices at the end of that year stood at 88 percent of pre-World War I levels, and farmers had accepted benefit payments totaling nearly two billion dollars. Prices rebounded highest in the South, especially for staple crops like cotton and tobacco, and farmers from Dixie took the lead in voting for mandatory crop restriction in the Bankhead and Kerr-Smith acts. A January 1936 Gallup poll showed only 41 percent of the national electorate in favor of the AAA's continuation, but in the South 57 percent voted for it. Moreover, southern farmers expressed alarm when the program seemed threatened by the courts.[38]

By late 1935 farmers had good reason to worry about the AAA's legal status. As a result of the earlier *Schechter* and *Hoosac Mills* decisions, businessmen assumed that processing taxes would be found unconstitutional, and over 1,100 of them filed suit against the AAA. By September 1935, officials estimated, these plaintiffs halted payment of processing taxes totaling one hundred million dollars. In January 1936 the U.S. Supreme Court found the AAA's action unconstitutional in *United States* v. *Butler*, holding that because the AAA induced farmers to regulate production, the processing tax constituted an improper exercise of power by the federal government and an impingement on the authority of state governments. "Agricultural production, if it exists at all," ruled the Court, "must under the Constitution, remain with the states rather than the federal government."[39]

Most southerners rued the AAA's demise. Members of the North Carolina congressional delegation excoriated the *Butler* decision as a "sickening and deadly blow," a "calamity" imposed on farmers by a "politically biased" Court. The Richmond *News Leader* expressed dismay at the Court's ruling and urged Congress to devise new legislation to obviate the effects of the decision. The Louisville-based

Farmers Home Journal accused the Supreme Court of being "nine cloistered old gentlemen who never ventured out of narrow academic society." Reacting with dispatch, Congress repealed the Bankhead and Kerr-Smith acts and considered replacement measures that omitted processing taxes and acreage restrictions. The Soil Conservation and Domestic Allotment Act, passed within weeks, emphasized conservation and the elimination of certain crops that depleted soils. According to the new law, farmers would receive bounties for introducing such crops as soybeans, legumes, and clover, withdrawing submarginal land, rotating crops, and employing other scientific agricultural methods. Much to the displeasure of many southerners, the act also stipulated that bounties would be mailed directly to sharecroppers and tenants.[40]

The implementation of the Soil Conservation and Domestic Allotment Act fell to the Soil Conservation Service (SCS), which had been created in 1935 within the Department of Agriculture. Hugh Hammond Bennett, SCS director and tireless champion of soil conservation since 1903, appealed to Congress for a national program. His pleas eventually carried the day, largely because of the dust storms billowing across the region of the Great Plains that came to be called the Dust Bowl. Hammond argued persuasively that the causes of the great disaster in Oklahoma, Kansas, and Colorado—the absence of grasses left nothing to hold the topsoil when winds blew—existed also in his native South, where generations of planting cotton and tobacco in open rows with heavy rainfall resulted in widespread erosion. By 1940 all southern states adopted legislation for soil conservation districts to cooperate with the SCS. Although the turnover came slowly and favored crops like cotton and tobacco remained on many farms, a greater diversification of southern farming resulted. Soybeans, sorghum, livestock forage, kudzu, trees for turpentine and pulpwood, and a host of other plants became viable cash crops in the South.[41]

Despite its long-term benefits, soil conservation immediately contributed to the problem of agricultural surpluses. When farmers rejected submarginal land and planted new crops in improving soil, yields increased. As the experts at the land grant colleges had counseled, these changes enhanced productivity in the abused southern soils. Unfortunately, glutted markets meant lower prices. A record cotton harvest in 1937, for example, led to a drop in price to 8.4 cents per pound, down from 12.3 cents in 1936, and the surpluses satiated the market for years thereafter. With soil conservation apparently a double-edged sword, southern congressional leaders Marvin Jones of Texas and John H. Bankhead, Jr., of Alabama renewed the call for mandatory production controls. In 1938 a second Agricultural Adjustment Act allowed soil conservation payments but made them subject to acreage restrictions. The new AAA established compulsory marketing quotas contingent upon the approval of two-thirds of farmers growing a particular crop and, to avoid any legal snares, assessed no processing taxes. It also included Henry Wallace's Ever Normal Granary, providing for crop insurance and storage of commodities until prices rose.[42]

The New Deal's attempts to restore farm income achieved modest success by decade's end. Improved farming methods and good weather produced bountiful harvests despite acreage reductions. National farm income rode a roller coaster, from seventy-nine billion dollars in 1929 to thirty-nine billion in 1933 and sixty-six billion in 1939. This was a partial recovery, to be sure, but not parity. In the South the story was much the same. Farm income in 1932 dipped to 37 percent of 1929 figures and by 1939, after additional fluctuations, reached 58 percent of pre-Depression levels. Unable to restore commodity prices completely, New Deal programs became most important in the long-term conduct of southern farming. Innovations adopted in the 1930s radically altered the face of the southern countryside and the lives of the people engaged in agriculture.[43]

In one of its most significant achievements, the New Deal brought electricity to isolated farmers and revolutionized their lives in the process. Power companies, maintaining that the cost of providing service to the very few potential customers in the rural countryside was prohibitive, usually did not stray far from lucrative city markets. In 1930 electric power served only about 10 percent of American farmers and about 3 percent in the South; in Mississippi fewer than 1 percent were so fortunate. Because of electric power, city dwellers by the 1930s enjoyed such amenities as street lighting, elevators, radios, street railways and subways, motion pictures, and electric fans. By contrast, farmhouses usually lacked indoor plumbing, refrigerators, washing machines, sewing machines, and electric lighting. Farmers relied principally on mules and their own energy to activate equipment and frequently commenced their predawn chores by the light of kerosene lamps. Women washed their clothes and their children outdoors and spent an inordinate amount of time and energy lugging buckets of water to the house from the nearest streams or wells. Hauling water consumed hours daily, with an average family of five needing two hundred gallons per day.[44]

Excessive cost explained the absence of rural power. In Canada and in Europe, where 90 percent of the farmers in some countries enjoyed electric power, cooperatives provided the answer. In the

United States, where the construction of distribution lines cost two thousand dollars per mile, groups of farmers could ill afford rural electrification on a grand scale. By 1935 approximately fifty electric cooperatives existed, typically with memberships of one hundred to two hundred families. In many instances groups of farmers cooperatively shared the cost of building the facilities, then ceded them to power companies for operation and maintenance. Without government assistance, the piecemeal electrification of the countryside would have taken a century to complete.[45]

Franklin D. Roosevelt became interested in public power upon discovering that his electric bills in Warm Springs, Georgia, totaled four times his bills in Hyde Park, New York. As governor of New York he had fought unsuccessfully to build a hydroelectric plant on the St. Lawrence River and in 1931 had persuaded the state legislature to pass a bill creating the New York Power Authority as a regulatory agency. President Roosevelt avidly supported the Tennessee Valley Authority's creation to serve seventeen counties in Alabama, Tennessee, Mississippi, and Georgia and, along with the Farm Bureau and the National Grange, pushed for rural power for the rest of the nation. In 1935 Congress appropriated $4.8 billion for rural power, and Roosevelt created the Rural Electrification Administration (REA) by executive order. Morris L. Cooke, a former trustee of the New York Power Authority, became its first administrator.[46]

At first Cooke hoped to work closely with private power corporations, but he found that the passage of the Wheeler-Rayburn Bill, which dismembered public utility holding companies, left a residue of hard feelings among power executives toward the New Deal. Lacking the financial support of the business community, Cooke turned to the use of cooperatives. The REA provided federal loans payable over twenty-five years at low interest rates, and farmer cooperatives responded with a flood of applications. Originally chartered as a temporary agency, the REA became permanent in 1936. By 1939 the REA had funded over 400 cooperatives serving 268,000 households, and after the Second World War the pace quickened. Typical was the situation in Virginia, where in 1934 only 7.6 percent of farms had electricity; by 1939 over 21 percent did, and by 1949, 91 percent did.[47]

Many proponents of rural electrification argued that it would save the family farm, stanch the flow of farmers from the country to the city, and usher in a new golden age of agriculture. It achieved none of these goals, and rural power did not halt the nation's urbanization and industrialization. Rescuing the farms from the dark ages did, however, relieve much of the drudgery of rural life for men and women and make farming a much less difficult occupation. Moreover, for the dwindling numbers of people who remained in rural areas, radio and, later, television, brought them closer to mainstream American culture. Throughout the South, still the nation's most rural region, farmers experienced sudden and startling change because of the REA.

In other ways New Deal programs accelerated changes in the rural South that had been ongoing for generations, usually by supporting the groups standing to benefit from these developments. The AAA, CCC, and other farm agencies, which worked closely with local authorities charged with administering programs, lacked both the mandate and the desire to disrupt socioeconomic hierarchies. Thoroughly aware of southern political realities, New Deal administrators—many of whom were themselves large landholders—understood the necessity of knitting close relationships with the gentry. Politically and economically powerless, tenants, sharecroppers, and day laborers, especially blacks, wielded little influence in New Deal councils. In Washington, the agricultural establishment, ranging from the Department of Agriculture to Edward O'Neal's Farm Bureau and the powerful committee chairmen on Capitol Hill, resisted liberals' desire to aid the rural poor and limited the effectiveness of such programs as the RA and FSA.

Landowners prospered, and the landless suffered under the AAA. One year, for instance, the Delta and Pine Land Company in Mississippi, reputedly the South's largest plantation, received benefit payments from the federal government totaling $114,840, and the Banks and Danner farm of Crittenden County, Arkansas, received $80,000. Under the operation of the Bankhead Cotton Control Act, as well as the Agricultural Adjustment Act, the largest plantations had the most incentive to curtail production. Similarly, no leveling occurred along Tobacco Road, where large producers profited most and warehouses maintained their lucrative role as economic intermediaries. Little wonder indeed that southern landowners consistently voted for mandatory crop restrictions, for as a result they received government subsidies, moderately higher commodity prices, continued control of a docile labor force, and capital for new machinery.[48]

Some New Dealers lamented the favoritism federal programs bestowed upon the well-to-do but could never muster the influence to redress the inequities. Tenant resettlement and purchase programs never enjoyed the funding necessary to affect anywhere near a majority of those eligible for aid, a situation that finally drove

Rexford Tugwell, the visionary agrarian reformer and advocate for the rural poor, out of government service. Conservatives' labeling of such programs as "collectivistic," "socialistic," and "communistic" kept them vulnerable throughout the 1930s to budget cutbacks and even liquidation. The FSA granted loans to a grand total of forty-six tenant farmers in Virginia: one cynic computed that it would take four hundred years to achieve complete land ownership in the commonwealth. Indeed, the neediest farmers seldom received RA and FSA rehabilitation loans, which statutorily were reserved for the debtors likeliest to repay them. Efforts to aid small farmers, like the Bankhead-Jones Act, the FSA, and crop insurance, came belatedly in the last years of the decade, as the New Deal foundered politically and funding evaporated. The onset of World War II diverted federal money into military coffers, and poverty programs dropped further on priority spending lists.[49]

The New Deal affected the poor most by helping to push them off the land. Tenancy peaked in the South in 1930–35, then dropped steadily. Especially in the cotton kingdom, less so in tobacco and rice counties, thousands of landless workers found themselves unemployed and without hope of finding a new place. Initially wage laborers replaced sharecroppers, equaling their numbers by the early post-World War II years and doubling them by the late 1950s. At the same time, however, the number of wage earners decreased as the number of tractors, harvesters, and mechanized pickers mushroomed. Farm machinery replaced hired help. Agricultural historian Gilbert C. Fite remarked: "As the cost of credit declined in relation to the cost of labor, farmers turned to machines."[50]

In the 1920s farmers had begun buying more and more tractors. The number in ten cotton states nearly quadrupled during the decade. Yet the number of farmers making that investment remained modest because of low market prices, the absence of capital, high credit rates, and cheap labor. AAA benefit payments, pocketed by landlords and usually not shared with workers, provided the capital, and thousands of farmers throughout the South used this rare opportunity to buy the tractors they had long desired. Each tractor replaced several families, so that the 111,399 tractors bought in the cotton states in the 1930s displaced an estimated one to two million people. Purchases occurred most often in the flatlands of Texas and Oklahoma and the deltas of Arkansas and Mississippi, where the machines could move unimpeded. By the later years of the decade technological refinements resulting in smaller, more maneuverable tractors made possible the extensive use of the machines on the hillier topography of the Southeast.[51]

To a great extent tobacco farming remained labor-intensive, and the highly mechanized rice farms changed little during the 1930s. Cotton, however, long so resistant to machinery, slowly succumbed to technological breakthroughs. Throughout the decade John D. and Mack Rust improved the speed of their primitive cotton harvester, and in the 1940s the International Harvester and Allis-Chalmers companies began producing spindle pickers. Other innovations included cotton strippers and flame cultivators; improvements in ginning the cotton and cleaning the machinery followed as well. Although machinery never took complete control over cotton farming, it did displace thousands of workers in what had once been a virtually machine-free environment.[52]

The mechanization of farming, made possible chiefly by New Deal largess, accompanied changes in land use. The cotton kingdom shrank, as southern farmers followed the lead of New Deal planners and agricultural experts. Cotton remained the leading cash crop, but corn, peanuts, tobacco, soybeans, rice, sugar, citrus fruits, and peaches all gained ground. The sale of livestock, especially poultry, cattle, and hogs, similarly increased. Finally, farmers responded to the plaintive urgings of extension agents by reducing their cotton acreage and diversifying. By 1959 cotton amounted to more than half of all crops harvested in just eleven counties in four southern states. Government's impact on cotton was immediate, on other commodity cultures less so. Tobacco farming saw fewer evictions and less mechanization until the postwar years; rice farmers also withstood the depopulation pressures until the 1950s.[53]

The New Deal reduced the number of farmers on southern land, resulting in an enclosure movement. Those who had access to federal government funds took advantage of their opportunities and consolidated their positions; tenants and day laborers lacked those alternatives. Southern farmers who survived the Depression generally owned larger holdings, grew a greater variety of crops, employed fewer workers but more machinery, incorporated more scientific know-how, and looked to government for subsidies in their quest for parity. New Deal programs pushed southern farmers along the road to agribusiness and, overall, made the region's agriculture more efficient. In doing so, the New Deal contributed to the destruction of sharecropping, an exploitative system that had plagued the South since Reconstruction. Lamentably, Franklin Roosevelt and Henry Wallace gave short shrift to the poor farmers and tenants caught in the advance of progress. That was the dark side of an otherwise laudable enterprise.

4

RELIEF AND EMPLOYMENT

> I am not saying that all of Mr. Roosevelt's plans are
> sound and right, but as long as he has the national
> grab-bag open and as long as all other states are grab-
> bing, I'm gonna grab all I can for the State of Texas.
>
> —Governor W. Lee ("Pappy") O'Daniel, 1938

The arrival of Franklin D. Roosevelt and his New Deal resulted in a significant increase in the federal government's involvement in local relief. Through the Federal Emergency Relief Administration's direct relief measures and through public works administered by the FERA, the Civil Works Administration (CWA), and, most important, the Works Progress Administration (WPA), nearly two billion federal dollars made their way to the South. This certainly constituted a deviation from the limited involvement of the Hoover administration and provided desperate southerners with much-needed resources. But while President Roosevelt's offers of assistance met with eager acceptance, southern attitudes toward public welfare changed slowly. The New Deal provided the wherewithal for beleaguered communities to survive hard times. Just as surely, however, long-standing attitudes regarding self-reliance, limited government, and balanced budgets persisted; social welfare matters continued to command a low priority throughout the South. The insistence of the federal government that southern communities establish permanent social welfare institutions for care of the indigent produced grudging compliance. Change came only after fierce resistance and was often not evident until years later. Yet if not for the intrusion of New Deal agencies, these breakthroughs would have been even more delayed.[1]

As the Hundred Days of feverish legislative activity unfolded, the uncertainty of Roosevelt's obscure and often contradictory campaign rhetoric gave way to concrete legislation. The president's programs designed to stimulate economic recovery generated considerable comment, none more so than the pathbreaking National Industrial Recovery Act (NIRA). Passed by Congress as an alternative to Alabama senator Hugo L. Black's bill, which reduced work weeks in all industries to thirty hours, the NIRA sought to stabilize business with codes of fair competitive practice. In each major industry, representatives of management, labor, and government drafted codes regulating production, wages, and working conditions. Patterned after the trade-association movement favored by Herbert Hoover, the NIRA went beyond the former president's concept of voluntarism by authorizing the National Recovery Administration (NRA) to establish legal compliance standards for those companies that elected to participate.[2]

NRA chief Hugh S. Johnson enlisted existing trade associations to initiate the program, and with the cooperation of the Cotton Textile Institute, the textile industry completed the first code of fair practice. The new agreement brought standard hours for industry workers down from fifty or fifty-five to forty, set minimum weekly wages of twelve dollars in the South, eliminated child labor in the mills, prohibited plant operations for more than eighty hours per week, and adopted the NIRA's section 7(a), which guaranteed labor the right to collective bargaining. Overproduction of textiles had glutted markets for years, and the industry's severe economic problems accounted for its willingness to embrace the NRA's formula for industrial cooperation.[3]

At the other extreme, the coal industry fought for months before signing a code and then signed only after intercession by the president. Like the textile industry, coal companies suffered from excess output and mounting surpluses; unlike textiles, the lack of successful trade associations and the inability of warring owners to find common ground forestalled cooperation. Because of the different types of coal mined in various areas of the country, codes had to be developed for five separate regions. Labor strife and persistent legal battles initiated by mine owners plagued the coal codes during the life of the NRA. Subsequent federal laws like the Guffey-Snyder Conservation Acts of 1935 and 1937 suffered similar difficulties, and the Appalachian coalfields remained bloody battlegrounds throughout the decade. Nevertheless, the NRA's lasting contributions to coal mining included the banishment of child labor and the institution of safer working conditions and a standard thirty-five-hour work week.[4]

At the outset, most southern communities greeted the NRA with enthusiasm. In Louisville the American Business Club sponsored a three-hour Roosevelt Recovery Parade with 175 floats and marching bands to demonstrate support for the new program. The Lexington American Legion staged a similar gala, in which an estimated thirty thousand people marched. By Labor Day approximately eighteen thousand businesses had signed the codes in the Bluegrass State. In Atlanta more than five thousand local firms, employing nearly fifty thousand workers, obtained the blue eagle insignias awarded for NRA participation, leading the chamber of commerce to proclaim the enrollment drive a great success. The New Orleans post office reported that it had not received enough blue eagle emblems from Washington to satisfy the demand by eager retailers; Houston went the Crescent City one better, boasting that its supply disappeared within the first four days of issue. The Nashville Chamber of Commerce reported that 70 percent of the city's employers signed an NRA agreement. Over thirty thousand Virginia businesses subscribed to the codes, and the Dallas Chamber of Commerce responded so quickly and energetically that NRA chief Hugh Johnson singled out the organization for commendation.[5]

By late 1933, however, optimism began to fade as problems surfaced. Paramount was the ineffectiveness of the compliance boards. Throughout the nation NRA offices reported rising disenchantment among those who adhered to the codes, while violators, whom the compliance boards largely ignored, grew increasingly brazen in their disregard for authority. By August violations of the lumber code reported in the South accounted for one-third of the cases examined by the NRA's compliance division. Kentucky's representative on the national code committee for editors and publishers reported that only 155 of the state's 265 printers were adhering to NRA standards. The Birmingham Chamber of Commerce, designated by the administration to monitor compliance, performed its task indifferently; local sources quoted chamber leaders as saying publicly that they did not intend to "insist too strong just at present" that code provisions be observed. Some firms continued to display NRA emblems despite negative compliance rulings; other companies, including the powerful New Orleans Steamship Association, which controlled the lion's share of shipping commerce in the city, simply never bothered to sign a code at all.[6]

In the oil-obsessed states of Texas, Louisiana, and Oklahoma, particular attention focused on the NIRA's section 9(c), which prohibited interstate commerce of oil illegally produced under state laws. Most local oil companies favored the "hot oil" clause, at least at first, because it guarded against overproduction and consequent profit losses. But some oilmen objected heatedly to the oil code itself, which granted to oil administrator Harold L. Ickes additional powers beyond those delineated in section 9(c)—including authority to prorate production. Especially vociferous, independent oilmen inveighed against government interference in free enterprise. The failure of the NRA enforcement procedures resulted in rampant violations of the hot oil clause, and by January 1934 over one hundred Texas renegades were selling the illegal crude across state lines. By the time the U.S. Supreme Court struck down the NRA oil provisions in January 1935, most oilmen had soured on federal regulation of hot oil. These same critics applauded the U.S. Congress's rapid adoption of the Hot Oil Act of February 1935, written by Texas senator Tom Connally, which re-created the NIRA's section 9(c) without the onerous oil code additions. Oilmen wanted protection against hot oil, but they opposed authority for distant government bureaucrats to regulate the industry as a whole.[7]

Within a year dissatisfaction with the NRA pervaded industries throughout the South. Dixie merchants complained about the laxity of enforcement and the insensitive bureaucracy that seemingly produced little but red tape. Workers complained that the NRA favored business: in one notable case, the agency upheld the firing of a Lumberton, North Carolina, man who refused to evict his son from their home for joining a union. Producers criticized the ruinously high wages mandated by the NRA; for example, southern lumber interests bitterly protested the 100-percent increase in hourly wages from twelve to twenty-four cents mandated by the lumber code. Mostly they railed against an excessive centralization and what they perceived to be inattentiveness to the needs of southern business. The Southern States Industrial Council, chartered in 1934 to oppose the NRA, complained to the Senate Finance Committee about the need for different wage scales for North and South, the dearth of southern representatives on the national code authorities, and the desire for autonomous local code authorities to regulate local industries. Also, many white southerners feared that NRA-imposed wage rates would result in equal pay for black workers. The Albany, Georgia, *Herald* complained: "Codes, codes, codes! Everybody had a code or is just about to adopt a code or, in case of stubbornness, will eventually have a code thrust upon them. Any day now we expect a new stanza to be added to the Negro spiritual: 'I gotta code, You gotta code, All of God's children got codes.' "[8]

In the 1935 case *United States* v. *A.L.A. Schechter Poultry Corporation*, the U.S. Supreme Court declared the NIRA unconstitutional. The justices ruled unanimously that much of the activity regulated by the NRA was not "interstate" and did not, therefore, fall under Congress's power to regulate commerce. Also, the Court found the NIRA's delegation of legislative power to the executive unconstitutional. In subsequent years such "sick" industries as oil, coal, and textiles organized "little NRAs" to regulate production, but at the time of the organization's demise few southerners expressed regret. In fact, so many businesses were blatantly ignoring NRA codes that the *Schechter* decision merely made official a situation already commonplace throughout the South. At the very least, southern metropolitan newspapers rued the NRA's ineffectiveness; some, like the Atlanta *Constitution*, charged that the NRA "retarded the return of prosperity."[9]

For all of its unpopularity, however, the NRA exerted a profound impact on the South. Such industries as textiles and coal mining eradicated child labor just as they reduced hours and improved working conditions. As economic historian Gavin Wright has demonstrated, the NRA achieved what many southern businessmen feared: it closed the wage differential between North and South. While northern pay scales generally remained static, federal laws like the NIRA and later the Fair Labor Standards Act boosted southern wages to unprecedented levels. NRA codes had the greatest impact on low-wage industries, so that poorly paid southern workers prospered to a degree unequaled elsewhere. Wages stipulated by NRA codes, even at their seemingly modest rates, set significantly higher levels throughout the South. The NIRA's passage owed, at least in part, to the desire of northerners to eliminate the South's low costs of production based upon low wages. Even though the abrogation of the NRA removed the statutory restrictions on low wages in the South, says Wright, "the important point is that these reductions were never really reversed." With the NRA, the federal government checked the expansion of low-wage industry in the South and laid the foundation for uniform national labor markets.[10]

Of most immediate concern in the South, however, were unemployment and the resultant relief crisis. In May 1933 Congress created the Federal Emergency Relief Administration, (FERA), authorizing the allocation of five hundred million dollars for direct and work relief as well as transient care. The federal government provided funds for distribution by state and local governments, with emphasis on decentralization. To encourage the continuation of existing relief efforts, the FERA would award grants to states according to their expenditures. The FERA administrator, New York social worker Harry Hopkins, would also retain funds for discretionary use. At his urging, southern states scrambled to assemble emergency relief administrations of their own to distribute the federal largess to local and county agencies. True to the spirit of the enabling legislation, local ERAs analyzed conditions, requested funds, and supervised programs.[11]

From its inception in July 1933 to 1935, when the federal government turned relief of the unemployables over to state and local authorities, the FERA aided thousands of jobless people in the South. During that time it spent nearly $1.5 billion in Texas, $35 million in Kentucky, and $26 million in Virginia. Work relief not only created temporary jobs for the indigent but also benefited southern communities in numerous other ways. In Kentucky the FERA funded canneries that processed produce and then distributed the canned goods to needy families. Houston workers cleared bayous and repaired streets. In Birmingham workers built four new sewage disposal plants and repaired miles of sewer lines. Atlantans constructed Chandler Airport and Grady Memorial Hospital. The FERA renovated Key West, Florida, transforming it, with the help of a highway connecting the keys to the mainland built by the Public Works Administration (PWA), into a thriving resort. In all locations, workers paved roads, dug ditches, and performed hundreds of other menial tasks that enhanced the health and appearance of the cities. Perhaps best of all, although Congress mandated that state and local governments contribute to the FERA's operation, the federal government ended up paying most of the bill.[12]

First on behalf of the FERA, and later on behalf of other federal relief agencies, Harry Hopkins waged an ongoing struggle with state and local officials in the South to force them to pay a greater share of the relief cost. He told FERA administrators: "Every department of government that has any taxing power left has a direct responsibility to help those in distress." Hopkins encountered stiff resistance in many states throughout the nation, as governors and legislators extolled the virtues of rugged individualism and warned against extensive federal intervention. In the South especially, politicians unfurled the banner of states' rights and claimed that their region's poverty precluded more substantial relief allocations. Instead, southern states accepted FERA funds while simultaneously cutting relief rolls, or more often, they simply limited the amount of relief provided their citizens by spurning matching grants. While the average FERA monthly stipends for families exceeded $15.00 nationally, Louisiana paid the most of any southern state, $13.89. Mississippi paid only $3.96. As a result, southerners received considerably fewer dollars than they might have. The South, with roughly one-fourth of the country's population, received one-seventh of the FERA's outlay; by 1939 the South accounted for one-sixth of FERA, CWA, and WPA expenditures.[13]

When obstreperous state officials refused to alter their tight-fisted policies, Hopkins "federalized" relief in several southern states; that is, he chose new administrators and instructed them to allocate all federal funds as directed, thus assuring that governors and mayors exercised no influence over relief. Oklahoma governor William ("Alfalfa Bill") Murray refused to abide by FERA regulations even if it meant losing federal funds, a foreboding prospect in the eastern part of the state, where 70 percent of the population qualified for assistance. Murray denounced Roosevelt to FERA regional administrator Aubrey Williams as the "syphilitic son of a bitch who has sent you down here to police me and my state." Governor Murray and his successors, Ernest W. Marland and Leon Phillips, repeatedly cut state relief allocations and limited revenues by trimming taxes on oil and natural gas production. In 1934 Hopkins federalized relief in Oklahoma, but the state never increased its contributions.[14]

In Georgia, Governor Eugene Talmadge emerged as one of the nation's most outspoken opponents of federal relief. Talmadge insisted that farmers sorely needed help, but city dwellers were "bums" and "chiselers." In a widely quoted remark he suggested that the best way to handle relief applicants would be to "line them up against a wall and give them a dose of castor oil." Outspokenly critical of all New Deal programs, the governor said that NRA and TVA were "all in the Russian primer and the President has made the statement that he has read it twelve times." In a thoroughly tasteless gibe at Roosevelt's physical handicap, Talmadge added: "The next President who goes to the White House will be a man who knows what it is to work in the sun fourteen hours a day. . . . That man will be able to walk a two-by-four plank, too."[15]

Hopkins purged the Georgia Relief Commission of Talmadge's cronies and installed Gay Shepperson as the state's relief administrator. According to WPA field representative Allen Johnstone, Talmadge refused to let Shepperson do her job. Johnstone reported that "days and weeks of delay interrupt the organization and interpretation. Appointments are held up. The Governor insists on signing every check. Wants to know the name and address of every person on staff and almost the name and address of every person on relief. Harasses the administration by continued criticism." Presidential emissaries advised Talmadge that his incessant sniping hurt the state, but the combative governor persisted.[16]

Conditions improved somewhat when avowed New Dealer E.D. Rivers replaced Talmadge in 1936, but the state legislature undermined Rivers's blueprint for a "Little New Deal." In 1935 Rivers, then Speaker of the Georgia House of Representatives, introduced a series of bills to enable the state to acquire federal funds more readily. When Talmadge vetoed them all, Rivers broke with his former ally and launched his own gubernatorial campaign. After his election Rivers pushed through the state legislature a bill expanding the authority of the Georgia Department of Public Welfare, empowering it to administer the WPA and other federal programs. The recalcitrant legislature refused to levy new taxes, however, and the lack of adequate revenue attenuated Little New Deal programs. By 1938 the state's refusal to provide matching grants led President Roosevelt to terminate all federal funds.[17]

Hopkins intervened most forcefully in Louisiana, where Senator Huey Long controlled the state's relief apparatus. In August 1933 Hopkins visited New Orleans and praised the "apparent lack of politicization of relief in Louisiana," yet in October he completely revamped the Louisiana Emergency Relief Administration to keep Huey Long from gaining access to federal funds. FERA regional administrator Aubrey Williams removed the entire Long-controlled state board and appointed as the new executive director Harry J. Early, who had directed the Community Chest and had overseen federal relief distribution in Birmingham. This worked temporarily, but as the political war between Long and New Orleans mayor T. Semmes Walmsley for control of the city intensified, Hopkins intervened again in 1935. He federalized the entire Louisiana relief structure, removing all state control, and named an outspoken critic of Long, Frank Peterman, as the state's FERA administrator. Predictably, Long objected vehemently, calling Peterman a "crook" and a "tin-horn railroad lawyer." The controversy subsided with Long's death later that year, and federal control loosened thereafter.[18]

Although Hopkins intervened so blatantly in just a few states, he worked ceaselessly to force other troublesome governors and legislatures to provide more funds for relief. He became so irate at the inaction by Kentucky governor Ruby Laffoon that he traveled to Frankfurt to address the state legislature personally and lobby for a tax increase to fund relief. The legislature enacted a small levy on beer and liquor, but within a year the relief allocations ceased again. In North Carolina, Governor John Ehringhaus refused Hopkins's offer for the federal government to absorb 75 percent of the state's relief bill. Ehringhaus argued that the state could not afford to pay the remaining 25 percent, yet when he left office in 1937 North Carolina sported a five-million-dollar budget surplus. FERA funds accounted for over 90 percent of Virginia's relief payments, but senators Harry F. Byrd and Carter Glass complained about the federal government's violations of state autonomy. Capable of increasing relief payments, the commonwealth continued to keep the monthly stipends ridiculously low. In defense, the state's welfare director said: "It takes people a long time to starve."[19]

Alabama governor Bibb Graves, ostensibly a loyal New Dealer, withheld a three-million-dollar appropriation acquired from a state gasoline tax as a bargaining chip in a struggle with the Jefferson County legislative delegation. The resultant lack of funds kept Birmingham from meeting Hopkins's demand for increased local and state contributions for relief. Frustrated by the recurring political gamesmanship, Birmingham's director of public welfare Roberta Morgan resigned in protest. Prior to quitting, Morgan had failed to endear herself to federal officials by her refusal to cooperate fully. FERA regional social worker Loula Dunn reported Morgan's intransigence, adding that "the old private agency attitudes and methods still prevail on the whole in the direction of the program, and I sometimes question how able we will ever be to make any real progress in Birmingham." FERA representative Elmer Scott similarly noted the desire of Houston's leaders to accept outside aid without shouldering any responsibilities: it shocked him "how parasitic a local community may become." In a moment of surprising candor, the Houston *Press* acknowledged the hypocrisy of its city's reliance on the dogma of states' rights, saying: "We recognize state boundaries when called on to give, but forget them when Uncle Sam is doing the giving." Threatening, cajoling, haggling, and occasionally intervening, Hopkins often coaxed additional support from southern states but seldom to the degree he sought. The battle continued.[20]

By the last months of 1933, with winter approaching, it became evident that the FERA's resources would be inadequate and that additional federal assistance would be necessary. In November 1933 the Civil Works Administration (CWA) assumed control of work relief. Unlike the FERA, the CWA did not operate through state and local intermediaries but paid wages directly to workers. Created as a stopgap measure to help the unemployed through the winter, it disbanded promptly in the spring of 1934. During its brief existence, the CWA provided makeshift employment for four million men and women, with the federal government assuming 90 percent of the cost and the states 10 percent. Harry Hopkins and others in Washington urged Roosevelt to retain the CWA, but concerned that the program far exceeded its modest allocations, the president ordered its liquidation on Easter weekend. The FERA completed several unfinished CWA projects and resumed control of direct relief and work relief measures.[21]

In 1933, as part of the NIRA, Public Works Administration offices opened in the South. Unlike the other New Deal agencies concerned with unemployment, which concentrated on short-term, low-cost projects, the PWA awarded grants to cities for large-scale efforts. The cities had to augment these grants with sizable contributions of their own. With PWA projects, about 70 percent of funds went for materials, and 30 percent for wages; at the CWA, wages accounted for 80 percent of project expenditures. Since make-work was never the primary goal, the PWA directly employed relatively few men. Moreover, the agency hired indiscriminately, not just from the relief rolls, so it had only an incidental impact on gross unemployment figures. Nevertheless, the amount of money spent and the construction projects completed constituted an impressive achievement.[22]

From 1933 to 1938 southern states received over five hundred million dollars from the PWA. In Virginia the PWA built the Colonial, Blue Ridge, and Skyline parkways, military barracks, and ships, among its 740 projects. In Kentucky PWA labor used concrete, granite, and steel to construct the twenty-ton vault at Fort Knox. New Orleans city officials obtained PWA funding for sewerage improvements, restoration of the historic French Market, bridge construction, and a new city auditorium. Most important, PWA money built New Orleans's Charity Hospital, the second largest health care facility in the country. In Richmond PWA largess made possible the erection of the Virginia State Library and a bridge spanning the James River. In Memphis new buildings included John Gaston Hospital, a new grain elevator, dormitories at the University of Tennessee Medical School, and several public schools. In conjunction with the U.S. Army Corps of Engineers, PWA workers built Riverside Drive alongside the Mississippi River, providing residents of Memphis with a safe thoroughfare at the base of the bluffs downtown. In

Nashville the PWA built the Tennessee Supreme Court Building and the State Office Building and remodeled the state capitol. Along with the WPA, the PWA helped fund the building of a dam and a massive industrial water supply system for Birmingham.[23]

The PWA also made possible the construction of the first public housing projects in southern cities, indeed nationally. The PWA's housing division funded the construction of multifamily dwellings prior to 1937, at which time the United States Housing Authority (USHA) assumed control. In order to obtain federal funding, cities created local housing authorities that submitted detailed proposals for slum clearance and construction, then operated the housing projects on a nonprofit basis. Owing to PWA administrator Harold L. Ickes's excruciating caution and meticulous attention to detail, the agency constructed only 21,800 units in fifty-one projects. A 1935 U.S. District Court ruling in *United States* v. *Certain Lands in the City of Louisville* kept the federal government from condemning private property to build public housing, and construction ebbed until a later court decision upheld the government's power of eminent domain. Despite these deterrents, thirty-one states passed enabling legislation, and the pace of construction quickened under the USHA. As countless surveys showed, some of the nation's worst housing conditions existed in southern communities. Fittingly, it was a southern municipality—Atlanta—that pioneered in the assault on slum conditions.[24]

The drive to obtain federal funds for public housing in Atlanta began with the vision and commitment of one man, Charles F. Palmer. A real estate developer and president of the National Association of Building Owners and Managers, Palmer felt that "wiping out the slum area would enhance the value of our central business properties." Accordingly, he and several other like-minded architects, builders, and investors formed a corporation that initially invested $375 in a slum reclamation project. They chose as a preliminary site the notorious Techwood slum, a nine-square-block area of dilapidated housing for nearly one thousand white families located between the campus of the Georgia Institute of Technology and Atlanta's central business district. They also chose a second site in a black slum known as Beaver Slide near Atlanta University. On October 13, 1933, federal authorities approved the companion projects—Techwood Homes for whites and University Homes for blacks—as the first and second slum clearance projects to be funded by the PWA.[25]

The endorsement from Washington notwithstanding, opposition emerged almost immediately. Over one hundred real estate owners and brokers, many of them slum landlords, banded together under the sponsorship of the Atlanta Apartment House Owners Association to oppose construction of the projects. Calling Techwood Homes "Palmer's Paradise," they contended that "this queer alliance between Uncle Sam and Uncle Chuck" would be the ruin of the private housing industry. The opposition unsuccessfully sought an injunction to prevent construction, and on September 29, 1934, Secretary Ickes dynamited the first shack to initiate the slum removal campaign. Slightly over one year later President Roosevelt dedicated Techwood Homes, and in 1937 the University Homes project opened as well.[26]

Nevertheless, hostility toward public housing remained. On September 24, 1937, Mayor William B. Hartsfield vetoed a bill creating a local housing authority, saying: "Atlanta is not going to be a guinea pig in this matter." The following year, however, a group of hovels caught fire across the street from Grady Hospital, and the threat to the hospital reawakened public interest in the health and safety hazards posed by slum conditions. Reluctantly, the mayor bowed to public pressure and named a five-man housing authority, with Charles F. Palmer as chairman. From 1939 to 1941 Atlanta spent $16,856,689 to construct seven additional public housing projects, four for blacks and three for whites. The federal government provided loans for 90 percent of the sum; the city floated bonds for 10 percent. Atlanta thus achieved a national reputation as a spearhead in the public housing movement, although slum eradication went forward largely because of the generous assistance of the federal government. Mayor Hartsfield continued to stress that point, emphasizing that a balanced budget, not philanthropy, would remain Atlanta's first priority.[27]

Public housing advocates encountered steadfast opposition throughout the South. Subsequent to the establishment of the USHA, only Wilmington and Raleigh established local housing authorities in North Carolina; in Charlotte real estate interests succeeded in blocking such a proposal, and in Winston-Salem the board of aldermen passed a resolution denying the existence of any slums in the city. The Virginia legislature finally empowered municipalities to constitute local housing authorities in 1938, but the state's capital city declined to do so then. Richmond mayor J. Fulmer Bright argued that creation of such an agency "violates every principle of sound business, democracy, Americanism, individualism and other fine traits." In 1939 the city council narrowly passed a resolution authorizing a public housing authority, but Bright vetoed the measure. Finally, after the election of a new mayor, Gordon B. Ambler, the

Richmond Housing Authority came into existence in 1940. Demolition for the city's first public housing project, Gilpin Court, began in 1941, and the project was completed the following year.[28]

In other southern cities local housing authorities sporadically appeared and entered into partnership with the USHA. The program of constructing public housing provided jobs for the unemployed, razed hundreds of deteriorating buildings, improved living conditions for the new public housing residents, and generally elevated the quality of the housing stock in participating cities. In the long run, moreover, it paved the way for decades of subsequent public housing construction. Of course, not all champions of slum eradication operated entirely from altruism. The members of local housing authorities, typically prominent businessmen, thought of improved real estate values, potential industrial growth, and revitalized downtowns. Self-interest could operate in a variety of ways. In Dallas, for example, a crime wave persuaded the *Morning News* to renounce its earlier opposition to public housing. The marauding of Bonnie Parker and Clyde Barrow in northern Texas raised questions about the impact of environment, including housing, on sociopathic behavior. To assure public safety, the *Morning News* called for reform. For whatever reasons, southern communities grudgingly accepted the idea of public housing, and the generous terms offered by Washington made the decision less painful. Even so, worries about fiscal irresponsibility often gave way to concerns about the larger issue of expanding federal power. The decision to construct low-rent housing rested with municipal housing authorities, so that local control prevented federal incursions.[29]

Another work relief program, the Civilian Conservation Corps, originated with an experiment Roosevelt had launched as governor of New York. The CCC sent the urban unemployed into the countryside to perform a variety of conservation tasks—planting trees, draining swamps and marshes, building dams and reservoirs, and landscaping parks. As an avid outdoorsman, Roosevelt originally suggested the CCC and took a particular interest in its operation. The CCC enrolled unmarried men between the ages of eighteen and twenty-five for six-month enlistments, renewable up to two years, and paid them thirty dollars per month (the men kept five dollars, and the agency remitted the remaining twenty-five to their families). Although created to address temporary problems, the CCC existed until 1942. It employed 500,000 men in 2,500 camps at its peak. As head of the agency Roosevelt named Tennessean Robert Fechner, an American Federation of Labor vice-president. Fechner

made certain that the camps located in the South were rigidly segregated, and the CCC remained one of the New Deal's most popular
agencies in Dixie as well as nationally.[30]

Like the CCC, the Tennessee Valley Authority affected a minority of southerners directly but attracted much favorable attention.
In the 1920s discussion revolved around the fate of a dam and two
power plants erected near Muscle Shoals, Alabama, during World
War I for the production of explosives. These facilities also produced
synthetic nitrates for use in fertilizer, which could be of great value
in poor southern soils. Nebraska senator George W. Norris, the great
champion of public power, defeated attempts by private enterprises
to purchase the Muscle Shoals complex and unsuccessfully introduced six bills in Congress to allow the federal government to operate hydroelectric plants on the Tennessee River. Norris kept alive
the dream of public power in the seven states encompassing the
Tennessee River Valley until the election of Franklin Roosevelt,
whose plans for development included flood control, soil conservation, afforestation, industrial development, the generation of hydroelectric power, and the removal of submarginal agricultural land.
With the able assistance of Norris and Tennessee senator Kenneth
D. McKellar, Roosevelt's TVA legislation passed in Congress despite
the antagonism of private utility companies and others philosoph-
ically opposed to increased planning initiatives by the federal
government.[31]

The TVA scored several notable successes in one of the nation's
most backward, poverty-ridden areas. First, it erected sixteen dams
in the years 1933–45, which not only controlled the annual spring
floods that regularly devastated the river valley but also offered employment to thousands of area residents. Opening a nine-foot channel from Knoxville, Tennessee, to Paducah, Kentucky, the TVA
made that portion of the Tennessee River navigable for the first
time. Government agricultural specialists worked with farmers to
combat soil erosion and create watersheds. Implementing broad-
based regional planning that cut across state lines, the federal
agency landscaped parks, created rural libraries, and improved
school systems. By altering the water levels at the system's dams,
TVA eliminated malaria as a serious health problem. The disease
previously afflicted one-third of the region's population. Finally, the
TVA brought electricity to the Tennessee Valley, where only 3 percent of the population had access by 1933. The Electric Home and
Farm Authority also allowed people to buy electrical appliances at
affordable prices.[32]

The TVA stirred controversy in two southern cities, Memphis and Birmingham, which the voters resolved in markedly different fashions. In October 1933 TVA director David Lilienthal visited Memphis and promised, contingent upon proof that an adequate local market existed, to have the federal government erect transmission lines. The city had only to construct an electrical distribution system, for which it needed to acquire the permission of the voters to issue bonds. The promise of considerably cheaper electricity rates assured the success of the referendum, but Memphis boss Ed Crump desired an overwhelming margin of victory as an unmistakable endorsement of his long-standing opposition to private power interests. To capture voters' attention, Crump stalwarts held meetings, canvassed door-to-door, and even staged fistfights downtown to attract crowds for speeches. The voters returned a resounding eighteen-to-one (32,735 to 1,868) verdict, and Crump christened a downtown alley November Sixth Street to commemorate the day of the election.[33]

Despite the lopsided outcome of the referendum, the TVA did not commence operation in Memphis until 1939. The Memphis Power and Light Company joined eighteen other private utility companies in a suit against TVA. After years of litigation the U.S. Supreme Court affirmed TVA's constitutionality. For several years the city's attempts to purchase the power company's facilities broke down over the question of a fair price, and negotiations dragged on until a June 1939 settlement. One year later the municipally owned utility claimed a saving for the city's customers of $2.4 million over previous years. For Memphis, notwithstanding the protracted haggling, the results seemed well worth the wait.[34]

Although some New Deal programs wavered in the public's esteem, TVA's popularity never faltered in Memphis. Indeed, the authority became something of a sacred cow, and local politicians endorsed public power as a matter of course. Ed Crump quickly saw how such a popular program could be used against his opponents. He charged that former ally Gordon Browning, seeking reelection as Tennessee governor, had been disingenuous in his support of TVA over the years. During the 1940 presidential election Crump suggested that Wendell Willkie's connections to the private power industry be contrasted with Roosevelt's role in securing public utilities for the Tennessee Valley. Crump conceded that neither Browning nor Willkie lost solely because of the TVA issue, but he felt it was an important factor in both outcomes.[35]

The TVA's smashing success in Memphis contrasted sharply with its bitter defeat in Birmingham. David Lilienthal spoke in the

Alabama city to curry support for the construction of power lines to Muscle Shoals. The PWA would fund 30 percent of the cost and lend the city the rest of the necessary capital at 4-percent interest. Public power advocates jumped on the bandwagon, led by city commissioner Lewey Robinson, the Scripps-Howard Birmingham *Post*, and the Jefferson County chapter of the League of Municipalities. Opposition formed behind the two locally owned newspapers, the *News* and the *Age-Herald*, and the privately owned Birmingham Electric Company, which cut consumer rates 25 percent to soothe the local consumers. City commission president Jimmy Jones endorsed TVA before his reelection in August 1933, but thereafter he became a vocal and influential opponent. On October 9, 1933, the people of Birmingham voted no by a three-to-one margin in a public referendum on TVA power. Lower power rates, the threat of higher taxes, and antipathy for public ownership all seemed to account for the people's choice in the referendum. After the construction of the TVA-Guntersville Dam, the majority of the communities in the area—including Bessemer, Tarrant City, and Irondale—subscribed to public utilities, but residents of Birmingham persisted in their rejection of public power.[36]

Although most of the people in the Tennessee Valley enjoyed a number of benefits because of the TVA, modernization entailed some unfortunate developments as well. To create the system's lakes, new dams inundated farms, homes, and in some cases entire communities with water, and uprooted people frequently left unwillingly. Ironically, the TVA violated its own conservation aims by strip-mining coal to operate power plants. In later years the conversion to nuclear power necessitated the removal of outdated equipment at a cost of billions of dollars. Cries arose about fiscal mismanagement and poor planning. On balance, the TVA meant substantial progress for one of the South's most benighted areas, but such advances often came at considerable cost to the inhabitants and the environment.[37]

New Deal programs had a salutary impact on the South, but by 1935 the relief crisis remained just as menacing. The FERA, CWA, PWA, CCC, and TVA provided varying amounts of aid to the needy but fell far short of offering adequate relief. Therefore, in 1935, at President Roosevelt's urging, Congress passed the Emergency Relief Appropriation Act, creating the Works Progress Administration (WPA) to employ workers in greater numbers and at a higher wage than the relief rate. Recognizing that make-work often had little intrinsic value, Roosevelt nonetheless favored it to the dole. (At the same time the federal government created the WPA, it turned the responsibility for unemployment relief back over to state and local governments.) In state after state the WPA absorbed the work relief programs of the various emergency relief administrations and sent the unemployed to work repairing streets, digging ditches, painting buildings, and resurfacing sidewalks. Unlike the FERA, which worked through state governments, the WPA operated independently, awarding projects to local sponsors, who would often contribute to the enterprise.[38]

FERA administrator Harry Hopkins assumed control of the WPA and immediately encountered the same resistance from local authorities seeking to avoid contributing their share of the cost. Faced with the care of unemployables, state and local governments often intensified their opposition to paying for work relief. With the economy still mired in depression, they argued, they were even less able than before to spend precious tax dollars. Unmoved, Hopkins proclaimed that nothing had changed with the creation of a new agency. He said: "Lots of people don't like the idea of taking care of their unemployables, but there is no state in the union that hasn't the power to take care of their unemployed."[39]

The reluctance of southern cities to sponsor WPA projects curtailed employment opportunities. The percentage of the cost to be borne by the sponsor fluctuated and often could be negotiable, but Hopkins insisted on some local contributions. Residents of Atlanta and Birmingham voted down bond proposals necessary to fund public improvement projects. In the Georgia city a struggle ensued over the funding of a mammoth sewer project. The PWA's Harold L. Ickes argued that Atlanta had sufficient bonding power to finance most of the project, while Hopkins thought the city should have to pay only 17 percent of the cost. Roosevelt decided to match Atlanta's dollars with federal money. According to a disgruntled Ickes, "while Atlanta was amply able to finance the building of its own sewerage system, a substantial part of it was built as a WPA project at the expense of the Federal Government." Hopkins similarly charged Memphis with shirking its duty by failing to meet its share of relief costs. Mayor Watkins Overton argued that the city had more than done its share in 1931–32, before the federal government had become involved. Since that time, the mayor asserted, "it was definitely understood that the city of Memphis needed its funds to care for increased burdens on its institutions which provide for this entire section." Hopkins disagreed. In 1936 Baltimore emergency relief commissioner Howard

Beck reported twenty-five cases of starvation, but Mayor Howard Jackson continued to cut relief rolls.[40]

Southern agriculturalists frequently complained about federal relief. Florida truck farmers and citrus growers charged that CWA employment left no available labor for private industry and demanded that federal wage rates be lowered to the prevailing level of fifty cents per day. Cotton magnates protested that the WPA drained unskilled labor from the neighboring countryside, and they registered their indignation at WPA workers' refusal to relinquish their make-work to pick cotton. A North Carolina plantation owner grumbled: "Ever since federal relief . . . came in you can't hire a nigger to do anything for you. High wages is ruinin' 'em." The Wilmington, North Carolina, relief office withheld assistance to unemployed workers who refused to pick strawberries, even though the landowners paid starvation wages of thirty-five cents per day. The owner of a large Arkansas cotton plantation requested that the WPA suspend all work until the end of the harvest. The federal government kept the agency functioning initially, but several cities deleted many relief recipients from the welfare rolls and forced them to pick cotton. In 1936 Hopkins agreed to the termination of WPA projects in the South so that workers would be freed to harvest cotton. He urged cotton planters to pay the workers "standard wages" but left the question of remuneration to the landlords' discretion.[41]

Low pay plagued southern WPA laborers as well. To discourage workers from remaining on WPA rolls, federal wages needed to be higher than relief rates yet below prevailing levels in private industry. In much of the South, with wages below relief levels, this proved problematic. The federal government divided the nation into four regions to establish variable pay rates. The southern region received the lowest monthly pay rates, fourteen to thirty dollars for unskilled workers and thirty-five to sixty-eight dollars for skilled workers. Laborers in the Southwest, which included Texas, Louisiana, and Oklahoma, fared slightly better. In the most generously endowed region, the Northeast, skilled workers earned sixty-five to eighty-five dollars monthly, and unskilled workers received forty to fifty dollars per month. Government paychecks were inadequate everywhere in the nation, but in the South workers received from 33 to 65 percent of the national average "emergency standard of living expense" identified by federal authorities. New Deal officials reported that WPA wages for Atlanta's unskilled workers, adjusted for cost of living, constituted the lowest in the nation and that rates in other southern municipalities were comparable. Because of their concentration in agricultural and domestic occupations, southern women received especially low wages. Women cotton pickers in one Louisiana parish, for example, earned a yearly average of $41.67 (men earned $120.19).[42]

Yet for all its shortcomings, the WPA provided a wellspring of jobs for unemployed southerners as well as a host of construction projects and civic improvements. The lining of miles of ditches with concrete helped eradicate malaria as a major health problem and, by the estimate of a federal administrator, brought many physical improvements to the region thirty years before they would otherwise have been affordable. In Kentucky alone the WPA constructed more than nine hundred public buildings and improved fourteen thousand miles of roads. In South Carolina WPA and PWA funds made possible the completion of the Santee-Cooper project, a miniature version of the TVA. Atlanta's massive sewer system was the single largest WPA project in the South, employing thousands of unskilled workers for months. In Tampa, Florida, the WPA built a municipal airport, improved Bayshore Boulevard, and renovated several hotels. New Orleans boasted three new bridges over Orleans Canal, the repair of City Hall and City Hall Annex, the new half-million-dollar Municipal Stadium, and the restoration of historic Vieux Carre around Jackson Square. A great champion of historic preservation, Charleston mayor Burnet Maybank obtained a $350,000 WPA grant to transform a seedy flophouse into a replica of an eighteenth-century playhouse. The Dock Street Theater, constructed in part from portions of the city's old homes, became a thriving cultural center and tourist attraction. Baltimore built new bridges and improved harbor facilities. Historian David R. Goldfield noted: "The federal government paid for the capital facilities in southern cities that northern cities had paid for themselves in earlier decades and on which they were still paying off the debt. The almost-free modernization received by southern cities would prove to be an important economic advantage in subsequent decades."[43]

The WPA devoted 78 percent of its funds to construction projects using mostly unskilled labor, but Harry Hopkins also insisted that a number of community service programs be funded to employ women and white-collar workers. WPA employees counted livestock, stuffed mattresses, surveyed land, operated day-care facilities for children, wrote books in braille, administered vaccinations in hospitals and health centers, created museum exhibits, and cataloged archives—most notably the Southern Historical Collection at the University of North Carolina at Chapel Hill. The WPA Historical Records Survey preserved and organized county records, church files, and personal correspondence. In the Kentucky backwoods, librarians on horses and mules carried books in their saddlebags to isolated families. Indeed, the resourcefulness of local WPA offices created a myriad of different job possibilities for the small percentage of unemployed workers unable or disinclined to perform manual labor. Best of all, remembered a West Virginia preacher, New Deal aid absolved cash-poor mountain folk from having to sell illegal moonshine in violation of their religious principles.[44]

The WPA also offered employment for women, despite many people's feeling that a woman's place was in the home and not competing with men in the job force. To administer the Division of Women's and Professional Projects, Harry Hopkins chose Ellen Sullivan Woodward, a former Mississippi state legislator who had served as the FERA's director of women's work from 1933 to 1935. Despite Woodward's protestations, most women were classified as "unskilled" when they worked outside the home and therefore received the lowest wage rate, twenty to thirty cents an hour. Because of the seasonal nature of the men's construction projects, winter months became especially difficult for families; with an unemployed husband at home, wives could not be certified as household heads in order to be assigned to indoor projects.[45] Most women employed by the WPA performed household work, often in the sewing rooms that existed in virtually every community. One WPA official noted: "For unskilled men we have the shovel. For unskilled women we have only the needle." The clothing the women made went to indigent children, allowing many of them in particularly destitute rural areas to attend school. Women also worked in school lunchrooms, mattress factories, canneries, book binderies, and libraries. Fifteen thousand women between the ages of eighteen and twenty-five participated in the Household Workers' Training Program, learning to be maids, cooks, laundry workers, and dishwashers. Student maids in Memphis could look up to see a banner advising that "dishwashing is an ancient art but few are proficient at it," as they received instruction "that goes to make a well-rounded servant." Ninety-three percent of the women enrolled in the seventeen states and the District of Columbia that offered the domestic training program were black; in Louisiana and Mississippi all were. Although a few critics complained that such projects reinforced traditional race and gender roles, most women happily accepted the precious opportunity for a paycheck.[46]

As part of the WPA, the National Youth Administration provided two programs for young people. First, the NYA allocated money for indigent high school and college students to remain in school. Second, it offered vocational education and temporary employment for nonstudents. Under the leadership of Alabamian Aubrey Williams, the NYA displayed a particular sensitivity to the needs of blacks: the agency operated a Division of Negro Affairs under the direction of estimable black educator Mary McLeod Bethune. In the South NYA facilities remained segregated, but they served a much larger proportion of blacks than did other government endeavors. One of the most popular New Deal programs, the NYA gave young people assistance or training that frequently aided them for the rest of their lives. Lyndon Johnson, a Texas NYA administrator long before he became president, felt that "if the Roosevelt administration had never done another thing, it would have been justified by the work of this great institution for salvaging youth."[47]

Another New Deal innovation, Federal Project One, supported unemployed artists, actors, authors, and musicians. The largest number of people employed in Project One lived in the sprawling industrial cities of the Northeast, especially in New York City, and modest numbers were enrolled throughout the South. When southern cities sought to enrich their residents by staging Federal Music Project concerts or Federal Theater Project performances and found an insufficient number of unemployed musicians and actors, they imported them from New York or elsewhere. Some locations simply did not have enough unemployed people in the arts to sustain projects. Mississippi had no theater project, and a tiny art project survived in Greenville primarily because of the patronage of famed author William Alexander Percy. The Federal Art Project in Georgia employed just one artist during its existence. Relatively few men and women qualified for jobs in most of the projects, so their value lay in an enhanced cultural awareness sparked by touring exhibitions and performances and by arts education classes conducted in community centers. WPA artists also designed and painted hundreds of murals in post offices, courthouses, and other public buildings depicting scenes of local history.[48]

The Federal Writers' Project offered temporary relief to jobless authors and editors, some of whom, like Richard Wright, Ralph Ellison, and Eudora Welty, became famous novelists in later years. The FWP usually engaged in the production of reference materials. It published the American Guide Series, a collection of state and local histories, as well as compendiums of folk songs and folklore. In North Carolina, Tennessee, and Georgia, project interviewers recorded the recollections of sharecroppers, former slaves, and other common folk; much of this material was subsequently published in *These Are Our Lives.* Less important for the employment of large numbers of jobless writers, the FWP preserved information about southern history and culture.[49]

WPA programs existed to employ the able-bodied, and after 1935 care of the unemployable fell to state and local governments. To ease that burden and to respond to the rising political concerns about the care of the aged in the Depression, Congress passed the Social Security Act. Title I of the pioneering measure created compulsory old-age insurance, to which both employers and employees contributed. Other sections of the act fashioned unemployment insurance, jointly funded by the state and federal governments, and federal grants to the states for a number of welfare programs, including aid to dependent children, mothers, and the blind, as well as provision for public health. Southern congressional leaders, led by Virginia senator Harry F. Byrd, objected to many of the stipulations originally included in the Social Security Act and succeeded in altering the law prior to its passage. In particular, they feared the imposition of uniform welfare standards and administrative oversight by the Washington bureaucracy. If southern states conformed to national standards, the strain on poor state budgets and on traditional class and race relations would be disastrous, they felt. As the Jackson *Daily News* pointed out: "The average Mississippian can't imagine himself chipping in to pay pensions for able-bodied Negroes to sit around in idleness on front galleries." The exemption of farmers and domestic servants and the determination of the barest minimum welfare payments in the law that survived congressional alterations assuaged many southern dissidents.[50]

To be eligible to receive social security grants, southern states needed welfare boards to supervise local activities. In the first year only North Carolina, Alabama, and Mississippi qualified. In rapid succession, the other states formed the necessary boards, and by 1938 all southern states were receiving federal grants. But although southern states participated in social security programs, they limited coverage and benefits. In the South unemployed workers received fewer dollars and for less time than elsewhere in the nation. Fewer southerners received old-age retirement benefits in later years, because fewer had participated in the program, owing to the exemption of such occupational categories as farm laborer and domestic servant. Similarly, southern states paid lower benefits for public assistance than did other states. Sometimes the disparities were striking. In 1940 California paid monthly stipends of $37.95 for old-age assistance (Arkansas, $7.47), $48.02 to the blind (Mississippi, $7.95), and $45.00 for dependent children (Arkansas, $12.00). Poor southern states simply could not match maximum federal contributions.[51]

In 1935 Roosevelt predicted that the states would still, after the disbursement of WPA and social security funds, have approximately 1.5 million unemployables to support. The actual number finally left unattended—4.7 million—severely taxed state resources. By 1937 Kentucky, Maryland, and Mississippi transferred all relief obligations to local authorities; Florida, Georgia, North Carolina, and South Carolina paid only for administrative costs. The other southern states struggled to operate fully, and they did so only by keeping relief amounts small and limiting eligibility. The Houston *Chronicle* reported that the city's elderly without relatives lived on seventy-seven cents per week. A Memphis Council of Social Agencies study found that monthly relief income averaged $4.38 per person. Jefferson County, Alabama, recipients received $2.00 per month. In Atlanta monthly family stipends dwindled from $10.17 to $8.05 after the creation of WPA: bitter local unionists called this situation "legalized peonage." In Dallas in 1939, 8,939 persons received certification for relief employment, but only 4,973 obtained assignments. A local social worker noted that "a large though undetermined number of individuals in varying degrees of need were thus left unprovided for by any existing agency, public or private."[52]

Throughout the South the refusal to supplement federal spending underscored the unchanged priorities of community leaders. In 1934 the Charlotte *Observer* editorialized that federal relief was "unfair to citizens who must foot the bill and it is even more injurious to the quality of manhood among such beneficiaries of this mercy, leading it by subtle paths to the dreadful end of an imposed pauperization." The advent of New Deal relief and employment agencies reinforced city governments' aversion to spending their own money. For 1933 and the first nine months of 1934, Shelby County, Tennessee, depended entirely upon federal and state funds for its two-million-dollar emergency relief outlay. In 1937 it allocated 0.1 percent of its budget for welfare payments, while authorizing more money for the maintenance of public golf courses. Despite the continued demand for relief, Houston kept its spending down to "responsible" levels: the city ended 1935 with a $386,609 cash surplus, 1936 with an extra $75,000, and 1937 with a $13,000 cushion. By cutting operating expenses by over one million dollars, Dallas boasted a balanced budget for the rest of the decade after 1931. The historian of public welfare in Birmingham, noting the city's aversion to spending its money for indigent care after 1935, concluded that "local government abandoned its concern with welfare issues once it was no longer called upon to contribute local funds for this purpose."[53]

New Deal representatives frequently commented on the persistent attitudes concerning relief in southern communities. Louisiana relief director Harry J. Early told Hopkins that, regardless of federal policies, he denied farmers, sharecroppers, and tenants FERA and WPA employment, because the farmer could be self-sufficient "would he but apply himself." Lorena Hickok wrote Harry Hopkins about a conversation she had with a Birmingham steel executive who had opposed the New Deal consistently while basking in the recovery that he readily acknowledged resulted from federal government activities. At the same time he privately feared the devastation that the termination of federal programs would bring. Elmer Scott wrote Hopkins that "Memphis gave the distinct feeling that a warm welcome was extended to government concerning itself with the plight of the unemployed, and paying the bills—as long as it is the federal government. The local city and county government thus also welcomes absolution from responsibility—moral or financial." Marion Alcorn told Aubrey Williams of a prominent New Orleans attorney who deplored the expanded relief role played by the federal government, saying: "He is an advocate of 'states rights' even while admitting that that may signify the 'right' to do nothing. What he fears is that as a result of this experience, the whole process of government may be centralized and the state's affairs will ultimately be administered by officials appointed at Washington. Regardless of the justification in his own mind of these fears, inquiry failed to reveal concrete evidence that he and others concerned were engaged in planning civic, political, and economic processes which would be the surest prevention of federal interference."[54]

Indeed, substandard pay rates, the implacability of state and local officials, the miserly contributions to public relief along with near absolute reliance on federal largess, and the testimony of New Deal officials all point to a dubious record on the part of southern communities. For the first time southern municipalities established permanent, publicly funded welfare bureaus, but, according to a study of Birmingham that seems accurate for the entire South, "not because of any conviction of the public at large that relief was a responsibility of the whole people rather than a philanthropy to be supported by a few individuals; rather . . . because of the availability of federal funds through a public department." Responding slowly and sparingly, local officials and charity-minded citizens kept their faith in a fiscal orthodoxy that preached the virtues of a balanced budget. The acceptance of New Deal funds provided a way to cling to these hallowed ideas while temporarily expanding relief coverage.[55]

Yet southern states had to implement some changes in order to receive federal funds. Without the impetus provided by social security, the modest investments in social welfare would not have occurred in the 1930s—nor would the foundation have been laid for further expansion of these services in later years. By 1940 southern state governments collectively spent 10.2 percent of their budgets on welfare, an unprecedented amount for the region, if small by national standards. To be sure, southerners remained skeptical of the need for substantial welfare spending, but for the first time public assistance institutions functioned in all the states and most cities. Grudgingly, tentatively, southern governments accepted commitments to the ideal of public welfare. In 1939 the Atlanta *Constitution* editorialized that financial exigencies should not determine "whether unfortunate men, women and children who, through no fault of their own, are unable to supply themselves with food, shelter and clothing shall be permitted to suffer." The public expression of such attitudes offers evidence of the New Deal's pioneering influence.[56]

5

LABOR AND THE NEW DEAL

Workers live in terror of being penalized for joining
unions; and the employers live in a state of mingled
rage and fear against this imported monstrosity:
organized labor.

—FERA investigator Martha Gellhorn,
November 30, 1934

Whether entirely intended or not, the New Deal had a profound
impact on labor unions, with such landmark pieces of legislation
as section 7(a) of the National Industrial Recovery Act (NIRA),
the National Labor Relations Act (NLRA), and the Fair Labor
Standards Act (FLSA). Labor's successes in the 1930s not only resus-
citated a listless American Federation of Labor but also led industrial unionists to break away from the craft union-controlled AFL
to form the Congress of Industrial Organizations. Both organizations won notable victories resulting in recognition, collective bargaining, and improved wages and working conditions, but they
met particularly stiff resistance in the tradition-laden South. Well-
publicized violence erupted in the coal mines of Harlan County, the
Piedmont textile villages, the cotton fields of plantation Arkansas,
and the big city factories. Determined to protect regional wage
scales, which presumably gave southern industrialists a competitive boost, and threatened by rumors of Communist influence and
racial mixing in the CIO, southern businessmen and government
officials curtailed civil liberties and employed violence on several
occasions. Organized labor fought hard for its successes in the
1930s but, even with New Deal backing, frequently settled for in-
cremental advances that paved the way for more substantial victories in the future.

The spark for union activity came from the NIRA's section 7(a), which guaranteed workers the right to organize and bargain collectively. Intense lobbying by the United Mine Workers had forced the inclusion of section 7(a), not any involvement by President Roosevelt, who did not foresee the impact of a collective bargaining provision. Union leaders did. AFL president William Green called section 7(a) labor's Magna Charta, and UMW president John L. Lewis referred to it as a second Emancipation Proclamation. Particularly skillful in exploiting the new law, the UMW bombarded workers with the slogan "The President wants you to join a union." Business leaders heatedly disagreed and worked assiduously to block union recruiting efforts. Indeed, company unions won the competition with the AFL for new members in 1933. The initial popularity of company unions ebbed, however, and hundreds of thousands of workers flocked to struggling unions in the coal, textile, auto, and other mass-production industries.[1]

The optimism of labor unionists notwithstanding, the NIRA's section 7(a) proved to be an imperfect tool for empowering workers. The NRA's inadequate enforcement provisions led businesses to disregard unfavorable rulings, and a spate of strikes nationwide resulted in 1933–34. When management used strikebreakers, court injunctions, and other time-honored antiunion tactics to win, disgruntled workers began to drift away from the newly expanded unions. In August 1933 the NRA endorsed "proportional representation" on the shop floor, repudiated closed shops, and endorsed company unions. Businessmen challenged the legality of the National Labor Board (NLB), an agency created to arbitrate labor disputes, and ignored its findings. In June 1934 Roosevelt signed an executive order creating as a successor to the ineffectual NLB the National Labor Relations Board (NLRB). Like its predecessor, however, the NLRB foundered, hamstrung by industrial obstructionism, NRA impotence, and litigation to specify its power. Not until the U.S. Supreme Court found a second NLRB constitutional in 1937 would the full force of government authority underscore the right of workers to organize and bargain collectively.[2]

Meanwhile, labor organizers struggled in the South during the NRA years. Particularly disheartening, the AFL's United Textile Workers (UTW) suffered a dramatic setback in the southern Piedmont. By June 1934 cotton textile production operated at only 72-percent capacity, and mill owners responded with stretch-outs, layoffs, and wage reductions. When the UTW requested the preservation of current wage rates and an end to the stretch-outs, the industry cut production further and refused to recognize the union. By August, wildcat strikes involving twenty-three thousand workers in Alabama and two thousand more in Georgia forced the timid UTW to call a special convention in New York City. The five hundred delegates, spurred on by southern firebrands, voted on August 15 to conduct a general strike. Fatalistically, UTW president Thomas McMahon said: "President Roosevelt is the only person in God's green world who can stop a general strike." Roosevelt declined to intervene, and the general strike commenced on September 4, 1934.[3]

The largest strike in the nation's history to that time, the action involved an estimated four hundred thousand workers, about half of them in the South. UTW organizers spread the word to isolated mill villages by the use of fast-moving automobile caravans called flying squadrons. Mill owners deployed armed guards and deputized workers at plant gates, and violence inevitably followed. The bloodiest encounter took place at Honea Path, South Carolina, where police and strikebreakers killed seven strikers. The governors of Alabama, North Carolina, South Carolina, and Georgia called out the state militias to restore order. In Atlanta, where strikers closed all ten of the city's cotton mills, police teargassed a thousand picketers who refused to disperse. The strike raged in the midst of the state's gubernatorial primary, an unpropitious moment for incumbent Eugene Talmadge, who promised: "I will never use the troops to break up a strike." On the very night of the primary, however, Talmadge mobilized the state's entire four-thousand-man National Guard and declared martial law. Guardsmen beat and bayoneted the strikers, then sent them to a makeshift internment camp at Fort McPherson. The governor released the 16 women and 119 men picketers, who had been kept in a barbed-wire enclosure for several days, when the strike ended.[4]

By the third week of September the strike began to unravel. The UTW, lacking funds to aid the strikers, saw hungry workers drift back to the mills. President Roosevelt appointed a special mediation board chaired by John G. Winant, the former governor of New Hampshire. On September 20 the Winant board issued its report, criticizing the textile code authority's bias against unions and calling for the establishment of a new, presumably fairer Textile Labor Relations Board. Roosevelt appealed to the union to end the walkout with the Winant report as the basis for a settlement. Eager for any face-saving opportunity, the UTW did so on October 3. The union leadership grandly proclaimed the strike a success, but no one could deny that the workers returned to the mills entirely on the owners' terms. In its brief existence, the new textile code authority proved as much a paper tiger as its predecessor. Thoroughly discredited, the UTW lost members by the thousands as mill owners ignored the strike settlement and reclaimed the control over working conditions prevalent before the brief outburst.[5]

Despite apparent success in the coal mines, the UMW found section 7(a) disappointing as well. Within two years of the NRA's enactment, the union enrolled 95 percent of the nation's miners of anthracite and bituminous coal. NRA codes raised wages about 5 percent, but southern mine owners frequently ignored the agreements. In 1933–35 the Bituminous Coal Labor Board considered ninety-one complaints from Harlan County, Kentucky: it deemed only seven worthy of formal hearings and found against the mine owners six times. The owners refused to comply, and nothing changed.[6]

Under the leadership of William Mitch, the UMW deployed black and white organizers in the coalfields of northern Alabama and enlisted almost all miners under NRA provisions. The union reserved the offices of vice-president and secretary for blacks in all their locals, and this biracialism prompted fierce opposition from mining concerns. Charles DeBardeleben's Alabama Fuel and Iron Company discharged UMW members and coerced workers into signing petitions that repudiated union membership. In 1935, when Alabama miners walked out in conjunction with a nationwide strike, mine owners near Birmingham refused to approve the settlement accepted everywhere else. Dynamite concealed by company guards at the approach to the DeBardeleben mines exploded, wounding several picketers and killing one. A grand jury indicted thirteen men, but the Alabama Fuel and Iron Company remained nonunion, and the strike ended with the UMW accepting far less than they won elsewhere. The UMW still had not obtained a closed-shop contract, and many discouraged miners deserted the organization for company unions.[7]

Especially threatening to southern mine owners was the International Union of Mine, Mill and Smelter Workers (usually known simply as Mine Mill), a predominantly black organization with a history of unusual militancy in the red ore mining areas of northern Alabama and southeastern Tennessee. Mine Mill locals agreed to divide offices equally between the races: the president and treasurer would be white, the vice-president and recording secretary black. Vigorous resistance to the union generally perceived as a champion of racial equality recurred throughout the decade: in 1934, for instance, Jefferson County, Alabama, deputies using machine guns killed two Mine Mill members, injured several others, and bombed homes of blacks. NRA code authorities could do nothing to stop the violence against such unpopular "radical" unions.[8]

By 1935 the NRA's impotence produced a call for stronger legislation to protect unions. Senator Robert F. Wagner of New York, labor's foremost champion in Congress, introduced in February 1935 the National Labor Relations Act. The Wagner Act created a new NLRB with the power to supervise elections for determining the workers' representatives in collective bargaining and to protect unions from coercive management practices determined to be illegal. Roosevelt showed no interest in the bill and offered no support until its passage by the Senate. After the NRA's demise at the hands of the Supreme Court, the president's backing of the NLRA increased, and the House of Representatives approved the bill by acclamation. Senators Joe Robinson of Arkansas and Pat Harrison of Mississippi and congressmen Howard Smith of Virginia and Eugene Cox of Georgia worked in Congress to limit the NLRB's authority, but like their fellow southerners, they voted for the bill in its final, unsatisfactory form. Undoubtedly, many Democrats remained loyal to the president and voted for the bill believing that the NLRA would meet the same fate as the NIRA. To many people's surprise, however, the Supreme Court upheld the NLRA's constitutionality in the 1937 *NLRB v. Jones and Lauchlin Steel Corporation* case.[9]

Ironically, just as new legislation gave unions unprecedented protection, long-gestating tensions in the AFL surfaced, with portentous results. Insurgent unionists devoted to the recruitment of industrial workers in mass-production industries chafed under the conservative AFL leadership, which was still devoted to the preservation of traditional craft distinctions. Led by the UMW's John L. Lewis, Sidney Hillman of the Amalgamated Clothing Workers, and David Dubinsky of the International Ladies' Garment Workers' Union, these dissident unions formed the Committee for Industrial Organization. The AFL's executive council suspended these unions, and the full AFL membership voted in convention to eject them. The ten pariah unions, already actively organizing industrial workers throughout 1936, officially formed the Congress of Industrial Organizations (CIO) in 1937 with John L. Lewis as president.[10]

In order to organize the vast numbers of nonunion industrial workers, Lewis challenged the previously unassailable corporate giants in the auto and steel industries. The CIO directed most of its efforts at the midwestern industrial belt but campaigned in the few southern manufacturing centers as well. In fact, the first sit-down strike in the auto industry occurred in Atlanta, predating the more famous Flint, Michigan, episode by several weeks. Only a handful of workers had joined the United Auto Workers (UAW) in Atlanta's Fisher Body and Chevrolet plants before November 1936. Precipitated by management's threat to fire two workers for wearing union buttons, the sit-down strike lasted only one night, and picketing commenced outside the next day, when General Motors agreed not to resume production before a strike settlement. The UAW held out for over three months in the unusually snowy winter of 1936–37, as membership in the union rose steadily. The Atlanta *Constitution* condemned the tactic of the sit-down strike and praised the AFL for its refusal to employ it. The strike ended in union recognition, largely as a result of the victory over General Motors in Flint.[11]

Without question, organized labor's greatest breakthrough in the South occurred in Birmingham in 1937, when the U.S. Steel Corporation, parent company of the Tennessee Coal and Iron (TCI) firm, signed a collective bargaining agreement with the CIO-affiliated Steel Workers Organizing Committee (SWOC). This action brought more than twenty thousand steel workers in Birmingham and its suburbs under union-management agreement, a remarkable achievement given the persistence with which the city's steel interests had previously resisted union encroachments. In 1933 TCI announced its plan for "employee representation" that adhered to NIRA guidelines but, according to unimpressed unionists, only created company unions. Following several years of bitter fighting, Myron C. Taylor, U.S. Steel's chairman of the board, offered terms to John L. Lewis, and in Birmingham TCI disbanded its company union. In 1941 SWOC obtained exclusive bargaining rights within the city's steel industry.[12]

Although obtaining recognition from the city's leading employer constituted a notable achievement, it would be wrong to conclude that resistance to industrial unionism toppled along with TCI. U.S. Steel's Birmingham branch capitulated, because its corporate management decided that the national economic climate dictated a settlement. In 1936 U.S. Steel made its first hefty profit since 1929, and Taylor decided to avoid any production losses because of strikes. The time was right for U.S. Steel to deal with the unions. Immediately, however, the chairman of Republic Steel rushed to Birmingham to affirm that his company had no intention of following TCI's example. The city's police chief announced his intention to quash all strikes and responded to the criticism his remarks provoked by saying, "communist ravings from New York are like so much water on a duck's back." In 1937 James Simpson, a state senator from Birmingham, wrote and helped steer through the Alabama legislature a bill prohibiting picketing; in 1939 he rewrote the state's unemployment compensation law to disallow benefits for striking workers. If anything, TCI's pathbreaking concession seemed to stiffen resistance among business leaders. In 1940 the Birmingham Chamber of Commerce grudgingly admitted that unions had made some gains in their city of late but countered that "the district is still open shop and indications are it will remain so."[13]

Indeed, CIO unions achieved few easy victories in the South during their early years. Historian George B. Tindall concluded, "Their Southern campaigns assumed . . . the character of guerilla actions punctuated by occasional victories." Opposition in the South to the CIO emanated from a number of factors, one of the most important being the unions' putative racial liberalism. For several reasons the AFL never threatened racial inequality as the CIO brashly did. A loose confederation that granted its members a great deal of autonomy, the AFL continued its subservience to the aristocratic craft unions, and its indifference to industrial unions excluded most black workers. The CIO's targeting of the mass-production industries meant that it would have to recruit blacks, and its leadership early on voiced a firm devotion to biracialism. Such CIO unions as the UMW and the SWOC established laudable records in actively recruiting black members, but other unions implemented official policies on racial equality less scrupulously. Even so, southerners clearly identified the CIO with a racial policy inimical to regional customs. Memphis boss Ed Crump articulated the passionate feelings of many in the South when he announced: "We aren't going to have any CIO nigger unions in Memphis. They can do what they want in Detroit, Chicago, and New York City, but we aren't going to have it in Memphis."[14]

Southern opposition to trade unions also derived from an agrarian heritage that lacked a tradition of organized labor. To many in the South collective action meant communism, and talk of a strong left-wing presence in some CIO unions underwrote the opposition to organizing efforts. In a region where sharecropping prevailed in agriculture and a similar kind of paternalism characterized textile villages, workers frequently deferred to the local gentry. Membership in a trade union tore at the fabric of personal relationships in a closely knit society. The concentration of factories in small towns and rural settings, not in more cosmopolitan urban environments, underscored community cohesiveness and magnified the opposition to outlanders peddling the exotic doctrines of unionism. The fear and suspicion of outsiders impressed CIO organizer Lucy Randolph Mason, who related this example: "I recall an instance in Alabama when an Alabamian refused to join a union because its leader was 'a foreigner,' but when it was revealed that the 'foreigner' was born in the neighboring county, he said triumphantly—'I knew he was a foreigner—and he was, born outside of this county.' "[15]

Mason enjoyed some success as a roving ambassador for the CIO because southerners did not perceive her as an outsider. A descendant of such famous Virginians as George Mason, John Marshall, and Robert E. Lee, she used her status as a native daughter of the South to gain access to the inner circles of the communities she visited on behalf of the union. Motoring throughout the southern states in her famous blue Plymouth coupe, Mason brought an image of respectability to the CIO's organizing efforts and helped somewhat to discredit the critics who railed against Communist intrusion. Even so, as she readily admitted, Mason could not dispel totally the animus against unions as an alien force in the South.[16]

Scattered throughout the region, a number of worker education centers contributed to labor's image as a subversive force striving to gain a foothold in a hostile environment. The Highlander Folk School in Monteagle, Tennessee, served as the CIO's principal leadership training center. Its emphasis on worker democracy and support of liberal causes brought reproach from southern politicians. Founded by two YWCA workers, the Southern Summer School for Women Workers convened each summer after 1927 in the North Carolina mountains and provided women who worked in the textile, garment, and tobacco industries with the principles of labor insurgency. Its flourishing alliance with the CIO later in the decade cemented the school's reputation as a radical force bent on subverting interrelated labor and gender relationships. Largely as a result of such institutions, some women assumed a prominent role in the South's inchoate labor movement.[17]

The high visibility of Lucy Randolph Mason and the Southern Summer School notwithstanding, the role of women in southern labor remained limited. Unions often encouraged women to join picket lines and attempted to focus press attention on women strikers, believing that such publicity would cultivate sympathy for the workers and offset more damaging reports of violence by men, but seldom invested them with much authority. Leadership positions in the unions infrequently went to women. The CIO organized women's auxiliaries to support male workers in the auto, steel, rubber, and coal industries. Excluded from becoming union members, women found themselves providing aid during strikes, serving as labor ambassadors to their communities, and inculcating union values in their families. In short, women's positions in the labor movement mirrored their roles in southern society, where they were expected to nurture and support but not lead.[18]

The prevalence of fundamentalist religion also predisposed southerners against organized labor. Evangelical Protestantism's emphasis on deferred gratification and the acceptance of suffering in this life bred submissiveness. As paragons of their communities, preachers often sounded the warnings against the CIO's sacrileges. The union's alleged Communist connections also displeased the clergy. Some ministers imbued with the spirit of the Social Gospel found it possible to combine Christianity and union organizing, but most southern preachers agreed with the Greenville, South Carolina, evangelist who said that "CIO" stood for "Christ is Out."[19]

In many southern communities virtually all religious, civic, and mercantile institutions united against unionism and the economic problems it threatened to bring. A Tupelo, Mississippi, newspaper editor advised mill workers, "If you join the CIO, you will be endorsing the closing of a factory." Local authorities, including elected officials and judges, served at the pleasure of the leading industries, which often paid all or part of police chiefs' salaries. Lawmakers at the state and local levels passed repressive laws, suspending habeas corpus, prohibiting picketing, condoning illegal searches and seizures, and limiting free speech and other forms of expression. A subcommittee of the Senate Committee on Education and Labor, chaired by Robert M. La Follette, Jr., of Wisconsin, originally formed to investigate civil liberties violations against the Southern Tenant Farmers' Union, cited southern firms for spying and strikebreaking. The American Civil Liberties Union listed eleven major "centers of repression" in 1937: six—Harlan County, northeastern Arkansas, Tampa, Atlanta, Birmingham, and New Orleans—were located in the South. The following year's list included Memphis and San Antonio while omitting Arkansas, Atlanta, Birmingham, and New Orleans. The extensive persecution of labor organizers, many imported from outside the region after achieving impressive results elsewhere, gave the South a fearsome reputation by the late 1930s.[20]

In Memphis, boss Ed Crump marshaled the forces of his powerful political machine to oppose industrial unionism. Crump used the radical specter of the CIO to lure industry to his city, promising that local authorities would keep the dreaded unions from gaining a foothold there. Several firms built large plants in Memphis after receiving the promise of the local chamber of commerce, as well as the covert assurances of the city administration, that the CIO's absence would be perpetual. When the Firestone Rubber Company's executives considered locating a factory in Memphis, for example, they voiced concerns about labor unions to the city government. Firestone president F. F. Doyle wrote Mayor Watkins Overton that "we do not believe in any form of self-government in our shops." The mayor, in turn, told Crump: "I am afraid Firestone won't expand much here if the CIO gets busy. . . . We will have to form a definite policy of some kind." The company's move to Memphis followed shortly thereafter. To ensure the continued absence of "outside agitators" among its work force, Firestone required that all job applicants provide proof of birth in Shelby County. To demonstrate their gratitude to the hospitable Crump machine, Firestone representatives exerted considerable pressure on their employees to vote the "right way"—even providing company transportation to the polls on election day.[21]

The inevitable clash between Memphis's community leadership and the CIO began in the clothing industry, where the International Ladies' Garment Workers' Union (ILGWU) launched an organizing drive in 1937. Successful strikes at the Tri-State Dress Manufacturing Company, the Kuhn Manufacturing Company, and the Nona-Lee Company led to union recognition and collective bargaining authority for the ILGWU. The union's success in wringing closed-shop status from the three textile companies, despite the ill will of local authorities, may have seemed a notable achievement at the time, but the victory was a limited one. The total number of workers profiting from new contracts numbered only about 150. For the CIO truly to represent Memphis's industrial labor force, it would have to penetrate the larger plants—especially the auto-related concerns, such as Ford and Firestone. At the entrances to these plants, Ed Crump, Mayor Overton, and police chief Will Lee drew a line and took their last stand.[22]

The UAW dispatched veteran organizer Norman Smith to Memphis, and immediately city officials demanded that he leave. In the local press Mayor Overton proclaimed the city's position:

Imported CIO agitators, communists and highly paid professional organizers are not wanted in Memphis. They will not be tolerated. Their tools are violence, threats, sit-down strikes, destruction. They demand the American worker to submit or starve. They seek strife and conflict. They care nothing for Memphis—only to use us if they could. The City Government favors fair wages and right working conditions for the laboring man. We will oppose CIO violence, threats, and un-American policies from start to finish. Let them go elsewhere, if anyone wants them. We don't, and we won't tolerate them.[23]

Three days later Smith fell victim to a vicious beating at the hands of unknown assailants. The UAW and the ACLU registered strenuous protests, but despite the identification of the thugs by several eyewitnesses, the police failed to make any arrests. A few days later, notwithstanding the nationwide furor aroused by the incident, six men clubbed Smith with pistols and an iron hammer following his release from the hospital. Again the UAW protested to Memphis officials, again Mayor Overton issued a high-minded denunciation of violence, and again the guilty remained at large. When Smith recovered sufficiently, the UAW recalled him to its national headquarters—a move symbolic of the union's failure to penetrate the Ford plant. Within a few months Crump triumphantly boasted that "everyone has forgotten the CIO down this way. Don't hear anything about it." Indeed, the 1930s ended with the UAW no closer to representing Memphis's industrial work force.[24]

In 1940 the relative calm of the preceding few years evaporated as the United Rubber Workers (URW) singled out Memphis's Firestone plant, the nation's largest unorganized rubber factory, for an organizing campaign. The URW's George Bass received the same sort of welcome afforded Norman Smith: a crowd of two hundred men attacked him as he distributed leaflets at a Firestone plant entrance. Only the intercession of a sympathetic bystander, who drove his car through the throng and carried the helpless victim to a nearby hospital, saved the organizer's life. Local officials subsidized the efforts of the URW's competitor, the AFL's white-only Rubber Workers National Council, for the exclusive right of representation. In a vote split almost exactly along racial lines and amid rumors of gross election improprieties, Firestone employees rejected the URW by a narrow margin in favor of the AFL affiliate. At the close of 1940 the CIO's failure to organize the Firestone workers, punctuating the equally fruitless efforts at Ford, kept most of Memphis's unskilled workers free from the influence of industrial unionism.[25]

Memphis authorities' aversion to unionism extended beyond factory workers to include the discontented Arkansas sharecroppers who formed the Southern Tenant Farmers' Union (STFU). Socialist

Norman Thomas's role in founding the union, along with the STFU's policy of granting positions of authority in its hierarchy to black members, damned the organization in the eyes of Memphis officialdom. The assistant publisher of the Memphis *Commercial Appeal* wrote Thomas that the only excuse for being a tenant farmer was "lack of intelligence or ambition to be anything else." Many sharecroppers driven from Arkansas plantations for union activities settled in Memphis, only to be arrested for vagrancy and sent to the Shelby County Penal Farm. Arkansas planters, looking for non-union labor, loaded up dozens of workers each morning in Memphis and trucked them across the Harahan Bridge to work in the fields. When the STFU assembled picket lines on the bridges, Memphis police arrested the strikers. STFU leaders living in Memphis found themselves the objects of police harassment, and one union official, a University of Tennessee Medical School professor, found his faculty position in jeopardy. In 1937 the STFU's membership voted to join the United Cannery, Agricultural, Packing and Allied Workers of America, a CIO affiliate. The city formally refused to recognize the union.[26]

In Dallas, resistance to organized labor emanated from respectable, influential businessmen's groups committed to the preservation of open shops. The chamber of commerce boasted that Dallas "was one of the first open shop cities of the country" and advertised nationally the virtues of the city's docile labor force, saying: "The percentage of foreign born is negligible. From the vast labor resources Dallas industries may draw an unlimited supply of native, intelligent labor, easily trained, loyal and efficient." The chamber's Open Shop Bureau took an active role in politics, supporting candidates of antiunion persuasion. The Dallas Open Shop Association, founded in 1919 by a coterie of local businessmen, guaranteed the solvency of all its members in case of work-stopping strikes through the use of its rumored two- to three-million-dollar reserve fund. Further, it subjected any member who knowingly hired union workers to a three-thousand-dollar fine. The business community's success in safeguarding the open shop resulted in total capitulation by the local AFL leadership: the Central Labor Council even offered to help the chamber of commerce keep the CIO out of the community.[27]

The Dallas *Morning News* consistently took a hostile position toward labor unions, opposing section 7(a) and the NLRA. Moreover, the newspaper flaunted its own noncompliance with New Deal labor laws, refusing to pay its employees time-and-a-half for overtime work. In short, the paper continued to treat its workers in the frankly paternalistic way it always had. It guaranteed employees a certain wage in its contracts with them and disregarded federal requirements for minimum pay. No one at the *Morning News* punched a time clock, federal strictures notwithstanding. The company felt so strongly about management's right to deal freely with its own workers that it successfully withstood legal challenges by the U.S. government, first in the Fifth Circuit Court of Appeals and finally in the U.S. Supreme Court. The victory of the Dallas *Morning News*, one of the most influential newspapers in Texas, lent special authority to the paper's regular antiunion fulminations.[28]

As in other southern cities, violence against union organizers in Dallas was frequent, brutal, and shockingly open. In 1937 the UAW initiated a campaign to organize a local Ford factory. Several union members, labor lawyers, and sympathizers suffered beatings near the automobile plant and downtown in broad daylight. Socialist Herbert Harris was knocked out, stripped, tarred and feathered, and deposited on a downtown street. A few days later several men took a UAW attorney from a downtown drugstore and beat him savagely. Police did nothing. In 1939 and 1940 the UAW filed charges of unfair labor practices against Ford with the National Labor Relations Board, which charged company officials in Dallas with "brutality unknown in the history of the Board." They were brutal, but effective: the 1930s ended with Ford still free of UAW representation.[29]

Similar violence flared when textile unions sought to penetrate the substantial Dallas clothing industry. Hat, Cap, and Millinery Workers vice-president George Baer lost sight in one eye when three men wielding blackjacks pummeled him on a busy downtown street. Baer identified his attackers, but police took no action. Sporadic violence interrupted an ILGWU strike in which hooligans stripped ten women picketers before a crowd of hundreds in the central business district. The bitter strike dragged on for over eight months before collapsing in defeat. By 1940 several hundred garment workers belonged to two ILGWU locals, representing the signal accomplishment of labor in the city. "Nonetheless," wrote labor historian George Green, "the union rated Dallas as the only Southwestern city with a considerable dress production market that was still unorganized."[30]

Strikes also flared in the region's oil fields, the most protracted occurring against the Mid-Continent Petroleum Corporation in Tulsa, Oklahoma. Oil field workers demanding higher wages, a more formal seniority system, and an arbitration procedure for grievances struck on December 22, 1938. Governor Ernest W. Marland called out the Oklahoma National Guard, which forced picketers to relocate three blocks away from oil refinery entrances. When an unidentified striker dynamited a pipeline outside the city, hostilities increased between workers and unsympathetic townspeople. Twenty-four-hour picketing continued uninterrupted until the Tulsa local of the Oil Workers International Union reached a settlement with the company on March 22, 1939. Field workers returned to their jobs, and management promised not to punish strike leaders and to consider establishing an arbitration apparatus in the future. Characteristically, the months-long strike resulted in a restoration of earlier conditions.[31]

Because of the importance of shipping to their economies, Gulf port cities experienced most labor activity over control of the docks. Bowing to pressure from hundreds of inactive white dockworkers, the New Orleans City Council adopted an ordinance stipulating that only certified registered voters be employed on the waterfront. Black longshoremen, most of whom were disfranchised, descended upon city hall to protest. One disapproving newspaper editorial cautioned that "thousands will seek to recapture the right in the only way left open . . . by registering and voting in our elections." The U.S. Court of Appeals ordered city officials to justify the ordinance and, unmoved by Mayor T. Semmes Walmsley's arguments, enjoined the city against enforcement. Undaunted, the city commission passed a new ordinance requiring a two-year-old poll tax receipt as a precondition for employment, thus achieving the same result. The New Orleans Steamship Association balked at compliance and, to circumvent section 7(a) of the NIRA, organized separate company unions for whites and blacks. The AFL created segregated locals of the International Longshoremen's Association (ILA) and tried to subsume the company unions, but the courts scotched the attempt. The docks remained effectively nonunion.[32]

In 1935 the ILA called a strike that idled 7,500 men in the Gulf Coast from Pensacola, Florida, to Corpus Christi, Texas. Business boomed in New Orleans, however, as police escorted strikebreakers to work and a federal district court banned the strikers. Violence resulted in three deaths in New Orleans and another three in Lake Charles, Louisiana, during the sixty-two-day work stoppage. The impotent ILA unions suffered a humiliating defeat, and the following year they had their charters revoked. In a move widely recognized as conceding defeat, the AFL made the company unions the official ILA locals. Thereafter, workers complained that management ignored the few collective bargaining agreements reached and that the unions took no action on the workers' behalf.[33]

In 1937 the Pacific Coast-based International Longshoremen and Warehousemen's Union (ILWU), a CIO affiliate, challenged the ILA in New Orleans for the right to represent the workers. The ILWU promised egalitarian racial policies and an aggressive negotiating posture. The Louisiana legislature responded with a resolution condemning the union as "communistic" and calling the unionization of blacks a grave threat to white supremacy. New Orleans police raided ILWU headquarters, arrested leaders, and destroyed membership cards. Employers temporarily raised wages to aid the ILA, and the NLRB's decision determining employee eligibility to vote in the representation election had the same result. Many black union leaders favored the ILA, because its support of segregated locals and job quotas assured that entrenched blacks would retain their positions of authority. Not surprisingly, given so much opposition, the ILWU lost the critical vote by a wide margin. By the end of the 1930s the 700 white members of the ILA worked regularly; the 2,100 black members, who paid higher dues, did not. Charges of corruption and graft continued against the black ILA local, and black longshoremen worked infrequently. Most important, the challenge of the CIO had been beaten back on Gulf Coast waterfronts.[34]

From 1931 to 1935 the Houston Ship Channel became the locus of periodic outbursts, as the ILA vied with numerous shipping concerns for collective bargaining authority and higher pay. Frequent episodes of gunplay resulted in several fatalities during the period, and the ILA enjoyed only moderate success. In 1934 a waterfront strike erupted into a gun battle, resulting in three deaths and three ILA members being charged with murder. The bitterest confrontations pitted the ILA against black strikebreakers, many of whom belonged to the Independent Lone Star Colored Longshoremen's Benevolent Association. Racial divisions and the fear of radicalism, combined with the fratricidal rivalry between the AFL and CIO affiliates for primacy on the docks, left far fewer southern longshoremen than their West Coast counterparts enrolled in unions.[35]

Textiles also remained an antiunion bastion, as impervious to CIO incursions in the late 1930s as to AFL efforts earlier in the decade. With over one million employees nationally, more than the steel or automobile industries, textiles continued to be an inviting target for unionists. The Cotton Textile Institute and independent mill owners attacked the NLRA, and their creation of inactive company unions made a sham of collective bargaining. The CIO's

Textile Workers' Organizing Committee (TWOC), the legatee of the AFL's teetering UTW, launched a southern campaign in 1937 under the leadership of Sidney Hillman of the Amalgamated Clothing Workers. In April the Marlboro Mills of Bennettsville, South Carolina, became the first southern factory to accept the TWOC as the workers' bargaining agent, and in the following five months the union negotiated contracts covering twenty-thousand workers. By October 1937 the TWOC claimed eighty-four thousand members, a remarkable number given the lack of interest evidenced earlier that year.[36]

In the fall of 1937 a nationwide economic collapse—the so-called Roosevelt Recession—hit the southern textile industry. Mills closed, workers lost their jobs, and the momentum built up by the union movement crashed along with the economy. At the same time an upheaval in the TWOC's leadership caused by Sidney Hillman's resignation owing to illness undermined the union's performance. Some dissident TWOC leaders broke away and revived the UTW, which the AFL rechartered in 1939. The end of the recession and the return of prosperity emboldened mill owners, who fought union organizing efforts with renewed vigor. From 1936 to 1939 nineteen union workers died at the hands of strikebreakers, special deputies, and law enforcement officials in the South. Sidney Hillman predicted that when unions succeeded in the textile industry, "every other industry will be organized in the South. That is why we are meeting . . . such vicious opposition from all of the southern Tories." The CIO desperately needed the kind of dramatic victory achieved in the massive northern auto and steel industries, but it could manage no such triumph in textiles, the touchstone of southern manufacturing.[37]

Violence and intimidation minimized labor successes throughout much of the South, but the heavy hand of repression finally loosened its grip on the coal miners in Harlan County, Kentucky. By 1935 UMW membership in the county, up to 5,000 during the NRA drive two years earlier, had fallen to 1,200. Mine owners maintained their hegemony under the auspices of the Harlan County Coal Operators' Association. "Reform" sheriff Thomas R. Middleton employed as deputies thirty-seven former convicts, who had committed an assortment of felonies, including murder, manslaughter, robbery, burglary, and grand larceny. From 1934 to 1937 Middleton managed to increase his bank account from ten thousand to one hundred thousand dollars on an annual salary of five thousand dollars, a clear indication to La Follette committee investigators that he was on the coal mine owners' payroll. A visitor to Harlan County wrote President Roosevelt in 1937 that "in that corner of Kentucky conditions can only be compared to Germany under Hitler."[38]

A 1935 UMW recruitment drive in Harlan County met with violent opposition and ended in failure. In 1937 the union tried again, just as the La Follette committee commenced its investigation of Harlan County. Despite the increased scrutiny, violence intensified: casualties included the father of three boys who had been subpoenaed as witnesses by the La Follette committee and a deputy who balked at the mayhem raging around him. The committee's highly publicized hearings on "Bloody Harlan" led to a political housecleaning and the abolition of private mine guards. A federal grand jury indicted forty-seven men for conspiring to violate the NLRA. Although the subsequent trial failed to convict the defendants, the promise of renewed prosecution compelled the coal operators' association to seek a settlement with the UMW. In 1938 the union signed a contract, the first ever in Harlan County's sordid history.[39]

In 1939 the coal operators' association refused to renew the contract, leading to a fifteen-week strike by the UMW. Kentucky governor Albert B. ("Happy") Chandler sided with the mine owners, calling out the National Guard to disrupt picket lines. The federal government supported the nine thousand striking miners; the WPA even distributed surplus food to them. The coal association capitulated and recognized the UMW as the sole bargaining agent for the miners, the final step in ending the reign of terror. The historian of labor's struggles in "Bloody Harlan" concluded: "Through the La Follette investigation, the conspiracy prosecution, and the NLRB's enforcement of the Wagner Act, the New Deal extended a new dimension of liberty to the Harlan miner."[40]

The federal government's overt assistance to the striking Harlan County miners produced one of the decade's great victories for labor in the South and underscored the importance of intervention from Washington. In the area of labor legislation, particularly concerning hours and wages, southern states still lagged behind, primarily owing to the fear of competition from other states. A. Steve Nance, the CIO's textile organizer in Georgia, observed that "the real threat to the American standard of living . . . [comes] from the poor whites of the South. They are terribly poor and terribly productive. They must be given some sort of standards or no other standards in America will survive." The Walsh-Healey Act in 1936 set standards for hours and wages for work under government contract, and reformers called for legislation regulating all employment. An editorial appearing in the Raleigh *News and Observer* prophetically warned that any state unwilling to adopt fair wages and hours legislation "may have decent standards imposed upon it."[41]

In 1937, after the Supreme Court found the NLRA and state minimum wage laws constitutional, Alabama senator Hugo L. Black introduced into Congress a bill mandating minimum wages and maximum hours, which was overwhelmingly defeated. A new version of the bill submitted the following year outlawed child labor in most industries, set maximum hours at forty-four per week and minimum wages at twenty-five cents an hour (to become forty hours and forty cents an hour in three years), and stipulated time-and-a-half payment for overtime. According to public opinion polls, a majority of southerners favored such legislation, but the region's leadership rushed forward to condemn a measure that they saw as a grave threat to the low-wage system necessary for maintaining southern industry. South Carolina senator Ellison ("Cotton Ed") Smith charged: "Any man on this floor who has sense enough to read the English language knows that the main object of this bill is, by human legislation, to overcome the splendid gifts of God to the South." Southern lumbering interests spearheaded the opposition to the bill; the Southern Pine Association and the ad hoc Southern Pine Industry Committee spent two hundred thousand dollars annually to lobby against wages and hours legislation. Threatened by a southern filibuster, the bill's supporters agreed to a series of compromises. The Fair Labor Standards Act exempted from coverage such individuals as agricultural workers, retail and service employees, fishermen, and seasonal workers. More important to southerners, the altered bill permitted Labor Department advisory boards to rule on regional differentials but prohibited wage rates lowered solely because of region. With a number of southern congressmen dissenting, the FLSA passed in 1938.[42]

In 1940 the American Federation of Labor held the Southern Labor Conference in Atlanta. Hailed as the "largest assemblage of members of organized labor ever to meet in the south," it attracted union dignitaries from across the country.[43] In his nationally broadcast keynote address, AFL president William Green said:

We propose to help the workers of the South, to stimulate industry in the South and to benefit all the people of the South by applying, through organization, the principles of union-management cooperation. . . . The American Federation of Labor is a truly American organization. Its members are loyal, honest, devoted Americans. The American Federation believes in the institutions of private property.... We have never engaged in sit-down strikes, stay-in strikes or other revolutionary techniques. We freely concede the right of capital to a fair return on investments. We have not sent in outsiders to tell the workers of the South how to run their business.[44]

Green's affirmation of the AFL's role in labor relations and his thinly veiled criticisms of CIO tactics seemed appropriate at the end of the 1930s. The warm welcome afforded Green and the other AFL luminaries by Georgia governor E.D. Rivers and Atlanta mayor William B. Hartsfield underscored the degree to which the organization remained respectable and, therefore, acceptable to many southern leaders. Conversely, it also emphasized the degree to which the CIO's reputation suffered in comparison. Furthermore, it reflected the relative strength of the two labor federations in the South. In 1939 the CIO had only 143,600 of the South's 627,000 union members, 80,000 of them in the UMW. The AFL had more members (388,700) distributed in a wider variety of industries (146,000 in the railroad industry, 102,000 in the building trades, 30,200 in other transportation work, 23,700 in the food and tobacco industries, 21,700 in government, and 13,000 in printing trades, for example). The CIO challenged class and racial norms, provoking bitter resistance from southerners, and its gains came slowly and fitfully. At the end of the Depression decade, southern business and government leaders hated and feared the CIO as strongly as at any time since its inception. They opposed its growth just as vigorously.[45]

The CIO recorded some notable victories in the South—in the case of the Birmingham steel mills, because of a national agreement, but in other instances, such as in the Atlanta auto factories, owing to local efforts. Nonetheless, the major breakthroughs for the CIO in most industries came outside of the South. Success achieved earlier in other parts of the nation was forestalled in the South by the single-minded opposition of local authorities like Memphis's Ed Crump and organizations like the Dallas Open Shop Association. F. Ray Marshall concluded in his compendious survey of southern labor, "In spite of considerable ferment during the 1930s, southern union membership was concentrated mainly in the older AFL unions and the railway brotherhoods." In 1940 only 10.7 percent of the South's labor force belonged to unions, compared with the national percentage of 21.5. Labor's greatest success came in mining and durable goods manufacturing, its greatest setbacks in textiles. In North Carolina, the leading producer of textiles, only 4.2 percent of the nonagricultural labor force was unionized by 1939. In 1946 the CIO launched its massive Operation Dixie organizing effort, but it discreetly gave up in 1953, when the frustrating lack of membership gains persisted. For decades after the end of the Great Depression, workers in the South joined unions in fewer numbers than elsewhere in the nation.[46]

The South remained an antiunion stronghold, but organized labor made some inroads largely owing to the New Deal's influence. If the New Deal's legacy is not readily apparent in huge union membership increases, it can be detected in other areas—in the guarantee of collective bargaining that benefited some, if not all, workers; in the end to child labor, particularly in the coal mines and textile mills; in the exposure and ultimate elimination of the most onerous antiunion activities; in the elevation of southern wages closer to national norms; and in the reduction of wage differentials based on race. Without federal government involvement, without the NRA, NLRA, or FLSA, unions would surely have made even less progress, and the conditions endured by southern workers would have remained even more oppressive.

6

THE NEW DEAL
AND RACE RELATIONS

Now, while the Government is pouring millions of
dollars into the South, is the time for it to insist
upon the correction of some of the evils of the plantation system as a condition of government aid.

—Roy Wilkins, NAACP assistant secretary, 1934

Blacks in the South led a decidedly precarious existence at the outset of the Great Depression. Victimized by an omnipotent racial
caste system and saddled with the lowest paying jobs, blacks suffered disproportionately from the ravages of the economy's collapse.
Traditionally "last hired and first fired," they sustained unemployment rates consistently dwarfing those for whites. In comparison
with white residents, blacks were less likely to own homes—and
those who did had homes of less median value than homes of
whites—shared their living unit with more persons, and occupied a
higher percentage of dilapidated structures. Moreover, they endured
the indignities of a jim crow system of segregation still in its prime,
experienced political powerlessness based upon systematic disfranchisement, and, though lynchings occurred less frequently than in
the past, fell victim to a campaign of violence and intimidation designed to preserve white supremacy. The federal government supplied a modicum of relief, but always under the watchful eye of local
authorities. Federal largess helped a number of destitute blacks
make ends meet, a considerable accomplishment given the tenor of
the times, but augmented no changes in the racial caste schema.
The New Deal's muted influence in the 1930s laid the groundwork
for later assaults on southern racial inequality. The New Deal provided a necessary—if frustratingly small—first step on the road
to change.[1]

The Depression brought increased suffering to an already oppressed people. Over half the nation's blacks lived in the rural South in 1930, and 80 percent of them were sharecroppers, tenant farmers, or day laborers. The collapse of farm prices, evictions, and the lack of adequate relief uprooted approximately two million black farmers during the decade. In the 1930s four hundred thousand blacks migrated northward, but most remained in the South. Some black farmers stayed on the land, hunting, fishing, scavenging, or accepting charity from white landowners; others headed for the nearest village, town, or city, hoping for work or the financial assistance more readily available in urban areas. Unfortunately, the economic situation in southern cities was calamitous. In 1931 in New Orleans and Birmingham the jobless rate for black males was double that for white males. By 1932 blacks in Atlanta and Dallas constituted fully one-half of the cities' unemployed; in Houston and Memphis they comprised one-third. Memphis resident M. S. Stuart described a scene repeated all too often in southern cities: "I happened to pass one of the city's garbage dumps. I was astounded to see 25 or 30 colored men and women with rakes, hoes, and other digging tools, with buckets and baskets, digging around in the garbage and refuse for food and any other articles which they might be able to use."[2]

The widespread failure of black-owned businesses added to the crisis. By 1937 only two insurance companies and two banks owned by blacks continued to operate in Texas. In Memphis the Fraternal and Solvent Savings Bank and Trust Company, the "Million Dollar Bank for Negroes," failed in 1927, and the twenty-eight thousand depositors received 9.4 cents on the dollar from the bank's assets. Psychologically, noted Ralph J. Bunche, the Solvent Savings Bank's failure demoralized black businessmen, who saw its demise as "the symbolic closing of opportunities" for Memphis blacks. Between 1929 and 1935 in New Orleans, 482 black-owned retail stores went out of business; nearly 100 failed in Atlanta during the same time. Of several black-owned banks in the Gate City, only the Citizens Trust Company survived the crash of 1929. In Houston black workers were fired from their jobs as clerks in the City Market and replaced by whites; this substitution occurred in several private firms as well.[3] In 1933 the head of the Atlanta School of Social Work described the seriousness of the situation to NAACP chief executive Walter White: "White men have taken over such positions as elevator operators, tradesmen, teamsters, expressmen, bill posting, city sanitation wagon drivers . . . stewards, cooks, waiters and bell hops in hotels, hospital attendants, mechanics at filling stations, delivery boys from drug stores, and not infrequently such domestic service employment as chauffeurs, maids, and all around domestics."[4]

Jim crow also continued to predominate, as public accommodations remained separate and egregiously unequal. Public school systems kept black and white pupils strictly segregated and appropriated far fewer resources for the education of black students. In Birmingham, for example, white teachers earned an average annual salary of $1,466, and black teachers earned only $682. In New Orleans in 1938 a first-year white teacher with a bachelor's degree earned $1,000 per year, and a black teacher with the same qualifications, $909. A white teacher with ten years' experience received an annual salary of $2,200, and a black teacher, $1,440. In 1931 the maximum salaries paid Houston's black teachers equaled the minimum salaries paid white teachers. The annual per-capita cost of education for whites was $47.36; for blacks, $25.55. The Houston public schools operated kindergartens in the white schools only. Most striking, the value of property for the white schools stood at $16,544,902; for black schools, $278,068. The Atlanta Board of Education president reported in 1931 that white teachers' salaries were 30-40 percent higher than black teachers'. According to a report of the Atlanta public schools for the 1937–38 school year, the annual per-capita cost of educating blacks was $29.77; $91.29 was spent on each white pupil. The pupil-teacher ratio was 40.3 to 1 for blacks and 30.8 to 1 for whites.[5]

Jim crow laws separated the races in other public places as well. In South Carolina textile mills, laws prohibited blacks and whites from working in the same rooms or using the same stairways and windows. In Houston blacks had access to one of twenty-seven municipal parks and one of ten playgrounds. Atlanta blacks could use eight of thirty-three municipal playgrounds, two billiard rooms, and one golf course. Memphis blacks could visit the Overton Park Zoo one day a week, on "colored day." Southern cities mandated separate seating on public transportation, but they handled it in different ways. In Houston an ordinance required segregation on buses, but some drivers simply refused to accept any black passengers at all. In Birmingham streetcars, large movable partitions clamped on the backs of seats formed barriers between black and white seating areas. Atlanta taxicabs operated by whites refused to carry black passengers, so only "Harlem cabs" accepted black fares. On streetcars whites seated themselves from front to back, blacks from the rear forward. All trolley passengers entered at the front of the cars, but blacks exited through rear doors only.[6]

The list of places covered by jim crow restrictions ranged from libraries and hospitals to jails. A series of amendments to the Birmingham general code adopted in 1930 prohibited blacks and whites from gambling together and from eating in the same restaurants unless a solid partition at least seven feet high separated the races and each had a separate entrance from the street. In 1933 Houston city authorities rejected plans for a new Southern Pacific railroad station, because blacks and whites would use the same ramps to board the trains. In New Orleans black physicians could practice only at Flint-Goodridge Hospital; none worked at state-supported Charity Hospital, which segregated patients by wards. The Atlanta City Council passed a barbershop segregation law, preventing black barbers from serving whites. Some real estate agents protested, fearing loss of money if black-owned shops closed, and the Atlanta *Constitution* noted that blacks serving whites did not violate accepted customs. The city council reconsidered and adopted a weaker law that only prohibited black men who were barbers from serving white women and children.[7]

Residential segregation continued to be the rule, despite court rulings outlawing discriminatory municipal ordinances. Black residents continued to inhabit the least desirable areas of southern cities; these neighborhoods expanded when whites fled to the suburbs or distant fringes of the city and blacks replaced them. Thus Atlanta's West Side, South Memphis, Dallas's Oak Cliff, and Birmingham's "Tuxedo Junction" inched across the landscape as white residents left their homes. But racial turnover slowed and construction nearly ceased in the Great Depression years, so inadequate housing constituted a serious problem. Most black southerners crowded into rickety frame cottages, cabins, and shotgun houses made of undressed, unpainted lumber. A religious leader observed: "In many cases ventilation is unknown; in others there is nothing but ventilation."[8]

A spate of studies conducted in the 1930s revealed graphically the sorry state of the housing stock for blacks. According to a 1940 report, 80 percent of black families in North Carolina were "ill-housed," and in Atlanta's Beaver Slide neighborhood, investigators found 80 percent of the structures "in need of major repairs or unfit for human occupancy." One-fifth of the units occupied by white families needed major repairs or were unfit for use, while nearly three-fourths of all units occupied by blacks were in a similar condition. A Houston Housing Authority survey revealed that of the 16,581 families living in the most substandard dwellings, there were 6,939 white families, 7,869 black families, and 1,773 Mexican families. Houston's black neighborhoods lacked paved streets and sidewalks, and because of the inadequacy of the storm sewers, residents routinely took off their shoes and waded through the streets when it rained. In Richmond, according to a report of the Negro Welfare Survey Committee of the Council of Social Agencies, almost two-thirds of black residences required "essential repairs or alterations," and many older black neighborhoods lacked paved streets and sidewalks. In Birmingham approximately 30 percent of black homes had no sewer connections, and only about one of every twenty black residents owned a bathtub. The city never collected trash in many black neighborhoods, and streets were paved only if individual property owners paid to have it done. A Dallas housing survey reported that 86 percent of black homes were substandard, and a New Orleans investigation found the quality of black housing far inferior to that of white housing. Indeed, fully one-fourth of the Crescent City's black-owned houses had no running water. Given the squalor in which so many blacks lived, it was not surprising that they also had markedly higher mortality rates than did whites.[9]

Keenly aware of the inferior status imposed upon them, blacks found little hope for amelioration in politics. Primarily through the use of jim crow laws, but also through force and intimidation, southern states and localities disfranchised thousands of potential black voters. Southern state constitutions included literacy, property, and poll tax requirements as well as grandfather and understanding clauses. Few southern states employed secret ballots, so whites could monitor closely the voting of the few eligible blacks. In Texas, as in many other states, the white primary formed the major obstacle to black voting. In 1923 the state legislature revised the election laws to prohibit blacks' participation in Democratic primaries. When the U.S. Supreme Court ruled the statute a violation of the Fourteenth Amendment's equal protection clause in *Nixon* v. *Herndon*, the Texas legislature rewrote the law, deleting references to blacks and empowering the state Democratic executive committee to approve voting qualifications. In 1935 the nation's highest court approved this revision in *Grovey* v. *Townsend*, arrogating disfranchisement to the political party by virtue of its being a nongovernmental voluntary association. Not until 1944 did the Court rule the white primary unconstitutional, in the landmark *Smith* v. *Allright* decision. During the 1930s, efforts by blacks at contesting the Texas Democratic party's exclusionary policies fell short.[10]

Though hampered by the usual impediments—Georgia adopted the white primary and poll tax in 1909—Atlanta's blacks labored mightily to register voters and enjoyed somewhat more success in politics than did their peers in other cities. In 1932 Mrs. John Hope, wife of the president of Atlanta University, and NAACP chapter president A. T. Walden opened a citizenship school for blacks, teaching civics and the procedures for voter registration. In 1934 two organizations, the Atlanta Civic and Political League and the Colored Voters League, attempted to increase black voting. In local elections that year two blacks ran for office: Dr. B. M. Sherrard ran for a seat on the board of education, and Maceo Blackshear, district manager for the Afro-American Life Insurance Company, ran for alderman. In the election only 108 of 15,000 eligible blacks voted. Both candidates carried their home wards, but the city's at-large election proved their undoing.[11]

While Atlanta blacks cast no ballots in Democratic primaries, they could vote in general elections and, most important, in special elections on bond issues, where passage required a two-thirds majority of the number of registered voters. With turnouts consistently low for these contests, blacks could register in large numbers, ensuring that their votes would be needed to obtain the two-thirds majority, and then refrain from voting. In this way blacks blocked passage of a 1938 school bond for $1,265,000, of which only $137,500-$250,000 would have been spent on black schools. (The National Municipal League's Consultant Service recommended that $725,000 be allotted for black schools.) Approval of the bond required 22,700 votes, but only 16,000 voters went to the polls. A 1940 school bond of $1.8 million allocated only $100,000 for blacks, and it too failed, as half of the registered voters cast ballots. Despite these successes, the herculean efforts of the black community reaped limited rewards: the number of black registered voters increased only from 500 in 1930 to 1,500 in 1940, and fewer actually voted, because some were unable to pay their poll taxes.[12]

In a few southern cities political machines used black votes to enlarge their totals. In San Antonio, for instance, black gambler Charles Bellinger manipulated the black electorate for Boss C. K. Quin's Democratic organization. In Memphis Ed Crump used the state's poll tax (originally adopted in 1870 to disfranchise blacks) to his advantage by paying the levy for black voters, keeping the receipts until election day, and then distributing them to "reliable" voters. To the dismay of reporters and civic-minded bystanders, Crump operatives "herded" truckloads of blacks to polling places throughout Shelby County, provided them with poll tax receipts, and told them how to vote—frequently repeating the practice at several locations in the area. In a magnanimous gesture, Crump usually allowed blacks to vote for Republicans in presidential elections. But in the critical state and local contests, the outcomes of which had a direct bearing on the survival of Crump suzerainty in western Tennessee, election officials made sure that blacks voted the "right way."[13]

As long as these votes materialized, Crump ignored the Republican party's considerable vitality in Memphis's black community. At least he practiced benign neglect until Robert R. Church, Jr., the local black Republican leader and nationally renowned bellwether of the GOP's black-and-tan faction, ran afoul of the white power structure at the end of the decade. While Church was out of town, the city accused him of failing to pay property taxes and seized his real estate holdings, including his own house, and sold them at a tax auction. An expatriate from his native Memphis, Church settled in Chicago, and Crump purged the Shelby County Republican organization of its surviving leaders by driving them out of the city or seducing them into the new Beale Street Democratic Club. As the decade ended, Crump controlled the black vote more completely than ever.[14]

Blacks' political powerlessness reflected their vulnerability in all areas of life in the 1930s. Periodic violence and persecution of blacks unwilling to adhere to prescribed behavioral norms served as grim reminders of white supremacy. Although the Ku Klux Klan had disappeared in most localities by the mid-1920s, it continued to operate on a reduced scale in some southern cities in the 1930s. As late as 1939 the Atlanta Klan, six hundred strong, paraded in front of the offices of the Atlanta *Constitution* to protest the newspaper's editorial policies. For several months in 1930 another paramilitary group, the Black Shirts, led the crusade for white supremacy in Georgia's capital. The Black Shirts blamed unemployment on the competition from black workers and "served notice" on Atlanta businesses to replace black workers with white ones. When its leadership wound up in jail for passing fraudulent checks, driving drunk, and evading taxes, the organization died out—but not before it focused national attention on the New South city that later prided itself on being too busy to hate.[15]

Atlanta kept to center stage throughout the 1930s as the southern city most visibly engaged in the persecution of dissident blacks. The 1930 case of the "Atlanta Six" involved the arrest and prosecution of a half-dozen radicals guilty of fomenting unrest at an integrated unemployment protest. Specifically, the city charged the defendants with violating an obscure 1866 black code that prohibited "attempting to incite insurrection and circulating insurrectionary literature." The six eventually fled the state when released on bail, and they never came to trial. In 1939 the city finally dropped the charges as a result of a U.S. Supreme Court ruling in a related case. In the celebrated Angelo Herndon affair, Atlanta police arrested and severely beat the black man, an avowed Communist. Charged with violating the same 1866 statute, Herndon pled not guilty and initiated a five-year court battle. In 1937 the U.S. Supreme Court ended the byzantine legal proceedings by overturning a lower court's guilty verdict and sentence of eighteen to twenty years at hard labor. While civil libertarians and champions of racial equality hailed the Court's decision, the supposedly progressive Atlanta *Constitution* excoriated the judges and praised the conduct of the city's law enforcement agents.[16]

The decade's most infamous example of racial persecution in the South concerned the fate of the "Scottsboro Boys," nine black youths accused of raping two white women on a freight train near Paint Rock, Alabama, in 1931. An all-white jury convicted eight of the nine defendants and sentenced them to death after a farcically biased trial in Scottsboro, the Jackson County seat. When an appellate court reversed the verdicts, the state of Alabama initiated another prosecution that lasted for five years in various state and federal courts. While the NAACP and the Communist-affiliated International Labor Defense vied for control of the accused men's defense, the case became an international cause célèbre as a symbol of the South's unequal legal treatment of the races. In 1937 a final decision freed four men and sentenced the other five to lengthy prison terms. The last of the prisoners to be paroled left an Alabama penitentiary in 1950.[17]

The plight of someone like the Scottsboro Boys or Angelo Herndon might become a genuine cause célèbre, but for countless thousands of other blacks, arbitrary violence and subjugation remained everyday reminders of their inferior status. Police homicides proliferated, and "resisting arrest" became one of the leading contributors to the high mortality rate among blacks. Local courts sentenced blacks guilty of petty crimes to hard labor and punished vagrancy severely. Blacks in the Iron City referred to their hometown as Bad Birmingham, in deference to police commissioner Eugene ("Bull") Connor's brutal legions. When the Mississippi River flooded in

1937, Memphis police invaded Beale Street dance halls and theaters and forced black men dressed in their Saturday night finery to fortify the levee south of downtown. Watched by armed guards, these "conscripts" worked for hours until Boss Crump allowed them to leave. NAACP national secretary Walter White protested to Memphis mayor Watkins Overton but received no response. Though violent treatment of blacks occurred sporadically, blacks complained of their consistently humiliating treatment at the hands of local authorities. In all likelihood, the absence of even more violence testified to the fear and despair that pervaded the black communities.[18]

Faced with such debilitating circumstances, black institutions and individuals mustered their limited resources to combat the Depression. The National Urban League operated emergency relief kitchens, but most of its efforts during the Depression went into vocational programs to train maids, custodians, porters, and elevator operators. The Red Cross distributed surplus food and flour to needy blacks but had little money to sustain such enterprises. Frequently, spokesmen for city social welfare agencies addressed blacks about the value of self-reliance and the desirability of relying upon kith and kin rather than community resources. Limited local funds and the bulwark of custom, coupled with community demoralization, meant that any attempt to improve conditions for blacks would be an uphill battle. Most blacks had only the New Deal's relief and recovery programs to rely on.[19]

Problems surfaced, beginning with the National Recovery Administration, as the lack of enforcement of its "color-blind" provisions became widely known. Southern businessmen argued that whites had always received higher pay and called the prevailing NRA wage scale much too generous for blacks. Long before the U.S. Supreme Court dismantled the NRA, many employers simply disregarded the code's mandatory equal pay for the races. Southern businesses often ignored prevailing wage scales and set pay rates of certain groups at predetermined levels. When avoidance of the NRA's equal pay provision proved difficult, many employers fired blacks and hired whites or bought machinery. None of the NRA codes contained specific racial differentials, but local enforcement boards allowed the unequal pay practices to continue throughout the South. Refusing to condemn the inequity, President Roosevelt said: "It is not the purpose of this administration to impair Southern industry by refusing to recognize traditional differentials."[20]

The NRA also worked to the disadvantage of southern blacks in other ways. NRA codes exempted from coverage agricultural laborers and domestics, two categories that accounted for approximately three-fourths of southern black workers. More than one hundred codes contained wage variations based upon geographic location that, though ostensibly having nothing to do with race, effectively discriminated against blacks. Moreover, blacks suffered as consumers when the NRA's production agreements inadvertently resulted in higher prices. Thus, many harmful effects left blacks embittered against the New Deal's principal recovery program. Black newspapers called the NRA's blue eagle a "predatory bird" and sardonically concluded that the agency's acronym meant "Negro Run Around," "Negro Rarely Allowed," "Negro Removal Act," and "Negroes Ruined Again."[21]

Blacks engaged in farming looked expectantly to the Agricultural Adjustment Administration for aid but became equally disillusioned. The domestic allotment program benefited landowners, of whom few were black, and resulted in the dismissal of many black sharecroppers and tenant farmers: a total of two hundred thousand were uprooted by New Deal programs, according to Swedish sociologist Gunnar Myrdal. The AAA caused the rapid depopulation of southern farms but paid scant attention to the suddenly landless black masses. Although some AAA bureaucrats like Jerome Frank and Lee Pressman argued that the New Deal should employ agricultural reform to dismantle the South's entrenched system of racial inequality, higher-level administrators in the agency—southerners like Cully Cobb and Oscar Johnston—carried the day in favor of the landlords' interests. Secretary of Agriculture Henry A. Wallace showed no sympathy for the concerns of black farmers, declining to appoint a black adviser in his department as other cabinet members had done in theirs. Of the 52,000 people employed in the Agriculture Department by 1939, only 1,100 were black, and three-fourths of them were custodians. More critically, AAA administrators excluded blacks from serving on the county committees that applied agency policies and procedures. Blacks correctly perceived in the AAA a bureaucracy indifferent to their concerns and devoted to bolstering the position of the landed gentry.[22]

Nor did blacks enjoy better treatment from the Civilian Conservation Corps. Director Robert Fechner was a Tennessean firmly devoted to white supremacy and racial segregation. Fechner argued that "there is hardly a locality in this country that looks favorably, or even with indifference, on the location of a Negro CCC camp in their vicinity." He insisted on separate camps for the races in the South, although some integration occurred in New England, where the tiny black population made separate camps impractical. More-over, he ordered CCC officials to limit the number of black partic-ipants. In some southern cities white "enrollment councils" went door-to-door in black neighborhoods advising young men not to en-roll in the program. In Mississippi, a state in which blacks were in the majority, whites constituted 98.3 percent of CCC enrollment in June 1933. Georgia, Florida, Arkansas, and Alabama enrolled blacks only after the CCC threatened to withhold the states' allotments. Oklahoma maintained segregated camps, including separate facili-ties for native Americans. By the end of the first year, despite the federal regulations against racial discrimination, black enrollment in the CCC stood at about 5 percent nationwide.[23]

In 1934 Fechner ordered the repatriation of all blacks from camps outside their native states, their replacement by whites, and the enforcement of segregation in all CCC jurisdictions. The follow-ing year he added the restriction that blacks would be enrolled only when vacancies developed in existing black camps. Roosevelt con-curred but told Fechner not to mention his name. The president pri-vately criticized Fechner's heavy-handedness and sought to avoid controversy, but he supported the CCC's racial policies. Prior to the Second World War the number of blacks enrolled in the program never exceeded 10 percent of the total black population; considering the high incidence of poverty among black males, they were con-sistently underrepresented.[24]

Racial turmoil also surfaced in the Tennessee Valley Authority. The agency's commitment to "grass-roots democracy," in many ways a laudable attempt to ensure decentralized decision making, allowed local customs to prevail in the southern states touched by the Tennessee River. When the TVA compensated farmers for flood-ing their land for agency reservoirs, it followed the AAA's example and paid only the landowners, not sharecroppers and tenants. Black communities destroyed by the flooding received little assistance in resettlement (a shortcoming evident in white communities also), and the new town of Norris, Tennessee, prohibited black residents. The TVA further reenforced racial separation in its creation of sep-arate and unequal parks and recreational facilities in the area, as well as segregated schools for the children of TVA employees.[25]

Committed to employing blacks in numbers comparable to their percentage of the area's population, the TVA managed to meet this goal throughout most of the 1930s. Blacks usually found jobs in temporary positions, however, and in low paying, unskilled endeav-ors such as reservoir clearance, ditch digging, and the like. By far, most found employment as custodians. Such inequities led the NAACP to conduct investigations in 1934 and 1935, and in 1938 NAACP spokesmen testified before the Joint Congressional Committee to Investigate the TVA. The black organization's staff members exposed incidents of discrimination, but the congressional committee only mildly chastised the TVA. In its defense, the TVA contended that it must adhere to regional racial customs to maintain amity with local authorities. To do otherwise would jeopardize the chances for a successful program that would benefit thousands of poor valley residents, black as well as white.[26]

New Deal housing programs also reenforced segregation in the South. The Home Owners Loan Corporation (HOLC) and the Federal Housing Administration (FHA) advocated the use of racially based restrictive covenants and "red-lining," a practice whereby federal agencies denied loans on mortgages to home buyers in black or integrated neighborhoods. The FHA decried the negative influence on real estate values of "inharmonious racial or nationality groups" and lent its support to residential separation. "For perhaps the first time," noted historian Kenneth T. Jackson, "the federal government embraced the discriminatory attitudes of the marketplace. Previously, prejudices were personalized and individualized; FHA exhorted segregation and enshrined it as public policy."[27]

The New Deal's inchoate public housing program also preserved racial segregation, first under the aegis of the Public Works Administration and later under the United States Housing Authority. The PWA's Harold L. Ickes reserved about half of the federal housing projects in the South for blacks, and PWA housing contracts required the hiring of black workers. Dozens of southern cities began construction of public housing projects in the 1930s, designating a substantial proportion of them for black occupancy. No question ever arose about the suitability of segregated housing units—no one, black or white, called for integrated projects—but implementation of the program aroused considerable controversy nevertheless. Construction delays developed when black projects were located too near white neighborhoods, and despite PWA and USHA contract stipulations that blacks be employed in construction, local authorities often failed to do so.[28]

The selection of tenants and the resettlement of residents displaced by public housing raised the question of whether the units truly helped those blacks most in need, the poorest denizens of the community. In Houston black homeowners had no recourse but to accept compensation at only a fraction of the value of their houses;

if they refused, the government leveled the structures anyway to make room for improvements. Houston blacks, led by the Reverend L. S. White, marched on city hall to protest, but Mayor Oscar Holcombe dismissed them curtly. Letters to President Roosevelt and USHA director Nathan Straus achieved nothing, and construction continued on schedule. Memphis city engineers found that federal housing projects provided aid to the "top of the bottom 30 percent of Memphians in terms of salary but not to the bottom 10 percent" and that most uprooted residents could not afford the supposedly low-cost housing units designated for them. Black residents of Atlanta's John Hope Homes earned an average annual salary of $735; the average for all blacks in the city was $576. In Birmingham public housing residents had to have a "steady income sufficient to meet the project rentals without denying themselves other essentials of life." Again, the poorest citizens hardly qualified.[29]

Site selection frequently proved problematic. Birmingham blacks protested their exclusion from decision making, especially regarding the construction of the Smithfield Court project, a residential complex for blacks. No blacks served on the PWA advisory board that chose the site or spoke at the groundbreaking ceremony. In Memphis authorities razed a black neighborhood to erect whites-only Lauderdale Courts and destroyed one of the city's finest middle-class black enclaves to build Foote Homes. In the latter case, a coalition of black property owners wrote to Mayor Watkins Overton that completion of the project would undermine the pride blacks felt in owning a home in a decent neighborhood. Area residents urged that the project be built a few blocks further south, and both of the city's daily newspapers published petitions signed by blacks and whites opposing the site choice. City officials refused to reconsider. The unilateral decisions about public housing confirmed what many blacks suspected—that the primary function of such housing was to maintain existing patterns of racial segregation rather than to address concerns about inadequate housing.[30]

Questions similarly arose about the discrepancy between the regulations governing federal relief dispensation and actual implementation. The Federal Emergency Relief Administration and the Works Progress Administration officially barred racial discrimination, yet local agents openly paid black workers less than whites. In 1935, for example, Atlanta's average monthly relief stipend to whites was $32.66, to blacks, $19.29; Houston gave whites $16.86 and blacks $12.67. Certification officials in Birmingham commonly turned down black applicants after intensive questioning found them "undeserving." Throughout the South officials registered blacks only when all white applicants had been provided for. In Bolivar County, Mississippi, the CWA foreman imported white workers from other locations even though eight hundred local blacks clamored for employment. Social security's exclusion of agricultural and domestic workers and its delegation of retirement pension funding to the states were similarly unwelcome developments. Howard University political scientist Ralph J. Bunche summed up blacks' disgruntlement, saying that the New Deal meant "the same thing, but more of it."[31]

Black women especially experienced a great number of inequities in New Deal programs. In some communities sewing project floors were segregated, whereas other southern cities located sewing projects exclusively for black women in black neighborhoods. Frequently black women lost their positions in sewing rooms and canneries and were forced to perform physically arduous labor in landscaping and construction. When awarded WPA jobs, the Birmingham NAACP charged, black women performed work on city streets normally done by men, such as rolling wheelbarrows and swinging picks and shovels. South Carolina officials forced black women relief recipients to do road work, and in Jackson, Mississippi, black women construction workers toiled under the supervision of armed guards. The Memphis NAACP inveighed against Civil Works Administration officials' practice of assigning black women to homes of personal friends for domestic work as a prerequisite for receiving aid. The Memphis branch of the National Youth Administration basically limited its job training programs for blacks to domestic work, in response to the cry that "good help" was becoming increasingly hard to find. The NYA did the same in other southern localities, consigning black women to low-level jobs offering scant hope for self-improvement.[32]

Blacks criticized Roosevelt not only for his neglect of racial discrimination but also for his unwillingness to endorse the greatest civil rights goal of the decade, an antilynching law. Enhanced economic competition during the Great Depression produced a recurrence of brutal lynchings: seven were reported in 1929, twenty-one were reported annually in 1930, 1931, and 1932, and twenty-eight were recorded in 1933. Jessie Daniel Ames led a spirited antilynching coalition composed of women's clubs, missionary societies, and other white women devoted to racial comity. Firmly limited to a policy of moral suasion, Ames's Association of Southern Women for the Prevention of Lynching rejected federal antilynching legislation and lost influence as other groups increasingly sought government involvement. Long engaged in litigation against the white primary and other discriminatory practices, the NAACP diverted its resources into the campaign against lynching. In 1934 the organization's efforts seemed to bear fruit when senators Robert F. Wagner of New York and Edward P. Costigan of Colorado introduced a bill in Congress that held state and local officials accountable for protecting prisoners and for prosecuting lynch mobs. The bill also provided for levying ten-thousand-dollar fines against counties where lynchings occurred. Even though the Senate Judiciary Committee favorably reported the bill, the president declined to support it publicly.[33] Twice that year Roosevelt told NAACP executive secretary Walter White that he personally approved of the measure but for political reasons could not make his feelings known. He said: "I did not choose the tools with which I must work. Had I been permitted to choose them I would have selected quite different ones. But I've got to get legislation passed by Congress to save America. The Southerners by reason of the seniority rule in Congress are chairmen or occupy strategic places on most of the Senate and House committees. If I come out for the anti-lynching bill now, they will block every bill I ask Congress to pass to keep America from collapsing. I just can't take that risk."[34]

Lacking the president's support, the bills never came up for a vote in the 1934 legislative session. Later that year public opinion throughout much of the nation demanded congressional action, after a crowd of four thousand enthusiastic onlookers cheered the grisly lynching of Claude Neal in Florida. In 1935 Congress gave antilynching fuller consideration, but a six-day filibuster by southerners again resulted in no vote being taken. Again Roosevelt kept silent. In 1936 and 1937 similar defeats ensued, and in 1938 fifteen southern senators filibustered for an incredible six weeks before Roosevelt asked for the bill's withdrawal and consideration of emergency relief legislation. In 1939 the president remained noncommittal even though his wife, Eleanor, publicly endorsed antilynching laws. The need for economic legislation and, by the end of the decade, military preparedness kept Roosevelt from alienating southern powerhouses on Capitol Hill. Black leaders understood the president's dilemma but grew impatient at his continued pleas for forbearance. Walter White wrote Roosevelt: "It is my belief that the utterly shameless filibuster could not have withstood the pressure of public opinion had you spoken out against it."[35]

Yet for all of its inadequacies, the New Deal became very popular with black Americans. The president's disappointing performance in the crucial antilynching crusade and his toleration of discrimination in government programs were offset by a number of more positive developments. As never before, federal government officials spoke out against racial inequality. Although the president hardly seemed to care at all about race relations, outspoken liberals in his administration—beginning with the first lady, Eleanor Roosevelt—left no doubt about their deep concern. Like her husband a product of an isolated, privileged upbringing in New York's high society, Eleanor Roosevelt cared little in her formative years about racial matters. Work for social welfare agencies in New York City later gave her empathy for the poor and downtrodden, and her developing friendship with Walter White and Mary McLeod Bethune, president of the National Council of Negro Women, brought her a fuller appreciation of the concerns of blacks. She became an unofficial ombudsman for blacks in the White House, championing their cause, arranging appointments for black leaders like Walter White with her husband, and constantly pestering the president and his top advisers about racial matters. While Franklin Roosevelt first thought of the political ramifications of all actions, Eleanor Roosevelt argued for justice and equality as the moral imperative. According to presidential speech writer Robert Sherwood, she acted as "the keeper of and constant spokesman for her husband's conscience."[36]

To the growing consternation of many southerners, Eleanor Roosevelt publicly advocated stringent measures to aid blacks. Her high profile in promoting civil rights made her the object of scorn and hatred among the most virulent southern racists, who spread rumors about "Eleanor clubs" fomenting racial mingling. Two incidents involving the first lady especially outraged her white critics. First, she sat in the "colored" section of the Birmingham auditorium at the 1938 national meeting of the Southern Conference for Human Welfare. When local police intervened to segregate the seating, she defiantly set her chair in the aisle between the white and black sides. Second, Mrs. Roosevelt resigned her membership in the Daughters of the American Revolution when the organization restrained black contralto Marian Anderson from performing in Constitution Hall; she subsequently helped to arrange another site for the concert. Such limited deeds may have produced insignificant advances for the nation's black population, but Eleanor Roosevelt's unprecedented actions won her—and her husband—the undying gratitude of black people unaccustomed to such symbolic gestures.[37]

Also renowned for his devotion to civil rights, secretary of the interior and public works administrator Harold L. Ickes had worked for racial change for decades as president of the NAACP chapter in his native Chicago. Shortly after arriving in Washington, Ickes desegregated public facilities in the Interior Department and later effected the same changes in the PWA. He hired many blacks in white-collar positions and integrated several northern housing projects and some southern national parks. At his insistence, the PWA set aside 50 percent of federally subsidized public housing in the South for blacks. As a result of Ickes's persistence, PWA funds totaling forty million dollars paid for the construction or renovation of eight hundred hospitals, schools, and libraries for blacks in the South. Ickes also established the office of race relations adviser in the Department of Interior and a similar position to monitor all federal agencies. He first appointed white Atlantan Clark Foreman and later Robert C. Weaver, a black economist, to fill that post. Ickes also helped create a special interdepartmental committee on Negro affairs that existed only for a short time. Although his efforts were frequently unpopular and he found himself accused of paternalism, Ickes never wavered in his commitment to desegregate his bailiwick.[38]

The highly visible efforts of New Dealers like Eleanor Roosevelt and Harold Ickes brought other liberals concerned about racial issues to Washington, including John M. Carmody of the Rural Electrification Administration, Nathan Straus of the United States Housing Authority, Hallie Flanagan of the Federal Theater Project, and W. Frank Persons of the Labor Department. Methodist clergyman Will Alexander, author of a highly regarded text on southern cotton tenancy and the founder, director, and chief spokesman of the Commission on Interracial Cooperation, succeeded Rexford G. Tugwell in 1937 as director of the Farm Security Administration. Alexander made do with an inadequate budget and clashed repeatedly with Congress, but under his direction the FSA established a sterling record for aiding blacks. The agency dispensed loans to blacks according to their proportion of the population, and by 1940 black families, most of whom lived in the South, occupied over half of FSA rental cooperatives and one-fourth of FSA homesteads. Alexander had no control over the amount of money allocated by Congress for rural relief—and it repeatedly proved inadequate—but blacks knew he would ensure that they received their fair share.[39]

Aubrey Williams, another white liberal southerner, used his positions of authority in various New Deal agencies to aid blacks. After serving as FERA field representative for the southwestern region, the Alabama social worker became deputy director of the

CWA and the WPA and director of the NYA. He mandated equal pay for the races in the South as well as in the North, funneled a substantial amount of funds to poor black colleges, and directed that skilled labor and preprofessional training programs be available to black as well as white youths. Williams's dogged determination to use the NYA to challenge southern racial traditions made him one of the most despised New Deal liberals, and southern conservatives successfully led the fight to deny his confirmation by Congress as head of the Rural Electrification Administration. Such opposition kept Roosevelt from nominating Williams to replace Harry Hopkins as WPA chief in 1938.[40]

Although New Deal administrators like Ickes, Alexander, and Williams lacked the authority to change the treatment of blacks in all areas of life and such agencies as the AAA, NRA, and CCC treated blacks as second-class citizens, the efforts of these liberals were noteworthy. In addition to the PWA, the FSA, and the NYA, the USHA became known for its nondiscriminatory racial practices. The USHA hired black workers on public housing construction projects and continued the PWA's policy of providing blacks with a significant portion of housing units. Despite its flaws, the WPA also received high marks from needy unemployed blacks. In 1939 the WPA provided the primary financial support for nearly 750,000 southern black families, as the agency joined agriculture and domestic work as their chief sources of income. In Virginia cities at one time more blacks than whites received relief. Harry Hopkins's attempts to equalize wages and include blacks in all WPA projects frequently met defeat at the hands of local administrators, but he never ceased trying. If blacks seldom received the relief their impoverishment dictated, greater numbers benefited from government aid than ever before. The bitter testimony of southern whites attests to the inroads made by the WPA. A southern landlord groused: "I don't like this welfare business. I can't do a thing with my niggers. They aren't beholden to me any more. They know you all won't let them perish." For southern blacks the New Deal agencies offered some alleviation of the situation imposed by the iron rule of local authorities.[41]

Blacks also lauded the New Deal's pathbreaking federal government employment policies. During the 1930s the number of blacks receiving paychecks from Washington tripled to about 150,000, owing in part to the abolition of the civil service regulation requiring job applicants to submit photographs. Although most blacks continued to occupy unskilled and semiskilled jobs, an unprecedented number of black lawyers, engineers, economists, and scientists appeared on the federal payroll. The appointment of blacks to higher government positions than in the past, coupled with the employment of racial advisers in some government departments, gave blacks higher visibility in Washington than ever before—a fact not lost on white southerners. Some complained acidly that "Negroes were taking over the White House." The existence of the "Black Cabinet," an informal group of advisers who met sporadically to exchange information and plot strategy, left these same southerners even more apoplectic. By the admission of its own unsettled, fluctuating membership, the Black Cabinet wielded very little influence in the highest councils of government. Its primary importance was symbolic, yet that symbolism spoke volumes, with starkly contrasting meaning to white and black southerners.[42]

As blacks came to see the New Deal as a generous benefactor, they began to alter their long-standing fealty to the Republican party. In 1932 Pittsburgh *Courier* publisher Robert L. Vann told black voters: "My friends, go home and turn Lincoln's picture to the wall. That debt has been paid in full." But not many blacks agreed with Vann, and despite Herbert Hoover's apparent indifference to their plight, more than two-thirds of black voters cast their ballots for the incumbent. In addition to his party affiliation, Roosevelt possessed other liabilities in the minds of black voters. His running mate, John Nance Garner, hailed from Uvalde, Texas, a town that supposedly barred blacks from even entering its boundaries. Roosevelt's boast that, as undersecretary of the navy in 1915, he had written Haiti's repressive constitution caused much concern as well. But dismissing their initial reservations, blacks responded favorably to indications that Roosevelt's administration would be an improvement over Hoover's. High-level appointments, more patronage for blacks, and increased relief in the New Deal's early days sent the president's stock soaring in black communities.[43]

In 1934 blacks gratefully acknowledged the new administration's pioneering innovations and voted Democratic. Franklin Williams, president of the Phelps-Stokes Fund, noted that "it was not civil rights" that dictated the voting shift of black Americans. "It was jobs." An embittered white Georgia politician put it differently: blacks, he said, voted Democratic "since Roosevelt became Santa Claus." Old-line black Republican stalwarts like Memphis's Robert R. Church, Jr., Henry Lincoln Johnson of Georgia, and Percy Howard of Mississippi continued to support the party of Abraham Lincoln and emancipation, but a younger generation of voters with less investment in the GOP found the Democratic party more inviting. Many of these younger black politicians saw little hope for advancement in the Republican hierarchy and forged careers in the more dynamic Democratic organizations, particularly in northern cities, where growing ghettos were already electing representatives to Congress.[44]

In 1936 blacks voted for President Roosevelt by a substantial majority, as much as 76 percent in the North. A few black newspapers declined to endorse the incumbent, but most of the influential dailies jumped enthusiastically on the Democratic bandwagon. In the southern states, where disfranchisement strategies kept an estimated 95 percent of eligible black voters from casting ballots, the swing away from the Republican party was less apparent. In the few cities where blacks voted in significant numbers—mainly in Texas, Tennessee, and North Carolina—the votes for Roosevelt materialized as they had in the North. In 1940 Roosevelt's margin of victory declined among virtually all voting groups, but less so with blacks than whites. Black voters supported the third-term candidacy strongly and established themselves as the most reliable constituents of the emerging Roosevelt coalition.[45]

The Roosevelt revolution in politics had less immediate impact in the South than elsewhere. By the end of the 1930s the number of black voters in twelve southern states examined by Ralph J. Bunche totaled only about 250,000. The number of whites voting Democratic remained much greater in the South, and the Republican party maintained some allure for blacks. In later decades, however, demographic changes significantly altered the calculus. Southern black migrants to northern cities reenforced Democratic voting tendencies, while blacks who remained in the South struggled to participate in party primaries and otherwise obtain a voice in party councils. Also enamored of Roosevelt and the New Deal, southern blacks became gradually more assertive and accordingly more influential. As a result, the allegiances of southern whites to the Democratic party faltered, and one-party dominance gave way to a more competitive two-party system.[46]

Just as the New Deal led to dramatic political changes, the initiatives of the federal government in the 1930s also spurred increased activity by civil rights groups. Organizations like the NAACP and the National Urban League led demonstrations, lobbied in Washington, and fought legal battles more often and with greater passion than before. Blacks in northern cities conducted rent strikes, boycotts, and "Don't Buy Where You Can't Work" campaigns and generally exhibited a boldness unmatched below the Mason-Dixon line. The New Deal's affirmation of racial justice stirred many whites in the "silent South," and abetted by southern white liberals, blacks challenged regional norms as never before. Blacks protested jim crow restrictions, police brutality, discrimination in relief appropriation, and economic exploitation. In Durham, North Carolina, for example, blacks picketed a grocery store to compel the reinstatement of recently released black workers. In nearby Greensboro, blacks boycotted a movie theater that showed films depicting blacks in unflattering roles.[47]

At a time when mass action carried considerable risk in the South, blacks more often chose courtrooms as the venues for challenging existing laws and customs. Although the legal challenge to white-only primaries fell short in the 1930s, blacks won some notable victories in the courts. The U.S. Supreme Court overturned the rulings of lower Alabama courts in the celebrated Scottsboro case, ruling that the black defendants had been denied equal protection of the law. The Court also ruled for a black litigant in *Missouri ex rel. Gaines* v. *Canada* in 1938, instructing the University of Missouri to admit a black student because the state offered no legal training for racial minorities. This decision paved the way for the ultimate destruction of segregation in public education. Of Franklin D. Roosevelt's eight appointments to the U.S. Supreme Court, only one—South Carolinian James F. Byrnes—opposed the battle against discrimination. The others helped lay the groundwork for the subsequent civil rights revolution. "What would culminate in the Warren Court," observed historian Harvard Sitkoff, "began in the Roosevelt Court."[48]

Indeed, much of the change in race relations that came in the 1950s and 1960s began slowly, cautiously, in the 1930s. These modest origins, what historian Bernard Sternsher termed a "prelude to revolution," made possible the truly remarkable alterations that followed. As in the later era of the Second Reconstruction, the federal government played the crucial role in instigating change. The New Deal's accomplishments were in many ways limited: federal agencies routinely supported discriminatory practices in the South and practiced more of the same. Occasionally, as in the case of the FHA, federal involvement exacerbated existing conditions. The majority of New Dealers, paralleling the attitudes of most white Americans in the 1930s, never cared deeply about the plight of blacks and considered the alleviation of racial inequality a low priority. Yet a group of liberal New Dealers took an interest in the plight of black

Americans, and their efforts made an impact. Most important, the New Deal insinuated the national government into the relationship between black and white southerners, with dramatic consequences in later years. That is why, despite Franklin Roosevelt's shortcomings, black southerners revered him and his New Deal. And that is why white southerners grew wary of the New Deal and deserted the president by the decade's end.

7

SOUTHERN POLITICS

I will have trouble with my own Democratic party
from this time on in trying to carry out further programs of reform and recovery.

—Franklin D. Roosevelt, 1935

Southern politics played an important role in the development
of the New Deal. Recognizing the importance of southern votes,
Franklin D. Roosevelt avidly courted Dixie's Democrats, and their
support was crucial in his nomination for president in 1932. Powerful southern Democrats in Congress made possible the passage of
much New Deal legislation, particularly in the "First New Deal" of
1933, but effectively blocked later laws they considered inimical to
their interests. By the end of the decade the same legislators helped
the president secure defense measures from a balky Congress wary
of military preparedness. The South benefited significantly from
New Deal programs as well, yet southerners formed the heart of the
conservative coalition that checked federal initiatives. Much of the
South's ambivalence stemmed from changes in the Democratic
party that threatened the region's prominence. The Roosevelt revolution transformed American politics, elevating the Democrats nationally while chipping away at the party's hold on the solid South.
Thus, political scientist Marian D. Irish correctly noted that
Roosevelt had both "his staunchest supporters and his strongest opponents within the ranks of his own party south of the Mason-
Dixon line."[1]

By the time he assumed the presidency, Franklin D. Roosevelt
had become a well-liked and well-respected figure in the South. As

assistant secretary of the navy under Woodrow Wilson, Roosevelt learned the importance of dealing with the powerful southern congressmen who controlled the military's purse strings. He observed the southern style of politics as practiced by Secretary of the Navy Josephus Daniels—a North Carolinian—and impressed congressmen with his administrative skills. After being stricken with poliomyelitis in 1921, Roosevelt took up residence in Warm Springs, Georgia, to use the warm water full of mineral salts for rehabilitation. The therapy never completely restored the use of his legs, but Roosevelt became partially ambulatory with the use of braces and crutches. Determined to continue the fight against polio, he invested two-thirds of his family fortune to establish the Georgia Warms Springs Foundation as a nonprofit clinic. He also purchased 1,200 acres of adjacent land and over the years grew a variety of crops and raised livestock there. Driving his specially built, hand-controlled automobile around the Georgia landscape, Roosevelt became well known throughout the state and acquainted himself with the land, people, and politics of the region. He became an adopted son of the South.[2]

During the 1920s, with Republican presidents ensconced in Washington, Roosevelt worked to heal the breach between the urban and rural factions of the Democratic party. More so than any other eastern politician, he traveled widely in the South and West to salve the hard feelings left from the fratricidal 1924 national convention. In that bitter conclave, rural supporters of California's William G. McAdoo and urban backers of New Yorker Al Smith fought to a stalemate before compromise candidate John Davis received the presidential nomination on the 103d ballot. In 1928 Smith won the nomination, but his parochial campaign focused almost entirely on the Northeast and Midwest and paid little attention to the South. His Roman Catholicism, opposition to Prohibition, apparent alliance with Wall Street, and urban provincialism contributed to an abysmal showing in Dixie. Indeed, the Happy Warrior managed to lose seven states in the solid South, and Republican Herbert Hoover won easily. Elected governor of New York in an otherwise disastrous year for Democrats, Roosevelt remained popular in the South. Though supporting Smith, Roosevelt disavowed the party's positions on many issues unpopular in the southern states—especially Prohibition. He continued to support "states' rights, local option." His 1930 reelection in New York left Roosevelt the front-runner in the South for the presidential nomination.[3]

In 1932 Roosevelt seemed the likeliest candidate to unite the party and return it to power in Washington, but Herbert Hoover's unpopularity because of the Great Depression encouraged many Democratic politicians to challenge the New York governor for the presidential nomination. Al Smith continued to command the loyalty of the big city masses, and others such as Maryland governor Albert Ritchie and former secretary of war Newton Baker waged aggressive campaigns. Most troubling for Roosevelt, the candidacy of U.S. Speaker of the House John Nance Garner of Texas threatened to erode his southern support. The party's rule that a candidate be chosen by two-thirds of the convention delegates kept Roosevelt from nomination through the first three ballots. At that point Garner realized that he lacked the national support to win and that his continued candidacy would only damage Roosevelt and aid Smith. So Garner, who controlled the large Texas and California delegations, released them to support Roosevelt and received as consolation prize the vice-presidential nomination. Southerners surely would have preferred a favorite son like Garner, but they settled for the second-best alternative. Ironically, considering later developments, Roosevelt enjoyed tepid support in the urban North and owed his nomination to the South.[4]

In 1932 Roosevelt campaigned energetically but offered the electorate few specifics. His speeches contained broad generalizations, suggesting that the Democrat had liberal leanings on many issues but could be counted on to manage the budget conservatively. On a few occasions Roosevelt made reference to a "new deal," but he never clearly defined what that meant in practical application. Certainly, many Americans voted against Herbert Hoover's failed policies as much as they voted for the Democrat's vague promises. Southerners liked Roosevelt and supported him out of party loyalty—not because of ideological commitment. His election left many southerners unsure of what to expect, yet a mood of jubilation reigned in the region. Their candidate had won, and the South had played a major role in the victory. As journalist W. J. Cash wrote: "For the South, in truth, it was almost as though the bones of Pickett and his brigade had suddenly sprung alive to go galloping up that slope to Gettysburg again and snatch victory from the Yankee's hand after all."[5]

When Roosevelt arrived at the White House in March 1933, the seniority system in Congress gave southerners a position of remarkable strength: they chaired nine of the fourteen most important committees in the Senate and twelve of seventeen in the House.

Moreover, Roosevelt could rely on a number of estimable southern Democrats to manage New Deal legislation on the floor of Congress. Senate majority leader Joe Robinson of Arkansas, minority leader since 1923, quickly showed his mettle by pushing the Emergency Banking Act through the Upper House in seven hours. Despite his own misgivings about the administration's measures, Robinson performed the same feats repeatedly in the New Deal's first months. Vice-President Garner presided over the Senate ably in the early years. Joseph W. Byrns of Tennessee, the new Speaker of the House, submerged his own conservatism and worked avidly to assure the passage of New Deal legislation—as did his successors, William Bankhead of Alabama and Sam Rayburn of Texas.[6]

A number of other southern Democrats held key positions in the seventy-third Congress. Mississippi senator Pat Harrison chaired the pivotal Finance Committee and took a leading role in passing the National Industrial Recovery Act, the Social Security Act, and several tax measures. South Carolina's James F. Byrnes served so effectively as Roosevelt's liaison in the Senate that presidential adviser Rexford Tugwell said: "I seriously doubt that any other man on Capitol Hill could have achieved the parliamentary victories realized by Byrnes." Robert Lee ("Muley") Doughton of North Carolina, chairman of the House Ways and Means Committee, piloted New Deal bills through with consummate skill. Before becoming Speaker of the House, Sam Rayburn chaired the Committee on Interstate and Foreign Commerce and helped steer to passage the Securities Act, the Securities Exchange Act, the Public Utilities Act, and the Rural Electrification Act.[7]

These southerners wholeheartedly supported the president in the spring of 1933 for several reasons. First came party loyalty. Democrats in Congress had been in the minority for a dozen years and had no intention of squandering their partisan advantage by challenging the president. Second, Roosevelt's popularity with the people preempted any obstruction by Congress. The gravity of economic depression demanded forceful action by the new chief executive, the people clamored for it, and lacking any contrary proposals of their own, congressional leaders gladly assented. Even archconservatives like North Carolina senator Josiah Bailey urged extraordinary action by the president. Third, the South stood to benefit from New Deal bills. Increased relief, construction, and employment seemed like a godsend to southerners, and if some defenders of states' rights questioned the extent of Washington's involvement, the opportunity to obtain federal dollars proved paramount. Finally, there was little in the legislative cornucopia of 1933 that caused southerners grave concern—no mention of civil rights, public housing, social security, wages and hours legislation, or utilities regulation. Suspicion that the New Deal might be too radical did not appear in most quarters for several years.[8]

Mayors, city councils, and city commissions, overwhelmingly composed of Democrats throughout the South, also pledged their fealty to President Roosevelt and observed what became a rite of political orthodoxy by affirming their support of the New Deal. Rhetoric aside, the attachment to Washington was partisan and practical, not ideological. Roosevelt reached a modus vivendi with the region's big city politicos as easily as he did for so many years with the gallused demagogues of the backwaters. As long as local leaders turned out the Democratic vote and kept their most odious practices within limits, New Deal officials kept their hands off local affairs. Much to the displeasure of many of his liberal supporters, Roosevelt allied with such infamous big city bosses as Chicago's Ed Kelly, Kansas City's Tom Pendergast, and Boston's James Michael Curley, allowing them to dispense patronage and other federal emoluments through city halls. As historian Lyle W. Dorsett noted, "Under the New Deal many welfare programs were financed in Washington, but they were *directed* at the local level." As long as they remained loyal, disreputable politicians could remain in the president's good graces.[9]

Boss Ed Crump in Memphis, one of the few southern cities ruled by a political machine, maintained a tenuous alliance with President Roosevelt throughout the 1930s. First as a congressman and later as a private citizen, the Memphis boss supported all New Deal measures. While serving in the U.S. House of Representatives, Crump voted for every law endorsed by the White House, remained unstinting in his praise of the New Deal, and argued that Roosevelt "has done more for the South than any President—aid to the farmers, public works, TVA." According to his biographer, Crump "liked the president's energy, flair, and forcefulness; he was especially impressed with the way in which Roosevelt had risen above his physical handicap." Also, "both were of the aristocracy of their particular regions, yet both came to be thought of as the benefactor of the 'little' man." Whatever the apparent similarities between the two men, self-interest bound them together. As the preeminent figure in Tennessee politics, Crump held the balance of power in the state. As the head of the national Democratic party and guardian of patronage, Roosevelt offered much to local politicians.[10]

Crump clashed with Roosevelt on occasion and balked at the more liberal New Deal experiments, but he remained loyal because of the largess afforded his machine and the autonomy he enjoyed in presiding over its distribution. City government appropriated very little money, but Crump was empowered to name local relief agents who took charge of dispensing federal funds. With roughly one-ninth of Tennessee's population, Shelby County received one-seventh of the WPA jobs. Over the years the combined enrollments of the FERA, CWA, WPA, and PWA brought thousands of jobs to Memphis—jobs that, though created and funded by the federal government, passed into the hands of the needy through the good offices of the Crump organization. Not only did the federal government make no effort to dislodge the local Democratic machine, but its generous patronage policy amounted to tacit approval of Mr. Crump and his minions.[11]

Because the machine ruled without viable opposition, it was impervious to exposés of electoral chicanery published by the crusading Memphis *Press-Scimitar.* Only the inconvenience and embarrassment of two U.S. Senate investigations aroused any concern. When Senator Gerald P. Nye, chairman of the Campaign Funds Committee, arrived in Memphis to conduct hearings on the 1930 gubernatorial primary, Crump conferred with another committee member, Senator Robert F. Wagner, and reported the results of that conversation to Tennessee senator Kenneth D. McKellar: "Wagner assured me that he agreed with me all along the line that nothing of a condemnatory report should be made regarding Memphis and I believe it will not be made. You can rest assured I will do everything possible to prevent it." Nye complained that poll tax receipts had been burned after the primary, ostensibly to save storage space in the courthouse, but he took no action. He also identified the Macon County and Memphis Republican primaries as the investigation's principal targets. At the conclusion of the hearings, Nye reported that the committee unearthed "no substantial grounds for the more serious charges" against the Democrats.[12]

In 1938 a much more exhaustive investigation of the Crump machine's alleged vote stealing occurred as a response to reports of irregularities in that year's senatorial primary. Senator David Walsh of Massachusetts accused the Crump organization of using federal jobs and relief to coerce voters, a practice he termed "gutter politics." When the six-man investigating committee came to Memphis, WPA administrator Harry Hopkins joined Mayor Watkins Overton in refuting the charges. In its report, the committee condemned the Memphis Democrats for illegally soliciting funds from WPA workers and relief recipients but added that the other faction engaged in similar practices elsewhere in the state. Both Crump supporters and opponents had purchased poll tax receipts in great numbers. Because both senatorial aspirants appeared guilty of corruption, the committee saw no merit in denying the Crump candidate his victory. These two investigations uncovered more than enough evidence to confirm the suspicions of electoral irregularities, but remarkably, the Senate committees took no action. Because the episodes received extensive coverage in the national media, the Bluff City's already sullied reputation, besmirched by reports of widespread gambling, prostitution, and violence, dropped even further in the public esteem. But it was no matter. Roosevelt's New Deal coalition still had room for Ed Crump's organization.[13]

In New Orleans Roosevelt again cooperated with infamous political machines, alternately supporting whichever Democratic organization held the upper hand. In the 1930 mayoral election the voters chose T. Semmes Walmsley, the scion of an old and respected New Orleans family and standard-bearer of the Old Regular (Choctaw) machine. Huey Long took virtually no part in the election, although he ordered his supporters at the eleventh hour to get out the vote for Walmsley (supposedly so the new mayor would be in his debt). At the insistence of local bankers, Walmsley consummated an alliance with the newly elected U.S. senator: the Old Regulars would support Long in return for his aid in securing a multi-million-dollar bond issue for the city. In a statement confirming his reputation as a political naïf, Walmsley said of Long: "You would have thought that he was the mayor of New Orleans, if you had seen the indefatigable way he took hold of the problems of New Orleans and worked to solve these problems."[14]

In 1934 the uneasy accord between Long and Walmsley dissolved, each accusing the other of treachery. Only the opposition of the Old Regulars kept the Kingfish from complete control in Louisiana, and in that year he fielded a candidate for mayor and four others for city commissioners. The January 23, 1934, election resulted in Walmsley's reelection, however, so Long began to use his dominance in the state legislature to wage political war against the New Orleans Democrats. As the Long-dominated legislators reduced aid to the state's leading city, the federal government also cut back its contributions to New Orleans as well as to other Louisiana communities. Mayor Walmsley issued several plaintive appeals to the president, affirming his loyalty to the New Deal and arguing that he and his city were being punished unfairly when Long alone should be disciplined. Although Roosevelt had no affinity for Long, he refused to intervene on Walmsley's behalf, and the battle for control of New Orleans continued.[15]

In 1935 the Louisiana legislature passed two laws limiting New Orleans's ability to obtain financial aid from the federal government without state approval. Another series of bills forbade the city from collecting real estate and personal property taxes—that power was assigned to a state tax collector—and from requiring manufacturers' licenses or levying paving assessments and liquor taxes. The financial situation for New Orleans could hardly have been more desperate. On July 10, 1935, Choctaw ward leaders voted thirteen to four to demand Walmsley's resignation; Long promised the thirteen that he would provide financial aid to New Orleans if the mayor capitulated. Three of the city commission's five members bolted from the Choctaws and enlisted in Long's camp. Walmsley still refused to resign, but the new Long majority on the commission assumed control of city government, and the Choctaws refused the mayor admission to their meetings. Deprived of patronage and cut adrift by his own party, Walmsley became a forlorn figurehead and finally resigned as mayor in 1936.[16]

After Huey Long's death in 1935, the men who inherited his organization, principally Governor Richard Leche and Lieutenant Governor Earl Long, chose Robert Maestri to succeed Walmsley. In a special election held in 1936, Maestri triumphed easily. At the same time the state's voters approved a constitutional amendment postponing the 1938 mayoral election to 1942, assuring Maestri an unprecedented six-year term. The new mayor's Italian immigrant grandfather had built a successful poultry business. He and his father added a furniture outlet near a notorious red-light district and sold their wares to prostitutes—thus, the millionaire mayor earned the sobriquet "Red Light Bob." As mayor, according to one observer, Maestri broke "laws, rules, and regulations with high-handed disregard" and became embroiled in an unseemly personal scandal: in 1937 he reached a settlement with the Internal Revenue Service over delinquent taxes, paid $134,000, and escaped indictment. Other scandals also sullied the mayor's reputation. Rumors implicated him in the 1939 Louisiana "hot oil" scandal and connected him with slot machine payoffs to New York racketeer Frank Costello. In many ways Maestri ended up an even more loathsome political figure than the much maligned Ed Crump.[17]

These embarrassments notwithstanding, Maestri earned a reputation as a sound manager of the troubled New Orleans economy.

Upon becoming mayor he borrowed $1.9 million from the state and donated a personal check for one hundred thousand dollars. Appalled to discover that New Orleans had no central purchasing system, he installed one, which resulted in a five-hundred-thousand-dollar annual savings for the city. At the same time he paved the way for reform of the city's antiquated tax collection system. Ending the practice of borrowing on anticipated revenue by collecting taxes at the first of the year, rather than in August, as had been done previously, reputedly saved the city four hundred thousand dollars annually. More important, Maestri and Governor Leche worked with dispatch to mend fences with Roosevelt, and federal dollars flowed once again into New Orleans. Roosevelt resumed relations with the eventual winner of the struggle for control of the city's Democratic leadership—despite its connections with Huey Long and its sordid reputation.[18]

Southern cities without political machines also found peaceful coexistence with the Roosevelt administration possible. In Birmingham, a fiercely conservative municipal government gave no evidence of New Deal influence. In 1911 the city had adopted a three-member commission form of government. Like other cities forsaking the traditional mayor-council arrangement during the Progressive era, Birmingham turned to the commission in search of efficient, businesslike management of municipal affairs. The men who sat on the commission came from the middle class, although they no doubt attended to the concerns of the city's preeminent industrial moguls, the so-called Big Mules. Between 1929 and 1941 the commissioners included a newspaper reporter, a former sheriff, the owner of a radio station, and Eugene ("Bull") Connor, a sportscaster who parlayed his popularity among area sports fans into a political career (and later, of course, into national prominence as the symbol of the city's commitment to white supremacy).[19]

Trucking executive Jimmy Jones won the commission presidency in 1925 and held the office until his death in 1940. His political career began in 1908 with his election as city clerk and tax collector in suburban East Lake. When the consolidation of Greater Birmingham eliminated his posts, he became, in turn, a clerk in the office of the city treasurer and city comptroller. In 1925 his bid for the commission presidency led to a runoff with former chamber of commerce president W. J. Adams, which Jones won with the crucial backing of the powerful Ku Klux Klan. Promptly renouncing the support of the hooded empire and his campaign manager, Horace Wilkinson, Jones drifted into the orbit of the more respectable if no less conservative Big Mules. He responded to the Depression by slashing city services and firing municipal employees—which earned him the approbation of his new benefactors.[20]

Jones and his two like-minded commissioners secured reelection easily in 1929, but in 1933 the election of two Horace Wilkinson allies to fill out the commission left the chief executive isolated and vulnerable. The next four years saw an ongoing struggle, as the two newcomers chipped away at Jones's power by transferring city departments from his jurisdiction to their own and by terminating the employment of city workers known to be his supporters. They also enjoyed some success in mitigating Jones's parsimony, most notably by limiting the layoffs of municipal employees. Wilkinson embraced the New Deal and became the chief dispenser of patronage in Birmingham. Jones continued to advocate severe economy measures and assailed the spendthrift New Deal policies. These positions were in line with those of the dominant steel interests, but Jones found the going treacherous.[21]

Led by Tennessee Coal and Iron's Charles DeBardeleben, Republic Steel's Wade Oldham, and Woodward Iron's H.A. Berg, the Big Mules fought back, formulating an extensive propaganda campaign, lobbying state newspaper editors, and financing the reactionary, anti-New Deal weekly magazine *Alabama*. Contributing to their efforts, a Birmingham grand jury found the two associate commissioners guilty of accepting bribes in the purchase of city equipment. The Birmingham *News* excoriated the men involved in the scandal and campaigned for the adoption of the city manager plan, but the citizenry saw fit only to remove the guilty officials. In the 1937 municipal elections Jones overwhelmed his opponents, and the voters chose two new associate commissioners, one of whom (Connor) had the backing of the Big Mules. Once again dominating the commission, Jones reaffirmed local government's defense of racial segregation, opposition to unions, and aversion to public housing, which, he argued, would undermine the private market for low-rent housing. Though he infrequently criticized the New Deal openly, Jones continued to represent the interests of those who did and to assert his independence from Washington.[22]

The Big Mules' opposition to Roosevelt and the New Deal went beyond support of Jimmy Jones. They bankrolled a faction of the Democratic party headed by state senator James Simpson, a corporation lawyer with well-known antilabor and anti-New Deal sympathies. Simpson never disappointed the industrialists, staunchly defending their views in the state capital and nurturing the careers of political neophytes like Connor, whose loyalty to the monied in-

terests never wavered. The Big Mules rued the fact that Alabama's
U.S. senators consistently voted for New Deal legislation, and they
unsuccessfully backed Thomas Heflin's attempt to unseat incumbent Lister Hill in 1938. As early as 1939 they supported threatened
insurgencies of southern Democrats against the national party's liberal policies, but these efforts similarly failed. The Birmingham industrial giants had to be content with control of the local polity.[23]

In Dallas, the goal of bringing local government more firmly under the control of the business community came to fruition in the
1930s. Agitation for better municipal government dated back to the
first decade of the twentieth century, when the nonpartisan Citizens Association was founded. Interest flagged, however, and by the
1920s the association had become dormant. In 1927 the Dallas
News published a series of muckraking articles exposing ineffi-
ciency in city government and proposing the city manager plan as
an alternative. In 1929 thirty men ran for mayor, and nine of them
constituted one-man "parties." The eventual winner, self-styled
populist J. Waddy Tate, lambasted the wealthy. He removed all
"Keep Off the Grass" signs from city parks and promised to allow
"plain folks" to camp there. Largely because of Tate's eccentric behavior, Dallas residents seriously began to consider the *News*'s arguments for political change. The remnants of the old Citizens
Association formed the Citizens Charter Association (CCA) in 1930
and joined the battle for new municipal government. Tate delayed
and dissembled, but he finally presented the question of charter
amendments to the people in a 1930 referendum. By a two-to-one
margin, the voters jettisoned the mayor-commission government
for council-city manager rule. Under the new system, the nine-
member council (six chosen from districts and three elected at
large) selected a mayor from its own ranks and appointed a city
manager. In the 1931 election all nine CCA candidates—including
the chairman of the board of the city's largest insurance company,
an oil company president, and other leading businessmen—won
landslide victories.[24]

In 1933 the CCA's slate of candidates ran unopposed, but resistance quickly formed among the ranks of the suddenly deposed politicians. They accused the CCA of being "organized . . . financed
and controlled by Wall Street trusts" and unsuccessfully sought the
recall of the new council. In 1935 an opposing faction, composed of
seasoned politicians and known as the Catfish Club, bested the
CCA's candidates to gain control of the city council. A haphazardly
planned counteroffensive by the CCA never got off the ground in

1937, and the brief reign of the business elite seemed finished. At that time, however, two hundred of the city's corporate presidents and chief executive officers formed the Dallas Citizens' Council to breathe new life into the dying CCA. In 1939 the candidates of the fledgling Citizens' Council parlayed rumors of graft in Mayor George Sprague's parks department into a resounding victory. The council's 1941 slate won without opposition, and its dominance of local government continued into the 1970s.[25]

The Dallas Citizens' Council sprang from the imagination of Robert Lee Thornton. A former tenant farmer who mismanaged several businesses into bankruptcy, Thornton finally struck it rich as a banker. Thornton was a maverick in the local business community: while other bankers avoided risky ventures, he had the prescience to invest in the automobile industry and gave hotel tycoon Conrad Hilton his first loan. He became one of the city's most visible and esteemed philanthropists, and in later years he was a four-time mayor who refused to keep a desk in city hall, instead continuing to operate from his Mercantile Bank office. By the mid-1930s he had grown tired of the local government's ineffectiveness and resolved to seize authority for the city's "natural leadership." In 1936 Thornton helped persuade the Texas Centennial Commission to hold its celebration in Dallas and then served as a member of the executive committee that planned and conducted the festivities. Serving on that committee convinced him that only a small, manageable group of the city's best people could make decisions effectively about such a massive undertaking as the Texas Centennial— or, for that matter, he concluded, govern the city. Therefore, Thornton set out to make the emerging Citizens' Council in the form best suited to getting things done.[26]

Thornton wanted to call the Citizens' Council the Yes or No Council, but others thought the title a bit unseemly and overruled him. Thornton did prevail on a number of other matters, though: he insisted, for instance, that membership be limited to chief executive officers of major corporations—no doctors, lawyers, clergymen, educators, or intellectuals who might temporize when prompt action was needed. Similarly, Thornton's no-nonsense attitude forced the exclusion of proxy voting. "If you don't come," the rough-hewn banker said, "you ain't there." The Citizens' Council, sometimes called Thornton's oligarchy, centralized power in open and complete fashion. A local newspaper observed: "In many cities, power descends from a small group of influential businessmen to the city council. What distinguishes the Dallas power group from others is that it is organized, it has a name, it is not articulately opposed and it was highly publicized." If anything, local autonomy, concentrated in the hands of a few influential citizens, increased during the Depression decade. The bureaucracy-laden state and federal governments had no truck with the "yes or no" men of Dallas.[27]

Altogether, municipal governments showed little evidence of federal intrusion, as firmly entrenched commercial elites continued to dominate local politics. In cities like Birmingham and Dallas the linkages between city halls and central business districts were a good deal more adhesive than any connections between city halls and Washington, D.C. In the machine-governed cities of Memphis and New Orleans, the New Deal made no effort to unseat the groups in power—despite inescapable evidence of corruption and scandal. Just as Roosevelt showed considerable forbearance in his association with a variety of allies in state and national politics, so too did he suffer in silence his relations with southern urban leaders. Moreover, the president acquiesced in the disfranchisement of black voters, one of the methods by which Dixie's Democrats kept the South a one-party region. Historian Richard Wade noted: "The New Deal might have produced a revolutionary rearrangement in formal governmental institutions and agencies, but it left most of the country's urban fabric intact." The same was true in microcosm in the South.[28]

At first, opposition to the New Deal came from only a handful of disgruntled southerners. Of the many conservatives in Congress, only three—senators Carter Glass and Harry F. Byrd of Virginia and Josiah Bailey of North Carolina—spoke out repeatedly against Roosevelt's policies in the halcyon early years of his presidency. Others may have shared this trio's sentiments but decided to keep their own counsel. Carter Glass became the first vocal New Deal critic and remained so throughout the decade, opposing virtually every administrative measure forwarded to Congress. He asserted the dubious constitutionality of the legislation, fearing the detrimental effects on individualism and states' rights, and decried the surrender of legislative authority to the executive apparent in 1933. He charged: "Roosevelt is driving this country to destruction faster than it has ever moved before. Congress is giving this inexperienced man greater power than that possessed by Mussolini and Stalin put together." Able to be magnanimous at a time when the Virginian stood nearly alone in his insurgency, Roosevelt cheerfully referred to Glass as an "unreconstructed old rebel."[29]

Harry F. Byrd, who came to the Senate in 1933, took longer to break with the president and never opposed New Deal measures as persistently as did Carter Glass. Byrd spoke out strongly against the Agricultural Adjustment Act and remained consistently critical of the administration's farm policies. Notorious for frugality in his earlier days as Virginia's governor, Byrd scored the New Deal for its spendthrift ways and feared the growing influence of the federal government in local affairs. Along with his fellow senator from the Old Dominion, he remained a nettlesome critic of the president after 1934.[30]

Josiah Bailey, an ardent Roosevelt supporter in 1932, soured quickly on the new administration and became one of the few congressional leaders to vote against the New Deal's two principal recovery measures, the Agricultural Adjustment Act and the National Industrial Recovery Act. Although he opposed a number of New Deal initiatives, Bailey remained at least nominally loyal to Roosevelt through 1934. After that time, however, he consorted openly with Glass, Byrd, and other emerging New Deal critics such as Georgia senator Walter F. George, Maryland senator Millard F. Tydings, and Rhode Island senator Peter Gerry. Like the other southern conservatives, Bailey explained his dissidence as opposition to centralized authority and concern about the preservation of liberty.[31]

Unlike the southern conservatives who pilloried the New Deal for tampering with time-honored customs, Louisiana senator Huey Long mounted early criticism of Roosevelt for his failure to effect enough change. Long had been prominent in his loyalty to Roosevelt at the 1932 Democratic convention, working overtime to keep delegations committed during the worrisome first three ballots, but he fell out quickly with the new president once the New Deal took shape. "Whenever the administration has gone to the left I have voted with it," Long explained in 1934, "and whenever it has gone to the right I have voted against it." A self-proclaimed tribune of the people, Long criticized the New Deal for catering to the rich and wellborn while failing to institute the kinds of sweeping reforms necessary to aid the poor. His Share-Our-Wealth program called for a limitation on personal wealth and a guarantee of a $2,500 annual income for every worker. By early 1935 Long boasted that he had chartered over twenty-seven thousand Share-Our-Wealth clubs nationwide, with a total membership of 7.5 million people.[32]

Openly ambitious, Long broke with Roosevelt and declared his intention to run for president in 1936. Democratic National Committee polls suggested that the Kingfish could possibly attract enough votes as a third-party candidate to throw the election into the House of Representatives, and administration officials began taking the flamboyant showman seriously. Roosevelt called him one of the two most dangerous men in America (Douglas Mac-Arthur, he said, was the other) and ordered the Internal Revenue Service to examine his income tax returns for possible illegalities. Long's assassination in September 1935 left his movement leaderless and silenced the New Deal's most vociferous critic. Long's southern congressional colleagues, conservative men of wealth and standing who found the Louisianan's rabble-rousing distasteful, did not mourn his passing.[33]

Most members of the southern political establishment continued to support the president and his policies, but disaffection grew with the New Deal. A tension developed between the desire for federal relief and the decreased dependence of the poor on local benefactors. The "county seat elites," dismayed at the apparent threat to their hegemony, rued the ubiquity of government intervention in local life. The NIRA revitalized an enervated trade union movement, and the actions of New Deal liberals in Washington challenged racial inequality, emboldening blacks to speak out against customary inequities. New labor standards threatened to raise wages and thereby unsettle class relationships. Creating stopgap measures to combat the Depression was one thing, but the New Deal seemed to entail much more than southerners originally perceived. The spate of legislation forthcoming from Congress in 1935, the "Second New Deal," included such troubling measures as the Wagner Act, the Social Security Act, the "soak the rich" tax, and the Public Utilities Holding Company Act. Southerners considered the wages and hours legislation a "sectional bill disguised as a humanitarian reform." How far did the New Deal intend to go?[34]

Southern apprehensiveness grew during Roosevelt's 1936 reelection campaign, as the administration openly courted black voters. White supremacists saw their fears being realized: northern blacks switched party allegiance by the thousands, and their growing numbers translated into greater influence in national party councils. Increased black suffrage in the South could only lead to greater independence and a lessening of white control. The inclusion of black voters strengthened the Democratic party nationally but promised only trouble for white defenders of the status quo in Dixie. Carter Glass warned his fellow southerners: "To any discerning person it is perfectly obvious that the so-called Democratic party at the North is now the negro party, advocating social equality for the races; but most of our Southern leaders seem to disregard this socialistic threat to the South in their eagerness to retain in power a Party which, to use a phrase of Mr. Roosevelt, 'masquerades as Democratic,' but is really an Autocracy."[35]

Events at the Democratic National Convention that year appalled southerners accustomed to much more solicitude for their desires. For the first time the convention permitted the seating of black delegates and welcomed black members of the press as well. When a black minister delivered the invocation at the start of a session, South Carolina senator Ellison ("Cotton Ed") Smith bolted for the exit, exclaiming: "By God, he's as black as melted midnight! Get outa my way. This mongrel meeting ain't no place for a white man!" Smith left again when black congressman Arthur Mitchell seconded Roosevelt's nomination, and the South Carolinian voiced his outrage at "any political organization that looks upon the Negro and caters to him as a political and social equal." Most troubling to southerners, the convention abrogated the two-thirds rule that had always given the South an effective veto against decision making by a simple majority.[36]

A group of disaffected Democrats deserted that year and formed a rump party, the Jeffersonian Democrats, devoted to the traditional verities of states' rights, white supremacy, and freedom from federal tyranny. The splinter group drew its leadership from the Southern Committee to Uphold the Constitution, which included Texas oil tycoon John Henry Kirby; the Reverend Gerald L. K. Smith, a former protégé of Huey Long's; Thomas L. Dixon, author of *The Klansman*; and Georgia governor Eugene Talmadge. Financial support came largely from wealthy right-wing northerners like Pierre du Pont and General Motors's Alfred Sloan. Skeptics believed that the group existed solely to further the presidential ambitions of Governor Talmadge, who presumably commanded a substantial following only in his home state, but some New Dealers expressed concern at the growing unrest throughout the South.[37]

In January 1936 the Jeffersonian Democrats convened their "grass-roots convention" in Macon, Georgia. Party officials sent invitations printed in red, white, and blue with a Confederate flag at the top to Democrats in seventeen southern states, predicting an attendance of ten thousand at the convention. Approximately 3,500 showed up, most of them Georgia farmers loyal to their governor. Each delegate received a copy of *Georgia Women's World* with a large photograph of Eleanor Roosevelt on the cover; the caption described the first lady "going to some nigger meeting, with two escorts, niggers, on each arm." Speakers denounced the New Deal vitriolically, none more intemperately than the Reverend Gerald Smith, who called the president a Communist, an atheist, and a cripple. The speakers' extremism resulted in a flood of negative publicity and the thorough discrediting of the movement. The convention broke up without formulating a ticket or nominating a candidate for any office, and the Jeffersonian Democrats quickly disappeared. Talmadge later that year lost in his campaign for the U.S. Senate to Richard B. Russell, a New Deal supporter.[38]

Roosevelt's landslide reelection and the Macon fiasco reaffirmed his great popularity in the South. Southern congressmen thus remained temporarily loyal to the president's policies, whatever their personal predilections. Unrest continued to simmer, however, and events after 1936 finally led to outright rebellion. The number of southern conservatives willing to challenge the president grew during the following years, so that by the end of the decade a coalition of southerners and conservatives sprinkled throughout the rest of the country brought the New Deal's legislative machinery to a halt. After Roosevelt's 1936 electoral triumph, Carter Glass concluded bitterly, "Why, if the President asked Congress to commit suicide tomorrow, they'd do it." The attitude he lamented, however, was changing.[39]

The rift with southern Democrats began with Roosevelt's daring plan to pack the Supreme Court in 1937. By narrow majorities the Court had declared unconstitutional such landmark New Deal bills as the National Industrial Recovery Act, the Agricultural Adjustment Act, and the Guffey Coal Act, as well as several state minimum wage laws. With decisions expected soon on the Wagner and Social Security acts, Roosevelt, who had been unable to appoint anyone to the Supreme Court during his first term, proposed the addition of new justices for each member over the age of seventy unwilling to retire (with a limit of six new appointments). Disingenuously, the president explained that the Court needed to expand so that it could address the growing backlog of cases that was accumulating at a disturbing rate. Almost immediately, the proposal generated an acrimonious debate. Court defenders warned against expanded executive power, the limitation of judicial independence, and the politicization of jurisprudence. Many Americans deeply revered the Supreme Court and opposed any tampering with its autonomy; others simply resented Roosevelt's contrived justification, calling it government by misdirection. For all these reasons, the court-packing proposal caused one of the severest controversies in Washington political annals.[40]

Public opinion aside, the court issue angered a great number of congressmen. Even the senators and representatives who eventually voted for the proposal did so with reluctance, and many were resentful. Conservatives rallied in opposition and found new resolve in their resistance to the New Deal. From the beginning, Roosevelt erred in not sharing his plan with congressional leaders until the last moment. The exasperated Speaker of the House William Bankhead said: "Wouldn't you have thought that the President would have told his own party leaders what he was going to do? He didn't because he knew that hell would break loose." Just before the press conference announcing his proposal, Roosevelt informed six key congressional Democrats, who offered no response and left the White House in shock. Breaking the silence on the drive up Capitol Hill, House Judiciary Committee chairman Hatton Sumners of Texas said: "Boys, here's where I cash in."[41]

The other members of the Democratic congressional leadership shared Sumners's anger but publicly supported the measure. Vice-President Garner held his nose and turned thumbs down during the bill's reading to the Senate but refrained from comment. When the Senate considered the bill, Garner went back home to Texas on "vacation." Senate majority leader Joe Robinson worked feverishly for the bill, partly out of partisan loyalty but also because he hoped to receive one of the six new Supreme Court justiceships. Sam Rayburn, William Bankhead, Pat Harrison, James F. Byrnes, and other top Democrats griped privately but went through the motions of support. Few of their southern compatriots did likewise, and many of them deserted the president for the first time. The veteran New Deal critics, Glass, Byrd, and Bailey, led the opposition, joined by Cotton Ed Smith, Millard Tydings, Thomas Connally, and Walter George. Josiah Bailey explained why the issue seemed such a threat to conservatives: "What we have going on in this country is a political revolution. . . . The President controls Congress and the people help him do it. He is now seeking to control the Court. . . . Give the President control over Congress and the Court and you will have a one man government."[42]

Opposition in Congress resulted in a deadlock. Joe Robinson's death on July 14 damaged the bill's chances, for many of the Democrats supporting the president's proposal had been doing so out of loyalty to the majority leader. After 168 rancorous days, the Senate voted by a seventy-to-thirty margin to recommit the bill to the Judiciary Committee, and any chance of reconfiguring the Supreme Court expired. More favorable Court decisions upholding New Deal measures and the rapid retirement of justices, allowing the president to shape a new majority, took some of the sting out of the congressional defeat. Nevertheless, Roosevelt's boast that he lost the battle but won the war missed the mark. Congress's victory solidified the nascent conservative coalition, linking disenchanted southern Democrats, alienated Progressives, and Republicans, and torpedoed the myth of Roosevelt's invincibility. Conservatives had experienced success, and they prepared for bolder action. Historian James T. Patterson summed up: "The President had gained a court but had begun to lose part of his Congress."[43]

Already strained relations with Congress deteriorated further in the summer of 1937, when Roosevelt intervened in the Senate's selection of a new majority leader. Insiders on Capitol Hill agreed that Mississippi's venerable Pat Harrison had the inside track until the president sent a letter to Congress indicating his preference for Alben Barkley of Kentucky. Harrison had almost always followed the administration's lead, but Barkley was a liberal who supported the New Deal out of genuine conviction. While the president denied any involvement, his aides lobbied aggressively for Barkley and offended a number of senators in the process. The vote went to Barkley, thirty-eight to thirty-seven; the narrowness of the victory provided another indication of the conservative coalition's growing strength. Roosevelt's intervention severed relations with Harrison, who proved a powerful addition to the bloc of southern Democrats no longer linked closely with the administration. Only a few days later Harrison gave his first anti-New Deal speech in the Senate, a ringing condemnation of a fair labor standards bill. In 1938–39 Harrison successfully opposed Roosevelt on several revenue bills and became a key figure along with James F. Byrnes in fighting to limit the increases in WPA funding requested by the White House.[44]

For the first time, Byrnes became active in Democratic southerners' opposition to the New Deal by challenging the administration's emerging labor policy. In particular, southern legislators objected to Roosevelt's refusal to condemn the suddenly popular sit-down strike. Fearing that the tactic successfully used against automobile factories in the North would be similarly employed in the South, they urged Roosevelt to demand enforcement of laws protecting property rights. In 1937 Byrnes attached to pending legislation an amendment prohibiting sit-down strikes in the coalfields. Presidential emissaries worked quietly behind the scenes to persuade Byrnes to rescind his amendment, but they failed. Instead, the stubborn South Carolinian expanded his proposal to include all sit-downs regardless of industry. Both houses of Congress bitterly debated the amendment, and Byrnes finally allowed a vote on the original bill only when the president agreed to an independent consideration of sit-down strikes by Congress.[45]

In 1937 southern congressmen took the lead in defeating or blunting a series of New Deal bills, beginning with a proposal for six "little TVAs," regional development authorities to be built on a much smaller scale than the Tennessee Valley project. Senators Byrd and Tydings obtained draconian cuts in Senator Robert F. Wagner's housing bill, limiting the total allocation for construction and the maximum amount allowed in any state—a direct attack on the large northern cities already planning to erect large numbers of public housing projects. A fair labor standards bill squeaked by in the Senate, but conservative southerners in the House voted it down. A lengthy filibuster forced Senator Wagner to withdraw his antilynching bill in the Senate. At the close of the combative congressional session in which he suffered a series of stinging defeats, the president struck back at conservatives by nominating Alabama senator Hugo L. Black to the U.S. Supreme Court. Southern Democrats decried the selection of the highly unpopular Black, the most liberal southerner in the Senate, and denied him the courtesy of automatic confirmation usually bestowed upon congressional colleagues. During the contentious confirmation hearings, reports surfaced of Black's earlier membership in the Ku Klux Klan. Nevertheless, Black survived the ordeal and took his seat on the Court. The furor only intensified the mounting enmity between Roosevelt and his southern foes.[46]

In November 1937 the president called Congress to a special session to deal with a deepening recession and to reconsider the many bills it had spurned earlier that year. The legislative deadlock persisted, and the special session produced virtually nothing—with the exception of the infamous "conservative manifesto." Convinced that Roosevelt intended to form a new party and run for a third term with the support of John L. Lewis and the CIO, Josiah Bailey organized the drafting of a document confirming conservative principles and, by implication, criticizing New Deal programs. Along with Bailey, who edited the manifesto, senators Millard Tydings of Maryland, Harry F. Byrd of Virginia, Royal Copeland of New York, Edward Burke of Nebraska, Arthur Vandenburg of Michigan, and Warren Austin of Vermont drew up a ten-point program for alleviating the recession based upon budget balancing and reduced relief spending. Before the authors could convince many of their peers to sign the document and condemn the New Deal publicly, news-papers broke the story of an incipient rebellion in Congress. Bailey then read the document to the assembled members of the Senate. Although many solons agreed with the content and tone of the man-ifesto, few risked signing it. Senators like Pat Harrison and James F. Byrnes, who opposed New Deal initiatives when it suited them, re-frained from a complete break with the Democratic administration. The authors of the conservative manifesto failed to generate an in-surrection, but the episode revealed mounting dissatisfaction within the party spearheaded by southern conservatives.[47]

Impeded by a series of setbacks and narrow victories in Con-gress, the New Deal's momentum slowed dramatically in the late 1930s. Once-loyal southern Democrats led the congressional oppo-sition that seemed to thwart Roosevelt's legislative designs as often as his measures became law. The Wagner-Steagall Housing Act passed in 1937 despite Harry F. Byrd's staunch opposition in the Senate, but only after construction allocations were severely cur-tailed and limitations on spending in individual states were estab-lished. In the 1938 congressional session Roosevelt's partisans succeeded in passing the Fair Labor Standards Act and raising the level of federal relief spending, but they failed to secure revision of taxation and reorganization of the federal executive branch. (In 1939 Senators Byrd and Byrnes again led the fight against executive reor-ganization, forcing the president to accept an attenuated version of the bill.) By 1938 the burgeoning conservative coalition had not es-tablished hegemony in Washington, but it found itself able to hold the president accountable as never before.[48]

The increasing effectiveness of the bipartisan opposition to Roosevelt on Capitol Hill owed largely to the persistent efforts of southern dissidents. Republican minorities produced dramatic vic-tories only because restive Democrats deserted their president. By 1938 Roosevelt's patience had dissipated, and he resolved to purge the disloyal members of his party running for reelection that year. Such a list did not include some of the most quarrelsome legislators, such as Josiah Bailey, Pat Harrison, Harry F. Byrd, and Carter Glass, but the opportunity to eliminate other foes and elect more liberal politicians remained. In that year's spring primaries, incumbents Claude Pepper in Florida and Lister Hill in Alabama, both avid New Dealers, won handily over conservative opponents. Encouraged by these outcomes, Roosevelt announced in June his decision to cam-paign for specific candidates in key Democratic contests later that year. Against the advice of many of his top political aides, Roosevelt prepared to intervene in state elections against fellow Democrats to a degree never attempted before.[49]

Roosevelt's support for liberal Democrats seemed to bolster the successful primary campaigns of senators Elmer Thomas in Oklahoma and Hattie Caraway in Arkansas, as well as Congressman Lyndon Johnson in Texas. With the president's backing, Senate majority leader Alben Barkley beat back the challenge of Kentucky governor Albert B. ("Happy") Chandler, and in New York James H. Fay unseated John J. O'Connor, conservative chairman of the House Rules Committee. But these contests took a back seat to the president's efforts to remove three particularly bitter southern antagonists, senators Walter George of Georgia, Cotton Ed Smith of South Carolina, and Millard Tydings of Maryland. The great purge would succeed or fail on Roosevelt's ability to sway the electorates in three solidly Democratic southern states where popular incumbents had displayed a mastery of sectional politics.[50]

Roosevelt launched his southern campaign on August 11 at Barnesville, Georgia. Ostensibly there to dedicate a new Rural Electrification Administration facility, he discussed the publication of the National Emergency Council's *Report on Economic Conditions of the South* and commented on its findings. The sixty-four-page report condemned economic colonialism, and the president proclaimed the South "the Nation's No. 1 economic problem." The solution, Roosevelt contended, was more New Deal legislation, an unlikely development with southern conservatives blocking the way. With Senator Walter George seated a few feet away on the platform, the president said that he and the Georgia senator "did not speak the same language." He concluded: "Therefore, accepting the request from many citizens of Georgia that I make my position clear, I have no hesitation in saying that if I were able to vote in the September primary in this state, I most assuredly would cast my vote for Lawrence Camp." The New York *Times* said that Roosevelt's endorsement of the little-known attorney amounted to a "second march through Georgia."[51]

In Greenville, South Carolina, Roosevelt endorsed Governor Olin Johnston in his attempt to unseat incumbent senator Cotton Ed Smith, and shortly thereafter he came out for liberal congressman David Lewis against Millard Tydings in Maryland. In these contests in Georgia, South Carolina, and Maryland, the president cut the flow of patronage to his opponents and dispensed campaign funds to his surrogate candidates. George, Smith, and Tydings avoided public confrontations with the president and denied that they had consistently opposed the New Deal. The senators' support of the administration never became as important an issue, however, as did their exploitation of the resentment against outside interference in state political affairs. Voters of all political persuasions bridled at this new "carpetbag invasion" and cast their ballots accordingly. All three incumbents won, and in Georgia Lawrence Camp finished a dismal third behind Walter George and Eugene Talmadge. Standing before a statue of Wade Hampton, exulting in his victory, Ed Smith proclaimed: "No man dares to come into South Carolina and try to dictate to the sons of those men who held high the hands of Lee and Hampton."[52]

The unsuccessful purge contributed to Roosevelt's mounting problems with Congress. The targets of the purge returned to Washington with heightened will to oppose the New Deal. Millard Tydings, whose dissension had been limited previously, became particularly vehement. Other Democrats who had not been directly affected disapproved of the president's involvement in state elections, many suspecting that they would have been targeted if they had run for reelection that year. The outcome of the contests in Georgia, South Carolina, and Maryland heartened southern conservatives and inflicted further damage on Roosevelt's withering prestige. After the president had made such an ill-advised foray into southern Democratic primaries, his calls for party unity seemed hypocritical and elicited only scorn from many former supporters. With the Republicans gaining eight seats in the Senate and eighty-one seats in the House in 1938, the Democrats suddenly had smaller majorities in Congress, and the bipartisan conservative coalition became more formidable.[53]

Southerners in Congress flaunted their independence from the White House openly in the late 1930s but remained loyal to the president on foreign policy matters. In his quest to revise neutrality legislation and to aid England against the mounting Nazi menace in Europe, Roosevelt relied on southern backing and enjoyed substantial support in Dixie. By all measurements, said political scientist V. O. Key, Jr., southern Democrats voted for interventionism more than any other group in Congress. The traditional southern advocacy of free trade dovetailed with Roosevelt's growing internationalism in the last years of the decade, and the deepening European crisis offered the prospect of greater profits for southern farmers. The war boom, already building despite American noninvolvement, brought the South military bases, defense contracts, and higher productivity in related industries. The South's martial tradition, patriotism, and party loyalty also helped to mend fences torn by years of skirmishing over domestic issues. As Roosevelt announced Dr. New Deal's replacement by Dr. Win-the-War, conservative southerners were pleased to vote for the diversion of federal funds from social welfare programs to expenditures to ensure military preparedness. Liberals went along reluctantly because of the need to strengthen national security.[54]

Although conservative Democrats predominated in the South, a few liberal voices could always be heard, and the New Deal increased their volume. With a sympathetic Democrat in the White House, the cautious group of liberals that historian Morton Sosna called the "Silent South" spoke out more often against the region's benighted practices. Some, like Will Alexander, Aubrey Williams, and Clark Foreman, went to Washington and exerted considerable influence in policy making. Most of the raised voices belonged to crusading journalists of the Upper South who used their newspaper columns to editorialize against the evils they abhorred. George Fort Milton of the Chattanooga *News*, Virginius Dabney of the Richmond *Times-Dispatch*, Mark Ethridge of the Louisville *Courier-Journal*, Jonathan Daniels of the Raleigh *News and Observer*, and Silliman Evans of the Nashville *Tennessean* most often wrote favorably of the New Deal. From colleges and universities such liberal professors as Walter Prescott Webb of the University of Texas and Edwin Mims of Vanderbilt University, along with University of North Carolina president Frank P. Graham, added their support to liberal reform. Organizations like the Southern Policy Study, the Fellowship of Southern Churchmen, and Jessie Daniel Ames's Association of Southern Women for the Prevention of Lynching worked for moderate reform, while a few—like the Highlander Folk School—pushed for genuinely radical change.[55]

The most prominent liberal organization to emerge in the South was the Southern Conference for Human Welfare (SCHW), which attracted middle-class reformers and labor unionists. In 1938 Roosevelt expressed his disapproval of poll taxes in a letter to Arkansas senator Brooks Hays, but he quickly denied any intention of pursuing federal legislation when Senator Pat Harrison expressed his displeasure. Roosevelt urged the SCHW to campaign against poll taxes, which it did unsuccessfully for several years. The SCHW held conferences and circulated information about the full range of problems plaguing southern life, including poverty, violations of civil liberties, lawlessness, inadequate social welfare, and substandard health, but it became best known for resisting segregation in its meetings. Such a volatile position on race scared off potential members, as did the presence of Communists, who, though prominent in the organization, never gained control of the leadership or determined policy. University of Virginia economics professor Wilson Gee correctly predicted that the SCHW "will stir up a great deal of enthusiasm and do some good work over a period of years, and then as is true of so many organizations of that nature, it will likely dwindle and pass off the stage."[56]

Some liberal politicians embraced the New Deal and challenged with limited success the conservatives who had long controlled the Democratic party in the South. Governors E.D. Rivers of Georgia and Ernest W. Marland of Oklahoma promised "Little New Deals" in their states but suffered repeated frustrations dealing with conservative legislatures. In South Carolina Olin Johnston bested noted race-baiter Cole Blease for the governorship, but Johnston's endorsement of the CIO proved politically damaging, and he lost in the 1938 senatorial race. Burnet Maybank, Johnston's successor in South Carolina, and Governor Dave Sholtz in Florida professed loyalty to New Deal principles and maintained reasonably good relations with state legislatures by attracting large sums of federal money for state improvements. A handful of unabashed liberals from the South won seats in Congress and allied with the president, including senators Lister Hill of Alabama, Alben Barkley of Kentucky, Theodore Bilbo of Mississippi, and Claude Pepper of Florida and congressmen Maury Maverick and Lyndon Johnson of Texas. Always a minority among their southern colleagues, they more often voted with northern Democrats to sustain New Deal advances.[57]

The small band of New Deal liberals in the South constituted a tiny minority: in historian George B. Tindall's apt phrase, they were "generals without an army." Overshadowed by their more powerful conservative colleagues, these highly vulnerable New Dealers generally survived on the political scene for only a short time. Claude Pepper retained his Senate seat until 1950, but others who remained outspoken did not fare as well. Some, like Olin Johnston and Maury Maverick, fell out of favor with the voters and lost elections; others, like Lyndon Johnson, read the changing political portents and altered their public images to appeal to increasingly conservative electorates. The band of New Dealers in the South shrank as the decade advanced.[58]

The small number of southern liberals not only enjoyed relatively little power but also tended to be, as historian Alan Brinkley has noted, "unliberal" in comparison with New Dealers from other regions. Purportedly liberal southern politicians professed fealty to the administration in Washington, but the actions of governors Dave Sholtz and Burnet Maybank left Harry Hopkins convinced that they were only interested in attracting federal money for their states. Liberal journalists supportive of Roosevelt's initial measures became unhappy with his continued calls for reform and, critical of his court-packing scheme and apparent sympathy for the CIO, deserted him by 1938. Speaking for many self-professed progressives, John Temple Graves II, syndicated columnist for the Birmingham *Age-Herald*, lambasted the Southern Conference for Human Welfare, trade unions, fair labor laws, and the excesses of northern liberals intruding in southern affairs.[59]

The limits of southern liberalism became apparent with the publication of the National Emergency Council's *Report on Economic Conditions of the South*, a document designed to sustain liberal faith in the New Deal. Southerners across the political spectrum denounced the report for perpetuating outdated stereotypes and complained about the North's continued condescension. When Roosevelt referred to the South as "the Nation's No. 1 economic problem," Arkansas senator John E. Miller countered that what the South needed was simply "to be left alone." The Atlanta *Constitution* observed that the report showed evidence of the "groundwork being laid" for "federal meddling" and warned that "no new reconstruction government is desired or will be tolerated." Much of the negative reaction stemmed from the document's release during the 1938 primaries, when liberal, as well as conservative, southerners resented Roosevelt's intrusion into local politics. John Temple Graves II noted: "The President has called the South a No. 1 economic problem and he has made it a No. 1 political problem."[60]

Southern liberals also frequently parted ways with their northern counterparts over the issue of race. Some southern congressmen, like Maury Maverick, the "Robespierre of the Rio Grande," spoke out forcefully against racial discrimination, but most remained silent on this most sensitive of topics. Numerous southern congressmen compiled records as loyal New Dealers, voting for an overwhelming percentage of the administration's proposals but against all civil rights legislation. As historian Chester M. Morgan has shown, Mississippi senator Theodore Bilbo engaged in the most scurrilous race-baiting in his campaigns and offended the sensibilities of even his fellow white supremacists with the viciousness of his attacks on black Americans, yet his voting record showed an unassailable devotion to liberal causes in all other areas. Bilbo supported Roosevelt on court-packing, labor legislation, public housing, and other controversial measures, when other "loyal" southerners deserted the administration. White supremacy was the litmus test of politics in the South, however, and liberals had no immunity from its power. Even those with a genuine desire to alter southern race relations feared that aggressive calls for reform would trigger violent retribution. So, at best, they counseled forbearance and bided their time.[61]

Although the New Deal stirred hope among liberals in the South, it fell far short of deposing conservative interests from their control of the Democratic party. Franklin Roosevelt remained personally popular throughout Dixie, but not enough so to dictate the outcome of state elections, as the events of 1938 clearly demonstrated. As the Depression decade advanced, the ranks of southern Democrats willing to challenge the president swelled, and these leaders became the heart of the conservative coalition that blunted the New Deal. With the shift in the administration's emphasis from recovery to reform, southern Democrats found it increasingly difficult to justify their unquestioning support. Resistance to change in certain key areas of southern life remained strong, apparently impervious to what political scientist V. O. Key, Jr., termed "weak forays against the established order."[62]

Yet the New Deal profoundly changed southern politics in an indirect and less obvious manner, by transforming the Democratic party nationally. The Roosevelt revolution forged a coalition that made the Democrats the majority party, a powerful electoral machine no longer desperately dependent on the solid South. Even if he had not received a single electoral vote from any of the eleven former states of the Confederacy, Roosevelt would have been elected in each of his four presidential campaigns. Moreover, the expansion of the Democratic party diluted southern influence. In 1918 the South controlled 26 of the 37 Democratic seats in the Senate, 107 of 131 in the House; by 1936 it had only 26 of 75 and 116 of 333 respectively. The emerging coalition in the North composed of a growing number of black voters and fueled by the votes and money of organized labor failed to develop similarly in the South but influenced southern politics nevertheless. The bitter southern opponents of the New Deal understood what these changes would mean in the future. Josiah Bailey showed foresight when he wrote in 1938: "The catering of our National Party to the Negro vote is not only extremely distasteful to me, but very alarming to me. Southern people know what this means, and you would have to be in

Washington only about three weeks to realize what it is meaning to our party in the Northern states."[63]

Finally, the transformation of the Democratic party resulted in electoral successes nationally but a weakening in the South. As the New Deal coalition nudged the Democratic party leftward, the more conservative Republican party, never previously considered a viable option to most white southerners, became more attractive. By the 1960s and 1970s the southern states were giving their electoral votes to Republican presidential candidates, and by the 1980s Republicans had become a force in state and local contests as well. A closed political system based upon white supremacy and deference to a traditional elite opened up. The New Deal contributed to the death of the solid South.[64]

8

CONCLUSION

In the coming days, and probably soon, [the South] is
likely to have to prove its capacity for adjustment far
beyond what has been true in the past.

—W. J. Cash, *The Mind of the South*, 1941

In December 1939 the citizens of Atlanta eagerly awaited the up-
coming world premiere of the film *Gone with the Wind*. Mayor
William B. Hartsfield had worked assiduously to convince Holly-
wood's moguls that Margaret Mitchell's hometown should be the
site of the eagerly awaited first showing. When a rumor surfaced
that the movie would open in New York City instead, Hartsfield
frantically contacted producer David O. Selznick for reassurances.
The night before the December 15 showing, Atlanta sponsored a ball
attended by Clark Gable, Vivien Leigh, and a throng of hoop-skirted
and tuxedoed revelers. The next day a crowd of forty thousand gath-
ered outside the Loew Grand Theater to catch a glimpse of the
MGM studio dignitaries and the two thousand members of the local
elite fortunate enough to be invited. Scalpers charged two hundred
dollars a ticket, an astronomical sum of money at that time, and
found customers eagerly willing to pay. The exuberance of the city
at the very end of the otherwise dismal 1930s seemed to symbolize
the rising wave of optimism that greeted the new decade.[1]

Throughout the South the arrival of the 1940s brought encouraging news about economic recovery. The coming of war ushered in
full employment and a welcomed prosperity. In suburban Atlanta a
huge bomber plant opened in Marietta, and a host of defense plants
within the city limits attracted an influx of skilled workers who laid

the foundation for other postwar industries. In Birmingham, freed from the freight rate differentials in 1938, defense backlogs totaled ninety million dollars. For the first time in memory, area steel mills operated at 100-percent capacity, and TCI announced an eighteen-month expansion that would boost pig iron production more than 20 percent. In countless cities the output of war materials increased dramatically as a variety of businesses converted to military production. The wartime-increased demand for petroleum products boosted the fortunes of Texas, Oklahoma, and Louisiana especially. Navy shipyards in Newport News, Norfolk, and Charleston sprang to life, as did private yards in Tampa, Houston, Mobile, Beaumont, Wilmington, Pensacola, and elsewhere along the southern coasts. The South's mild weather attracted military training camps necessary for a dramatically enlarged armed forces, and southern cities burst at their seams as people poured in from around the country. The bustle of renewed economic activity in the South provided an antidote to the torpor of the preceding years when belt-tightening and retrenchment had been the order of the day.[2]

The years after the Second World War brought more unsettling change to the South. The military presence continued in peacetime, and the Pentagon remained a leading employer. The sunbelt boom meant great population growth, principally in the region's burgeoning cities. A Second Reconstruction completed much the first Reconstruction had left undone a century before, and race relations changed irrevocably. Low-wage industries still predominated in some enclaves, but the South also attracted computer, aircraft, petrochemical, and other high-tech industries. Southern distinctiveness never disappeared entirely, but to a remarkable degree the region became more a part of mainstream American culture. For better or worse, the South's population growth, industrial and urban expansion, and economic integration with the rest of the nation constituted the most radical alteration in its history.[3]

The New Deal's role in this remarkable transformation was largely preparatory. The monumental changes were evident in some cases decades later, but the first crucial steps in new directions came in the 1930s. In the case of agriculture, the impact of New Deal programs such as the Agricultural Adjustment Act and the Soil Conservation Act was pronounced and immediate. The replacement of an archaic sharecropping system with agribusiness—along with the attendant displacement of a landless proletariat—changed the patterns of land use, reduced drastically the number of people living on the land, and benefited those wealthy farmers best suited to expanding their operations. The cotton kingdom declined in significance, replaced by an agricultural diversity never before achieved in the region. Mechanization, a key to development in agriculture just as in industry, became more feasible with the capital provided by the federal government, and the New Deal's most obvious immediate gift to the South appeared to be the tractor. Southern farming painfully divorced itself from backward practices commonplace for far too long and, because of Washington's influence, modernized much more rapidly than it otherwise could have.

As the New Deal dismantled plantation agriculture, it also undermined the paternalistic relationships between workers and employers that had long characterized southern industry. The southern factory, said journalist W. J. Cash, had long been "a plantation, essentially indistinguishable in organization from the familiar plantation of the cotton fields." In textile villages, mining towns, and lumber camps, federal government intrusion disrupted dependency relationships of long standing. Southerners continued in the 1930s and after to join labor unions less often than workers elsewhere in the nation, but the New Deal aided workers principally through the elevation of wage levels. The narrowing of regional wage variations began with the National Industrial Recovery Act, continued with the Works Progress Administration, and reached fruition with the Fair Labor Standards Act. Wages and hours legislation aided the southern worker tremendously. The result, as historian Numan V. Bartley noted, was that "the behavior of southern working people changed, and so too did southern society's attitudes toward work."[4]

Threatened by the loss of their low-wage advantage, southern entrepreneurs sought other means to maintain their competitiveness. The New Deal example of government planning inspired the idea of state-aided promotion. The North Carolina General Assembly made two appropriations totaling five hundred thousand dollars to tout the state nationally as a site for industry and tourism. In 1936 Mississippi created its Balance Agriculture with Industry program, an innovative attempt to attract capital from northern investors that other southern states quickly copied. By the 1960s the southern states competed fiercely to lure factories, branch offices, and corporate headquarters, and according to historian James C. Cobb, they enjoyed considerable success. Southern industrial productivity increased after the Second World War, and with the growing drive for economic growth came further denial of the rural agrarian past.[5]

The rapid growth of the urban South after the war also owed in part to the New Deal's influence. To accommodate the masses of displaced rural folk resettling in the cities, the federal government

built roads, housing, schools, and other public facilities. Its benefi-
cent taxing and lending policies made house purchases possible for
great numbers of working-class people who wanted to own their
own homes. Moreover, the federal presence reenforced the decentralization ongoing in American cities—regardless of location—and
thereby assured that suburbs flourished in the South as well as in
the North. Cities and their suburbs spread across the landscape,
eliminating large sections of the rural South and investing in the
bucolic areas that remained a new sophistication and urbanity.

To be sure, the South's persistent reverence for a bucolic ideal
and concomitant aversion for all things urban yielded gradually.
Southern politicians successfully exploited this animus against cities and worked hard to maintain the imbalances in state legislatures
favoring sparsely populated rural areas. Georgia governor Eugene
Talmadge boasted that he disdained votes from any towns large
enough to have streetcars and on the stump urged backwoods voters
to "come see me at the mansion. We'll sit on the front porch and
piss over the rail on those city bastards." Yet the cities' growth accelerated as more and more southerners left the small towns and
hamlets that had traditionally been the population centers. The
takeoff of Dixie's urban boom—what historian C. Vann Woodward
called the "bulldozer revolution"—came in the 1940s when the region's cities grew 36 percent, the fastest growth rate in the nation.
But if the 1940s saw the breakthrough, the federal government's expanding presence in the 1930s made it possible.[6]

As the region's population shifted to the cities, so too did the
balance of political power. The county courthouse elites lost out to
their big city counterparts, with the Democratic party still ruling in
both areas. The Republicans made few inroads into the solid South
in the 1930s, yet disturbing developments in the national Democratic party presaged monumental voter shifts in the future. The
Roosevelt coalition, as many southern conservatives clearly understood, both expanded the party's base nationally and lessened the
South's influence. Northern big city ethnics, blacks, liberals, and
others relied much less on southern Democrats for their previously
crucial contributions, and southern liberals, ostracized and powerless at home, found new respect and influence in Washington. The
conservatives' success in stalemating the New Deal in the late
1930s represented a bittersweet victory, for the days of glory for
southerners in their beloved Democratic party were slipping away.

The Democratic party's recruitment of black voters proved especially worrisome to white southerners who were committed to

black disfranchisement, poll taxes, and the other hallmarks of white supremacy. Under Roosevelt's cautious stewardship, the New Deal stopped short of challenging southern racial customs and generally deferred to the powerful southern congressional leaders who frequently controlled the fate of vital legislation. In any event, Roosevelt was no crusader for racial equality and had no hidden agenda to force integration on an unsuspecting South. Yet for all its moderation, the New Deal was progressive for its time, and southerners, sensitive to the slightest threat to the social order, reacted defensively. If Roosevelt kept a low profile, others in his administration did not: liberals like Eleanor Roosevelt, Harold L. Ickes, and Aubrey Williams made racial inequality an issue and put the federal government at the center of the agitation for reform. Hopeful and increasingly assertive, blacks lionized Roosevelt, shifted their allegiance to the Democratic party, and took the first hesitant steps down the long road to the civil rights movement of the 1950s and 1960s. The shattering of the southern system of apartheid took a heroic effort over many years, beginning with the modest, seemingly inconsequential advances of the 1930s.

In all these areas the New Deal's impact can readily be identified, but perhaps its greatest influence rested in a comprehensive challenge to the South's distinctive way of life. As late as the 1920s the region continued to display an economically and socially backward rural culture tied to sharecropping agriculture, de jure racial segregation, and political rule by courthouse elites. Resistance to modernization resulted in smaller cities, retarded industrial development, a modest investment in education, low wages, and a lower standard of living for most southerners. New Deal oral historians, photographers, and filmmakers exposed the poverty and pathology that were part of that culture, just as President Roosevelt articulated an unpleasant truth when he called the South the nation's number one economic problem. Resentful of what they perceived as unfair criticism from meddlesome outsiders and thoroughly steeped in long-standing values and norms, many southerners resisted new ideas stubbornly. Change came grudgingly, and though it was frequently not immediately evident, the New Deal marked the beginning of the end of southern exceptionalism.

Southern obeisance to states' rights and decentralized authority had long resulted in a fear of federal government intervention—a fear that such intrusion would undermine the foundations of a closed society. Ironically, the economic strictures brought on by the Great Depression made federal aid the South's only salvation. The

New Deal's major programs spent an estimated four billion dollars in the South, and much of this money came with no strings attached. The Roosevelt administration harbored no desire to attack the South's social structure, but the fears of many southerners were realized nevertheless. Southern leaders worked hard in the 1930s to preserve their way of life even as they accepted federal resources, and in many instances they enjoyed remarkable success. They could not, however, withstand all of the pressures for change. The New Deal disrupted, challenged, catalyzed. Its legacy can be seen in the remarkable years that followed.

NOTES

Chapter 1: ON THE EVE OF DEPRESSION

1. George B. Tindall, *The Emergence of the New South, 1913–1945* (Baton Rouge: Louisiana State Univ. Press, 1967), 111–12; Pete Daniel, *Breaking the Land: The Transformation of Cotton, Tobacco, and Rice Cultures since 1880* (Urbana: Univ. of Illinois Press, 1985), 35, 56, 92.

2. Tindall, *Emergence of the New South*, 112, 121 (Vance quotation), 122; Daniel, *Breaking the Land*, 56.

3. Tindall, *Emergence of the New South*, 130–34.

4. Gilbert C. Fite, *George N. Peek and the Fight for Farm Parity* (Norman: Univ. of Oklahoma Press, 1954), 150–62.

5. George W. West, "How the 'Forward Atlanta' Fund Has Helped Atlanta," *American City* 43 (Oct. 1930): 139; Charles Paul Garofalo, "The Sons of Henry Grady: Atlanta Boosters in the 1920s," *Journal of Southern History* 42 (May 1976): 190; James R. Thompson, "The Forward Atlanta Movement," M.A. thesis, Emory Univ., 1948, pp. 101–3, 127.

6. Don H. Doyle, *Nashville in the New South, 1880–1930* (Knoxville: Univ. of Tennessee Press, 1985), 192–97; Glenn Martin Runyan, "Economic Trends in New Orleans, 1928–1940," M.A. thesis, Tulane Univ., 1967, pp. 2, 3, 7; George H. Santerre, *Dallas' First Hundred Years, 1856–1956* (N.p., 1956); Dallas Chamber of Commerce, *Report of Industrial Dallas, Inc., 1928–1929–1930* (Dallas, 1931), 6–12; Irving Beiman, "Birmingham: Steel Giant with a Glass Jaw," in *Our Fair City*, edited by Robert S. Allen (New York: Vanguard, 1947), 100–101.

7. Tindall, *Emergence of the New South*, 74–75.

8. Solomon Barkin, "The Regional Significance of the Integration Movement in the Southern Textile Industry," *Southern Economic Journal* 15 (1948–49): 308; Jack Blicksilver, *Cotton Manufacturing in the Southeast: A Historical Analysis* (Atlanta: Georgia State College of Business Administration, 1959), 92–93; Robert H. Zieger, "Textile Workers and Historians," in *Organized Labor in the Twentieth-Century South*, edited by Robert H. Zieger (Knoxville: Univ. of Tennessee Press, 1991), 35–36.

9. Tindall, *Emergence of the New South*, 85–88.

10. Frank A. Howard, "Standard Oil Company, the Largest Industrial Investor in the South," *Manufacturers' Record*, Feb. 13, 1930, pp. 55–59; Rupert B. Vance, *Human Geography of the South* (Chapel Hill: Univ. of North Carolina Press, 1932), 344–50.

11. Tindall, *Emergence of the New South*, 78–80.

12. Ibid., 104–9.

13. Brenda Bell and Fran Ansley, "Strike at Davidson-Wilder, 1932–1933," in *Working Lives: The Southern Exposure History of Labor in the South*, edited by Marc S. Miller (New York: Pantheon, 1980), 79.

14. Vance, *Human Geography of the South*, 375–435.

15. W. J. Cash, *The Mind of the South* (New York: Knopf, 1941), 134; Roger Biles, *Memphis in the Great Depression* (Knoxville: Univ. of Tennessee Press, 1986), 14 (newspaper quotation), 15.

16. Tindall, *Emergence of the New South*, 212–14. Also see Pete Daniel, *The Shadow of Slavery: Peonage in the South, 1901–1969* (Urbana: Univ. of Illinois Press, 1972).

17. Walter White, *Rope and Faggot: A Biography of Judge Lynch* (New York: Arno Press, 1969), 19–21; Arthur Raper, *The Tragedy of Lynching* (Chapel Hill: Univ. of North Carolina Press, 1932), 480–88.

18. Tindall, *Emergence of the New South*, 170 (Byrnes quotation); Biles, *Memphis in the Great Depression*, 15 (newspaper quotation); White, *Rope and Faggot*, 205–25.

19. John Hope Franklin, *From Slavery to Freedom: A History of American Negroes* (New York: Knopf, 1947), 464 (*Defender* quotation); Tindall, *Emergence of the New South*, 148–49.

20. For a detailed, state-by-state discussion of the KKK in the South, see David Chalmers, *Hooded Americanism: The First Century of the Ku Klux Klan, 1865–1965* (Garden City, N.Y.: Doubleday, 1965).

21. Kenneth T. Jackson, *The Ku Klux Klan in the City, 1915–1930* (New York: Oxford Univ. Press, 1967), 242–43.

22. Pete Daniel, *Standing at the Crossroads: Southern Life since 1900* (New York: Hill and Wang, 1986), 95–96. Also see Suzanne Cameron Linder, *William Louis Poteat: Prophet of Progress* (Chapel Hill: Univ. of North Carolina Press, 1966).

23. Ray Ginger, *Six Days or Forever? Tennessee v. John Thomas Scopes* (Boston: Beacon, 1958), provides the best account of the trial.

24. Tindall, *Emergence of the New South*, 221.

25. George B. Tindall, "Business Progressivism: Southern Politics in the Twenties," *South Atlantic Quarterly* 62 (Winter 1963): 92–106.

26. Dewey W. Grantham, *The Life and Death of the Solid South: A Political History* (Lexington: Univ. Press of Kentucky, 1988), 78–101.

27. See Blaine A. Brownell, *The Urban Ethos in the South, 1920–1930* (Baton Rouge: Louisiana State Univ. Press, 1975).

28. Jacquelyn Dowd Hall and Anne Firor Scott, "Women in the South," in *Interpreting Southern History: Historiographical Essays in Honor of*

Sanford W. Higginbotham, edited by John B. Boles and Evelyn Thomas Nolen (Baton Rouge: Louisiana State Univ. Press, 1987), 483. On conditions in the textile mills, see George S. Mitchell and Broadus Mitchell, *Industrial Revolution in the South* (Baltimore: Johns Hopkins Univ. Press, 1930).

29. Bertha Hendrix, "I Was in the Gastonia Strike," in *Working Lives,* ed. Miller, 169.

30. Irving Bernstein, *The Lean Years: A History of the American Worker, 1920–1933* (Boston: Houghton Mifflin, 1960), 1–43.

31. Tindall, *Emergence of the New South,* 334–39; E. C. Wallis, "After Dallas Threw Off the Shackles of the Closed Shop," *Manufacturers' Record,* Feb. 13, 1930, pp. 53–54.

32. Daniel, *Standing at the Crossroads,* 100.

33. Twelve Southerners, *I'll Take My Stand: The South and the Agrarian Tradition* (New York: Harper and Brothers, 1930); Daniel, *Standing at the Crossroads,* 132 (Smith quotation); Tindall, *Emergence of the New South,* 579 (Jones quotation).

Chapter 2: DEPRESSION AND RESPONSE, 1929–1933

1. John L. Robinson, "Great Depression," in *Encyclopedia of Southern Culture,* edited by Charles Reagan Wilson and William Ferris (Chapel Hill: Univ. of North Carolina Press, 1989), 623; Douglas L. Fleming, "Atlanta, the Depression, and the New Deal," Ph.D. diss., Emory Univ., 1984, 47; Jesse O. Thomas, *A Study of the Social Welfare Status of the Negroes in Houston, Texas* (Houston: Webster-Richardson, 1929), 10.

2. Nashville *Tennessean,* Sept. 2, 1930; Dallas *Morning News,* Nov. 13, 1929; Lexington *Herald,* Oct. 26, 1929; New Orleans *Times–Picayune,* Jan. 1, 1930.

3. "Editorial," *Birmingham* 7 (Feb. 1931): 10; Atlanta Chamber of Commerce, "Sure, Business Will Be Good!" *City Builder* 14 (Jan. 1930): 18; Birmingham *Post,* Oct. 30, 1929; Dallas *Morning News,* June 23, 1930.

4. Fleming, "Atlanta, the Depression, and the New Deal," 190–91; Tindall, *Emergence of the New South,* 360–61; Robert F. Hunter, "Virginia and the New Deal," in *The New Deal: The State and Local Levels,* edited by John Braeman, Robert H. Bremner, and David Brody (Columbus: Ohio State Univ. Press, 1975), 118; Franklin Garrett, *Atlanta and Environs,* vol. 2 (Athens: Univ. of Georgia Press, 1969), 856; Dallas *Morning News,* Oct. 13, 1929; David R. Goldfield, *Cotton Fields and Skyscrapers: Southern City and Region, 1607–1980* (Baton Rouge: Louisiana State Univ. Press, 1982), 181; New York *Times,* Feb. 20, 1930.

5. Anthony J. Badger, *The New Deal: The Depression Years, 1933–1940* (New York: Farrar, Straus, and Giroux, 1989), 16–17; idem, *North Carolina and the New Deal* (Raleigh: North Carolina Department of Cultural Resources, Division of Archives and History, 1981), 2; Numan V. Bartley, *The Creation of Modern Georgia* (Athens: Univ. of Georgia Press, 1983), 173 (quotation).

6. Robert E. Snyder, *Cotton Crisis* (Chapel Hill: Univ. of North Carolina Press, 1984), 50, 107–13.

7. Glenn Martin Runyan, "Economic Trends in New Orleans," 2, 22.

8. Douglas L. Smith, *The New Deal in the Urban South* (Baton Rouge: Louisiana State Univ. Press, 1988), 18–19; Atlanta Chamber of Commerce, "Statistical Report, " *City Builder* 14 (July 1935): 20; Alice E. Stenholm, "Louisiana: Report of a Field Trip, December 5–12, 1931," State File: Louisiana, President's Organization for Unemployment Relief, Record Group 73, National Archives, Washington, D.C.; Don H. Doyle, *Nashville since the 1920s* (Knoxville: Univ. of Tennessee Press, 1985), 86.

9. Ronald L. Heinemann, *Depression and New Deal in Virginia: The Enduring Dominion* (Charlottesville: Univ. Press of Virginia, 1983), 34.

10. Birmingham Chamber of Commerce, "Industrial Information," *Birmingham Bulletin*, Dec. 19, 1932, p. 8; Marlene Hunt Rikard, "An Experiment in Welfare Capitalism: The Health Care Services of the Tennessee Coal, Iron, and Railroad Company," Ph.D. diss., Univ. of Alabama, 1983, pp. 275–76; Birmingham *Labor Advocate*, Dec. 19, 1931; "Hard Times Came Here First," program no. 8 from the "Working Lives" documentary radio series, produced by the Archives of American Minority Cultures at the University of Alabama; Blaine A. Brownell, "Birmingham, Alabama: New South City in the 1920s," *Journal of Southern History* 38 (Feb. 1972): 24 (quotation).

11. Dorothy Dell DeMoss, "Resourcefulness in the Financial Capital: Dallas, 1929–1933," in *Texas Cities and the Great Depression*, edited by Robert C. Cotner (Austin: Texas Memorial Museum, 1973), 119–21; WPA Writers' Project, *Houston: A History and Guide* (Houston: Anson Jones Press, 1942), 119.

12. Dallas *Morning News*, Dec. 11, 1931; William E. Montgomery, "The Depression in Houston during the Hoover Era, 1929–1932," M.A. thesis, Univ. of Texas, 1966, pp. 156, 173; J. F. Lucey to Walter S. Gifford, telegram, Oct. 27, 1931, State File: Texas, Box 247, President's Organization for Unemployment Relief, RG 73, NA.

13. State File: Georgia, Box 245, President's Organization for Unemployment Relief, RG 73, NA; Memphis *Commercial Appeal*, June 4–8, 1932.

14. Tindall, *Emergence of the New South*, 366–67; Stephen F. Strausberg, "The Effectiveness of the New Deal in Arkansas," in *The Depression in the Southwest*, edited by Donald W. Whisenhunt (Port Washington, N.Y.: Kennikat, 1980), 103; George T. Blakey, *Hard Times and New Deal in Kentucky, 1929–1939* (Lexington: Univ. Press of Kentucky, 1986), 10; Badger, *North Carolina and the New Deal*, 3; Bascom N. Timmons, *Jesse H. Jones: The Man and the Statesman* (New York: Henry Holt, 1956), 157–60.

15. "Conversations with Prominence: Null Adams of the *Press-Scimitar*," videotape, 1979, Memphis Public Library; Atlanta Chamber of Commerce, *Facts and Figures about Atlanta, 1935* (N.p., 1936), 22; Fleming, "Atlanta, the Depression, and the New Deal," 67–70.

16. Howard P. Chudacoff, *The Evolution of American Urban Society* (Englewood Cliffs, N.J.: Prentice-Hall, 1975), 210.

17. Tindall, *Emergence of the New South*, 371; Glenn Steele, "Family Welfare," U.S. Department of Labor, Children's Bureau, no. 209, 1932, p. 4; Alexander Kendrick, "Huey Long's Revolution," *Nation*, Aug. 22, 1934, p. 209.

18. Heinemann, *Depression and New Deal in Virginia*, 80 (quotation); Fleming, "Atlanta, the Depression, and the New Deal," 79.

19. Houston *Post*, Jan. 25, 1936, and Jan. 19, 1938; Walter E. Monteith to Robert M. La Follette, Jr., Dec. 28, 1931, *Congressional Record*, 72d Cong., 1st sess., 1932, vol. 75, p. 3238; Houston *Post-Dispatch*, Jan. 28, 1933 (Monteith quote), Mar. 30, 1930; Christopher Silver, *Twentieth-Century Richmond: Planning, Politics, and Race* (Knoxville: Univ. of Tennessee Press, 1984), 131; Danney Goble and James Ralph Scales, "Depression Politics: Personality and the Problem of Relief," in *Hard Times in Oklahoma: The Depression Years*, edited by Kenneth E. Hendrickson, Jr. (Oklahoma City: Oklahoma Historical Society, 1983), 8.

20. "PWA and Georgia: The State's No-Debt Policy Raises the President's Ire," *Newsweek*, Dec. 5, 1938, p. 12; Beiman, "Birmingham: Steel Giant with a Glass Jaw," 118; untitled, undated memorandum, James M. Jones, Jr., Papers, Department of Archives and History, Montgomery, Alabama; James M. Jones, Jr., to Robert M. La Follette, Jr., Dec. 24, 1931, *Congressional Record*, 72d Cong., 1st sess., 1932, vol. 75, p. 3100.

21. Houston *Post*, Jan. 25, 1936, Jan. 19, 1938; Montgomery, "Depression in Houston," 153; Roscoe C. Martin, "Dallas Makes the Manager Plan Work," *Annals of the American Academy of Political and Social Science* 199 (Sept. 1938): 65; Dallas *Morning News*, Apr. 28, 1932; Robert B. Fairbanks, "The Good Government Machine: Politics and Consensus Building in a Sunbelt City, 1930–1960," paper delivered at the twenty-third annual Walter Prescott Webb Lecture Series, Mar. 17, 1988, pp. 5–6; Dorothy Dell DeMoss, "Dallas, Texas, during the Early Depression: The Hoover Years, 1929–1933," M.A. thesis, Univ. of Texas, 1966, pp. 119–22.

22. Beiman, "Birmingham," 116; Montgomery, "Depression in Houston," 88, 161–65.

23. Houston *Post-Dispatch*, Jan. 19, 1932 (editorial quotation), Jan. 28, 1932 (Monteith quotation).

24. "Public Works Program, Memphis, Tennessee," Sept. 1938, Memphis Public Library; Thomas H. Baker, *The Memphis Commercial Appeal* (Baton Rouge: Louisiana State Univ. Press, 1971), 282; New Orleans *Times-Picayune*, Apr. 5 and Dec. 8–12, 1930; Goldfield, *Cotton Fields and Skyscrapers*, 180; Keith L. Bryant, Jr., "Oklahoma and the New Deal," in *The New Deal: The State and Local Levels*, ed. Braeman, Bremner, and Brody, 169–70.

25. Memphis Board of Commissioners, "Resolution," Dec. 3, 1935, Box 10, Folder 9, Watkins Overton Papers, Mississippi Valley Collection, Brister Library, Memphis State University; Memphis *Commercial Appeal*, Dec. 14,

1935 (quotation); Stenholm, "Louisiana: Report of a Field Trip, December 5–12, 1931."

26. John Williams, "Struggles of the Thirties in the South," in *The Negro in Depression and War: Prelude to Revolution, 1930–1945*, edited by Bernard Sternsher (Chicago: Quadrangle, 1969), 173; James M. Jones, Jr., to Hugo L. Black, telegram, Feb. 3, 1932, James M. Jones, Jr., Papers.

27. Sidney Fine, *Frank Murphy: The Detroit Years* (Ann Arbor: Univ. of Michigan Press, 1975), 299–300.

28. Montgomery, "Depression in Houston," 28–30; Atlanta *Constitution*, July 1, 1932; Roman Heleniak, "Local Reactions to the Great Depression in New Orleans, 1929–1933," *Louisiana History* 10 (Fall 1969): 302; Edward Shannon LaMonte, "Politics and Welfare in Birmingham, Alabama, 1900–1975," Ph.D. diss., Univ. of Chicago, 1976, p. 163; Warren Leslie, *Dallas, Public and Private* (New York: Grossman, 1964), 84–85 (quotation).

29. John W. Hevener, *Which Side Are You On? The Harlan County Coal Miners, 1931–1939* (Urbana: Univ. of Illinois Press, 1978), p. 16 (quotation); Tony Bubka, "The Harlan County Strike of 1931," in *Hitting Home: The Great Depression in Town and Country*, edited by Bernard Sternsher (Chicago: Quadrangle, 1970), 185–97.

30. New York *Times*, Apr. 3, 1932; Houston *Post-Dispatch*, Oct. 5, 1931; American Public Welfare Association, "Dallas Welfare Survey," 84; Dallas *Morning News*, Dec. 4, 1931; Dallas Community Chest, "Annual Report to Subscribers, December 1, 1932, to December 1, 1933," 1934, Western History Collection of the De Golyer Foundation, Southern Methodist University, Dallas, Texas.

31. C. S. Perry, "Telephone and Movies Help Unemployment Relief," *American City* 46 (May 1932): 115; Houston *Post-Dispatch*, Mar. 18 and Oct. 1, 1931; Montgomery, "Depression in Houston," 168.

32. Michael S. Holmes, *The New Deal in Georgia: An Administrative History* (Westport, Conn.: Greenwood, 1975), 17; "Community Team Work," *Survey*, Aug. 15, 1932, p. 378; State File: Georgia, Box 245, President's Organization for Unemployment Relief, RG 73, NA; Atlanta *Constitution*, Apr. 17, 1933; Fleming, "Atlanta, the Depression, and the New Deal," 110.

33. William Key, " 'Back-to-the-Farm' Movement Gives Aid to the Rehabilitation of Homes and Land as Well as People," *City Builder* 17 (Oct. 1932): 18–20; Atlanta *Constitution*, June 18, 1933; Everett R. Cook, *Memphis, Cotton's Market Place* (Memphis, 1942), 13; interview with Frank Ahlgren, Memphis State University Oral History Project, Mississippi Valley Collection, Memphis State University; Memphis *Commercial Appeal*, Jan. 1, 1940.

34. Dallas *Morning News*, Sept. 12, 1930; DeMoss, "Resourcefulness in the Financial Capital," 122; Memphis *Commercial Appeal*, Mar. 2, 1931; Ed Weathers, "Carnival Knowledge," *City of Memphis* 2 (Apr. 1977): 34–35.

35. Roberta Morgan, "Social Implications and the Human Side," *Journal of the Birmingham Historical Society* 1 (Jan. 1960): 11–14; LaMonte,

"Politics and Welfare in Birmingham," 174–76; "Service to Humanity: The Career of Roberta Morgan," Roberta Morgan Papers, Box 1, Folder 12, Birmingham Public Library Archives, Birmingham, Alabama; Rikard, "Experiment in Welfare Capitalism," 269–80; Lorena Hickok to Harry Hopkins, Apr. 1, 1934, Lorena Hickok Papers, Box 11, Folder "March–April 1934," Franklin D. Roosevelt Library, Hyde Park, New York.

36. Daniel, *Standing at the Crossroads*, 111; Strausberg, "Effectiveness of the New Deal in Arkansas," 102; Tindall, *Emergence of the New South*, 368.

37. Tindall, *Emergence of the New South*, 368–69; Lionel V. Patenaude, *Texans, Politics and the New Deal* (New York: Garland, 1983), 87–94; Smith, *New Deal in the Urban South*, 38–39; Roger D. Tate, Jr., "Easing the Burden: The Era of Depression and New Deal in Mississippi," Ph.D. diss., Univ. of Tennessee, 1978, p. 44; James T. Patterson, *The New Deal and the States: Federalism in Transition* (Princeton, N.J.: Princeton Univ. Press, 1969), 48.

38. Montgomery, "Depression in Houston," 154–55 (first quotation); Donald W. Whisenhunt, *The Depression in Texas: The Hoover Years* (New York: Garland, 1983), 9 (second quotation); Memphis *Commercial Appeal*, Mar. 12, 1933 (third quotation).

39. Tindall, *Emergence of the New South*, 373; Memphis *Commercial Appeal*, Mar. 2 and Aug. 19, 1930.

40. Smith, *New Deal in the Urban South*, 40.

41. Biles, *Memphis in the Great Depression*, 55 (McKellar quotations); Tindall, *Emergence of the New South*, 374; Smith, *New Deal in the Urban South*, 40 (Jones quotation), 41.

42. Tindall, *Emergence of the New South*, 357–59; Albert U. Romasco, *The Poverty of Abundance: Hoover, the Nation, the Depression* (New York: Oxford Univ. Press, 1965), 214–15.

43. See Frank Freidel, *F.D.R. and the South* (Baton Rouge: Louisiana State Univ. Press, 1965).

44. Tindall, *Emergence of the New South*, 387 (quotation from Texan); Freidel, *F.D.R. and the South*, 23–24.

Chapter 3: FROM SHARECROPPING TO AGRIBUSINESS

1. David E. Conrad, *The Forgotten Farmers: The Story of the Sharecroppers in the New Deal* (Urbana: Univ. of Illinois Press, 1965), 1–2; Pete Daniel, "The New Deal, Southern Agriculture and Economic Change," in *The New Deal and the South*, edited by James C. Cobb and Michael V. Namorato (Jackson: Univ. Press of Mississippi, 1984), 60.

2. Gilbert C. Fite, *Cotton Fields No More: Southern Agriculture, 1865–1980* (Lexington: Univ. Press of Kentucky, 1984), 113, 126; Tom Terrill and Jerrold Hirsch, eds., *Such as Us: Southern Voices of the Thirties* (Chapel Hill: Univ. of North Carolina Press, 1978), xiii.

3. Paul E. Mertz, *New Deal Policy and Southern Rural Poverty* (Baton Rouge: Louisiana State Univ. Press, 1978), 9; Jack Temple Kirby, *Rural Worlds Lost: The American South, 1920–1960* (Baton Rouge: Louisiana State Univ. Press, 1987), 56; Heinemann, *Depression and New Deal in Virginia*, 10–11 (quotation).

4. Daniel, *Breaking the Land*, 115.

5. Ibid., 83; Fite, *Cotton Fields No More*, 145 (first quotation); Theodore Saloutos, "Edward A. O'Neal: The Farm Bureau and the New Deal," *Current History* 27 (June 1955): 358 (second quotation).

6. Ronald A. Mulder, *The Insurgent Progressives in the U.S. Senate and the New Deal* (New York: Garland, 1981), 122.

7. Frank Freidel, "The South and the New Deal," in *New Deal and the South*, ed. Cobb and Namorato, 25; Tindall, *Emergence of the New South*, 392–93.

8. Roy V. Scott and J. G. Shoalmire, *The Public Career of Cully A. Cobb: A Study in Agricultural Leadership* (Jackson: Univ. Press of Mississippi, 1973), 171, 209; Gavin Wright, *Old South, New South: Revolutions in the Southern Economy since the Civil War* (New York: Basic Books, 1986), 226.

9. Holmes, *New Deal in Georgia*, 219; Conrad, *Forgotten Farmers*, 47.

10. Arthur M. Schlesinger, Jr., *The Age of Roosevelt: The Coming of the New Deal* (Boston: Houghton Mifflin, 1959), 235–55; Conrad, *Forgotten Farmers*, 49.

11. Conrad, *Forgotten Farmers*, 50, 61–63.

12. Blakey, *Hard Times and New Deal in Kentucky*, 115–16; Anthony J. Badger, *Prosperity Road: The New Deal, Tobacco, and North Carolina* (Chapel Hill: Univ. of North Carolina Press, 1980), 63–65.

13. Daniel, *Breaking the Land*, 135–51; Fite, *Cotton Fields No More*, 132–34.

14. Conrad, *Forgotten Farmers*, 39.

15. Ibid., 106–8.

16. Richard S. Kirkendall, *Social Scientists and Farm Politics in the Age of Roosevelt* (Columbia: Univ. of Missouri Press, 1966), 60–68.

17. President's Commission on Farm Tenancy, *Farm Tenancy, Report of the President's Commission* (Washington, D.C.: GPO, 1937); Mertz, *New Deal Policy and Southern Rural Poverty*, 13.

18. Fite, *Cotton Fields No More*, 152 (quotation from landholder); Daniel, *Breaking the Land*, 95 (Cobb quotation).

19. Kirby, *Rural Worlds Lost*, 64 (quotation); Theodore Saloutos, *The American Farmer and the New Deal* (Ames: Iowa State Univ. Press, 1982), 122.

20. Kirby, *Rural Worlds Lost*, 63.

21. Tindall, *Emergence of the New South*, 415–16.

22. Kirby, *Rural Worlds Lost*, 151.

23. Conrad, *Forgotten Farmers*, 85–95. Also see Donald H. Grubbs, *Cry from the Cotton: The Southern Tenant Farmers' Union and the New Deal* (Chapel Hill: Univ. of North Carolina Press, 1971); Leah Wise and Sue

Thrasher, "The Southern Tenant Farmers' Union," in *Working Lives*, ed. Miller, 120–22.

24. Conrad, *Forgotten Farmers*, 95–98.

25. Ibid., 123–25.

26. Scott and Shoalmire, *Public Career of Cully A. Cobb*, 231.

27. Ibid., 142–48.

28. Fite, *Cotton Fields No More*, 143.

29. Paul K. Conkin, *Tomorrow a New World: The New Deal Community Program* (Ithaca, N.Y.: Cornell Univ. Press, 1959), 130–42; Blakey, *Hard Times and New Deal in Kentucky*, 61–62.

30. Paul W. Wager, *One Foot on the Soil: A Study of Subsistence Homesteads in Alabama* (University: Univ. of Alabama Press, 1945), 45–50; Kirkendall, *Social Scientists and Farm Politics*, 71–73.

31. Kirkendall, *Social Scientists and Farm Politics*, 109–12.

32. Ibid., 115.

33. Ibid., 128, 129; Conkin, *Tomorrow a New World*, 183–84.

34. Kirkendall, *Social Scientists and Farm Politics*, 130–31; Tindall, *Emergence of the New South*, 426; Mertz, *New Deal Policy and Southern Rural Poverty*, 259–61.

35. See F. Jack Hurley, *Portrait of a Decade: Roy Stryker and the Development of Documentary Photography in the Thirties* (Baton Rouge: Louisiana State Univ. Press, 1972).

36. Christiana McFadyen Campbell, *The Farm Bureau and the New Deal: A Study of the Making of National Farm Policy, 1933–40* (Urbana: Univ. of Illinois Press, 1962), 28, 102.

37. Ibid., 50, 57, 157, 194 (quotation).

38. Ibid., 85–87; *New York Times*, Jan. 5, 1936.

39. Saloutos, *American Farmer and the New Deal*, 131–35.

40. Tindall, *Emergence of the New South*, 404–5; Blakey, *Hard Times and New Deal in Kentucky*, 117 (quotation).

41. Tindall, *Emergence of the New South*, 404–5.

42. Ibid., 406–7.

43. Ibid., 409; Saloutos, *American Farmer and the New Deal*, 256.

44. D. Clayton Brown, *Electricity for Rural America: The Fight for the REA* (Westport, Conn.: Greenwood, 1980), v–x.

45. Ibid., 5, 12–16; Saloutos, *American Farmer and the New Deal*, 209–10.

46. Saloutos, *American Farmer and the New Deal*, 211–13.

47. Brown, *Electricity for Rural America*, 65–75; Heinemann, *Depression and New Deal in Virginia*, 126–27.

48. Fite, *Cotton Fields No More*, 140.

49. Ibid., 147.

50. Kirby, *Rural Worlds Lost*, 64–69; Wright, *Old South, New South*, 232; Fite, *Cotton Fields No More*, 153.

51. Tindall, *Emergence of the New South*, 430; Daniel, "New Deal, Southern Agriculture, and Economic Change," 55–59.

52. Tindall, *Emergence of the New South*, 430–31.

53. Kirby, *Rural Worlds Lost*, 65–73; Daniel, *Standing at the Crossroads*, 123.

Chapter 4: RELIEF AND EMPLOYMENT

1. Tindall, *Emergence of the New South*, 476.

2. On the NRA, see Otis L. Graham, Jr., and Meghan Robinson Wander, eds., *Franklin D. Roosevelt, His Life and Times: An Encyclopedic View* (Boston: G. K. Hall, 1985), 275–77, and Bernard Bellush, *The Failure of the NRA* (New York: Norton, 1975).

3. John Kennedy Ohl, *Hugh S. Johnson and the New Deal* (DeKalb: Northern Illinois Univ. Press, 1985), 115–17.

4. Ibid., 133–36; Tindall, *Emergence of the New South*, 440–41.

5. Blakey, *Hard Times and New Deal in Kentucky*, 151; Atlanta Chamber of Commerce, "NRA Drive a Success, Says Chairman Robert F. Madox," *City Builder*, Sept. 10, 1933, p. 15; Smith, *New Deal in the Urban South*, 46; Houston Chamber of Commerce, "Chamber Welcomes NRA Responsibility," *Houston* 4 (Aug. 1933): 6; Doyle, *Nashville since the 1920s*, 87; Heinemann, *Depression and New Deal in Virginia*, 51; Dallas Chamber of Commerce, "Departmental Reports for 1933," *Dallas* 12 (Nov. 1933): 6.

6. James E. Fickle, *The New South and the 'New Competition': Trade Association Development in the Southern Pine Industry* (Urbana: Univ. of Illinois Press, 1980), 136; Blakey, *Hard Times and New Deal in Kentucky*, 153; E. Thomas Lovell, "Houston's Reaction to the New Deal, 1932–1936," M.A. thesis, Univ. of Houston, 1964, p. 24; *Southern Labor Review*, Aug. 9, 1933 (quotation); Smith, *New Deal in the Urban South*, 49–51.

7. Linda J. Lear, "Harold L. Ickes and the Oil Crisis of the First Hundred Days," *Mid-America* 63 (Jan. 1981): 4–12; Lovell, "Houston's Reaction to the New Deal," 34–46.

8. "Report from Hugh Humphreys to John Swope, March 2, 1934," Records of the NRA, RG 9, Public Attitude Reports, NA; Fickle, *New South and the 'New Competition*,' 131; John Dean Minton, *The New Deal in Tennessee, 1932–1938* (New York: Garland, 1979); Holmes, *New Deal in Georgia*, 185 (quotation).

9. Atlanta *Constitution*, May 29, 1935.

10. Wright, *Old South, New South*, 217–23.

11. Patenaude, *Texans, Politics and the New Deal*, 85–90.

12. Lionel V. Patenaude, "Texas and the New Deal," in *Depression in the Southwest*, ed. Whisenhunt, 92; Blakey, *Hard Times and New Deal in Kentucky*, 53; Heinemann, *Depression and New Deal in Virginia*, 76; Works Progress Administration, *Final Statistical Report on the Federal Emergency Relief Administration* (Washington, D.C.: GPO, 1942), 177–92; Smith, *New Deal in the Urban South*, 66–71; Tindall, *Emergence of the New South*, 476.

13. George McJimsey, *Harry Hopkins: Ally of the Poor and Defender of Democracy* (Cambridge, Mass.: Harvard Univ. Press, 1987), 54 (Hopkins quotation); Tindall, *Emergence of the New South*, 482.

14. Bryant, "Oklahoma and the New Deal," 173–74, 183, 189; John A. Salmond, *A Southern Rebel: The Life and Times of Aubrey Willis Williams, 1890–1965* (Chapel Hill: Univ. of North Carolina Press, 1983), 49 (Murray quotation).

15. Allen Johnstone to Harry Hopkins, Sept. 18, 1933, FERA State Files, 1933–36, Georgia 401.2-420 Field Reports (406), RG 69, NA; Jane Walker Herndon, "Ed Rivers and Georgia's 'Little New Deal,' " *Atlanta Historical Quarterly* 30 (Spring 1986): 98–99 (quotations).

16. Allen Johnstone to Harry Hopkins, Sept. 18, 1933, FERA State Files, 1933–36, Georgia 401.2-420 Field Reports (406), RG 69, NA; Clark Howell to Harold Ickes, Apr. 25, 1935, Franklin D. Roosevelt Papers, President's Personal File 604, Franklin D. Roosevelt Library.

17. "PWA and Georgia," 12; Herndon, "Ed Rivers," 99–103.

18. Betty M. Field, "The Politics of the New Deal in Louisiana, 1933–1939," Ph.D. diss., Tulane Univ., 1973, pp. 57–64; M. J. Miller to Aubrey Williams, Oct. 15, 1934, FERA State Files, 1933–36, Louisiana 403-420, Field Reports (406), RG 69, NA.

19. Blakey, *Hard Times and New Deal in Kentucky,* 49–51; Douglas C. Abrams, "North Carolina and the New Deal, 1932–1940," Ph.D. diss., Univ. of Maryland, 1981, pp. 83–84; William R. Brock, *Welfare, Democracy, and the New Deal* (Cambridge: Cambridge Univ. Press, 1988), 229; Heinemann, *Depression and New Deal in Virginia,* 84 (quotation).

20. LaMonte, "Politics and Welfare in Birmingham," 224–26; "Service to Humanity: The Career of Roberta Morgan," Roberta Morgan Papers, Box 1, Folder 12; Loula Dunn to Robert P. Lansdale, Oct. 19, 1934, FERA State Files, 1935–36, Alabama 401.3-420, Field Reports (406), RG 69, NA; Marion Alcorn to Aubrey Williams, Apr. 9, 1934, FERA State Files, 1933–36, Texas 401.2-410, Field Reports, RG 69, NA; Houston *Press,* Mar. 23, 1936.

21. Bonnie Fox Schwartz, *The Civil Works Administration, 1933–1934: The Business of Emergency Employment in the New Deal* (Princeton, N.J.: Princeton Univ. Press, 1984).

22. Graham and Wander, eds., *Franklin D. Roosevelt,* 336–37.

23. Tindall, *Emergence of the New South,* 474; Heinemann, *Depression and New Deal in Virginia,* 64; Division of Information, "Louisiana State Committee Report," Appraisal Report File, Box 191, RG 69, NA; New Orleans *Times-Picayune,* Jan. 16, 1940; WPA Writers' Project, *Houston: A History and Guide,* 120; City of Memphis, "Public Works Program, Jan. 1, 1928–Aug. 31, 1938," Watkins Overton Papers, Box 8, Folder 12; "Birmingham's Industrial Water Supply," *American City* 51 (May 1936): 66.

24. Graham and Wander, eds., *Franklin D. Roosevelt,* 187–88; John C. Petrie, "Survey Shows Housing Scandals," *Christian Century,* Feb. 21, 1934, p. 265; "Housing Authorities Describe Local Conditions Demonstrating Need for Slum Reclamation," *American City* 53 (Nov. 1938): 58.

25. Charles F. Palmer, *Adventures of a Slum Fighter* (Atlanta: Tupper and Love, 1955), 8–18; Mark B. Lapping, "The Emergence of Federal Public Housing: Atlanta's Techwood Project," *American Journal of Economics and Sociology* 32 (Oct. 1973): 380 (quotation); "Techwood Homes, Atlanta, Is a Working Reality," *American City* 51 (Oct. 1936): 58–59. Also see "Confidential Memorandum Regarding Dinner at White House, Monday Evening, May 17, 1937," Charles F. Palmer Papers, Box 22, Folder 12, Robert W. Woodruff Library, Emory University, Atlanta, Georgia.

26. Palmer, *Adventures of a Slum Fighter*, 20, 29, 137; Howard W. Pollard, "The Effect of Techwood Homes on Urban Development in the United States," M.A. thesis, Georgia Institute of Technology, 1968, pp. 20, 35; Michael L. Porter, "The Development and Amelioration of Housing Conditions in the Techwood Housing Area (1890–1938) and the University Housing Area (1930–1950)," M.A. thesis, Atlanta Univ., 1972, pp. 17–33.

27. Palmer, *Adventures of a Slum Fighter*, 229–37 (Hartsfield quotation on p. 229); Housing Authority of the City of Atlanta, "Rebuilding Atlanta: Second Annual Report, June 30, 1940," Charles F. Palmer Papers, Box 4, Folder 32; William B. Hartsfield to Jimmy Jones, July 18, 1938, James M. Jones, Jr., Papers.

28. Badger, *North Carolina and the New Deal*, 52–53; Silver, *Twentieth-Century Richmond*, 147–54.

29. Dallas *Morning News*, Apr. 3, 1934.

30. John A. Salmond, *The Civilian Conservation Corps, 1933–1942: A New Deal Case Study* (Durham, N.C.: Duke Univ. Press, 1967).

31. Richard Lowitt, "Tennessee Valley Authority," in *Encyclopedia of Southern Culture*, ed. Wilson and Ferris, 365–66.

32. Ibid.

33. Ralph C. Hon, "The Memphis Power and Light Deal," *Southern Economic Journal* 6 (Jan. 1940): 350; Watkins Overton to David Lilienthal, Sept. 17, 1934, and David Lilienthal to Watkins Overton, Sept. 19, 1934, both in Watkins Overton Papers, Box 11, Folder 30; Hugh Russell Fraser, "Memphis Votes for Cheaper Power," *Nation*, Nov. 28, 1934, pp. 615–16.

34. Robert A. Sigafoos, *Cotton Row to Beale Street: A Business History of Memphis* (Memphis: Memphis State Univ. Press, 1979), 189–90.

35. Lyle W. Dorsett, *Franklin D. Roosevelt and the City Bosses* (Port Washington, N.Y.: Kennikat, 1977), 44; Thomas H. Coode, "Tennessee Congressmen and the New Deal, 1933–1938," *West Tennessee Historical Society Papers* 31 (1977): 140; William D. Miller, "The Browning-Crump Battle: The Crump Side," *East Tennessee Historical Society's Publications* 37 (1965): 84–88; Ed Crump to Kenneth D. McKellar, July 23, 1940, Kenneth D. McKellar Papers, McKellar-Crump Correspondence, Box 4, Folder "1940 May–July," Memphis-Shelby County Archives.

36. "Public Utilities," *Newsweek*, Oct. 21, 1933, p. 20; "An Alabama Defeat for Public Ownership," *Literary Digest*, Oct. 28, 1933, p. 45; Birmingham *News*, Oct. 10, 1933, and Nov. 28, 1939; Birmingham *Age-Herald*, Aug. 12, 1939.

37. Michael J. McDonald and John Muldowny, *TVA and the Dispossessed: The Resettlement of Population in the Norris Dam Area* (Knoxville: Univ. of Tennessee Press, 1982).

38. Graham and Wander, eds., *Franklin D. Roosevelt*, 461–64.

39. David E. Rison, "Arkansas during the Great Depression," Ph.D. diss., Univ. of California, Los Angeles, 1974, p. 113.

40. Harry Hopkins and Gay Shepperson, memorandum of a telephone conversation, Aug. 8, 1935, Harry Hopkins Papers, Box 73, Folder "Georgia," Franklin D. Roosevelt Library; Harold L. Ickes, *The Secret Diary of Harold L. Ickes: The First Thousand Days, 1933–1936* (New York: Simon and Schuster, 1954), 409, 427, 582 (Ickes quotation); Watkins Overton to Hill McAlister, Aug. 30, 1933, Hill McAlister Papers, Box 47, Folder 7, State Library and Archives, Nashville, Tennessee (Overton quotation); Jo Ann E. Argersinger, *Toward a New Deal in Baltimore: People and Government in the Great Depression* (Chapel Hill: Univ. of North Carolina Press, 1988), 42–44.

41. Mertz, *New Deal Policy and Southern Rural Poverty*, 54; Memphis *Press-Scimitar*, Sept. 9, 1936, and Mar. 22, 1937; Tindall, *Emergence of the New South*, 478 (quotation), 479.

42. Donald S. Howard, *The WPA and Federal Relief Policy* (New York: Russell Sage Foundation, 1943), 84, 95, 178; Michael S. Holmes, "The New Deal in Georgia: An Administrative History," Ph.D. diss., Univ. of Wisconsin, 1969, pp. 213, 237; Susan Ware, *Holding Their Own: American Women in the 1930s* (Boston: Twayne, 1982), 31.

43. Douglas L. Fleming, "The New Deal in Atlanta: A Review of the Major Programs," *Atlanta Historical Journal* 30 (Spring 1986): 40; "Iron Man," *Time*, Aug. 17, 1936, p. 68; Estelle Marlowe, "Celebration Dedicates Symbol of City's Wealth and Spirit," *American City* 54 (June 1939): 127; WPA Writers' Project, *Houston: A History and Guide*, 120–21; Commission of Control for Texas Centennial Celebrations, "Monuments Erected by the State of Texas to Commemorate the Centenary of Texas Independence," Dallas Public Library; George H. Santerre, *Dallas' First Hundred Years*; City of Memphis, "Public Works Program, Jan. 1, 1928–Aug. 31, 1938," Watkins Overton Papers, Box 8, Folder 12; WPA Division of Information, "Louisiana State Committee Report," Appraisal Report File, Box 191, RG 69, NA; WPA Writers' Project, *The WPA Guide to New Orleans* (New York: Pantheon, 1938), 39; Argersinger, *Toward a New Deal in Baltimore*, 71; David R. Goldfield, "The Urban South: A Regional Framework," *American Historical Review* 68 (Dec. 1981): 1030.

44. Blakey, *Hard Times and New Deal in Kentucky*, 63; Kirby, *Rural Worlds Lost*, 57.

45. Martha Swain, "A New Deal for Mississippi Women, 1933–1943," *Journal of Mississippi History* 46 (Aug. 1984): 198.

46. Ware, *Holding Their Own*, 40 (quotation from WPA official); Blakey, *Hard Times and New Deal in Kentucky*, 61; Biles, *Memphis in the Great Depression*, 76 (banner quotations).

47. Tindall, *Emergence of the New South*, 495.

48. Smith, *New Deal in the Urban South*, 209–12; Swain, "New Deal for Mississippi Women," 208.

49. WPA Writers' Project, *These Are Our Lives* (Chapel Hill: Univ. of North Carolina Press, 1939).

50. W. Andrew Achenbaum, *Social Security: Visions and Revisions* (Cambridge: Cambridge Univ. Press, 1986), 18–23; William E. Leuchtenburg, *Franklin D. Roosevelt and the New Deal* (New York: Harper and Row, 1963), 131 (quotation).

51. Smith, *New Deal in the Urban South*, 156; Tindall, *Emergence of the New South*, 487–88.

52. Houston *Chronicle*, Nov. 30, 1935; Birmingham *News*, June 30, 1936; Roger Biles, "The Urban South in the Great Depression," *Journal of Southern History* 56 (Feb. 1990): 86 (first quotation); WPA Writers' Project, *Dallas Guide and History* (Dallas, 1940), 494, 495 (second quotation).

53. Anthony J. Badger, *North Carolina and the New Deal*, 46 (first quotation); Memphis *Press-Scimitar*, Feb. 18, 1935; U.S. Bureau of the Census, *Financial Statistics of Cities over 100,000 Population, 1937* (Washington, D.C.: Department of Commerce, 1940), 186–87; Houston *Post*, Jan. 25, 1936, and Jan. 19, 1938; New York *Times*, Aug. 13, 1934; LaMonte, "Politics and Welfare in Birmingham," 237 (second quotation).

54. Mertz, *New Deal Policy and Southern Rural Poverty*, 51; Lorena Hickok to Harry Hopkins, Apr. 8, 1934, Lorena Hickok Papers, Box 11, Folder "March–April, 1934"; Elmer Scott to Harry Hopkins, Apr. 15, 1934, Harry L. Hopkins Papers, Box 60, Folder "Tennessee Field Reports, 1933–1936," Group 24, Franklin D. Roosevelt Library; Marion Alcorn to Aubrey Williams, Apr. 14, 1934, FERA State Files, 1933–36, Louisiana 403–420, Field Reports (406), RG 69, NA.

55. Anita Van de Voorf, "Public Welfare Administration in Jefferson County," M.A. thesis, Tulane Univ., 1935, p. 99.

56. Tindall, *Emergence of the New South*, 490; Smith, *New Deal in the Urban South*, 164 (quotation).

Chapter 5: LABOR AND THE NEW DEAL

1. Irving Bernstein, *Turbulent Years: A History of the American Worker, 1933–1941* (Boston: Houghton Mifflin, 1971), 41.

2. J. Wayne Flint, "The New Deal and Southern Labor," in *New Deal and the South*, ed. Cobb and Namorato, 65–66.

3. James A. Hodges, *New Deal Labor Policy and the Southern Cotton Textile Industry, 1933–1941* (Knoxville: Univ. of Tennessee Press, 1986), 76–99; John Wesley Kennedy, "The General Strike in the Textile Industry, September, 1934," M.A. thesis, Duke Univ., 1947, pp. 25–27; Tindall, *Emergence of the New South*, 510 (McMahon quotation).

4. Hodges, *New Deal Labor Policy and the Southern Cotton Textile Industry*, 105–8; Atlanta *Constitution*, Sept. 5–23, 1934; John E.

Allen, "The Governor and the Strike: Eugene Talmadge and the General Strike, 1934," M.A. thesis, Georgia State Univ., 1977, pp. 2 (quotation), 3, 112–26.

5. Hodges, *New Deal Labor Policy and the Southern Cotton Textile Industry*, 111–18, 130.

6. Walter Galenson, *The CIO Challenge to the AFL: A History of the American Labor Movement, 1935–1941* (Cambridge, Mass.: Harvard Univ. Press, 1960), 194–95; Hevener, *Which Side Are You On?* 120.

7. Robert J. Norrell, "Caste in Steel: Jim Crow Careers in Birmingham, Alabama," *Journal of American History* 73 (Dec. 1986): 673; William Mitch to Hugh L. Kerwin, Aug. 8, 1933, Philip Taft Papers, Box 1, Folder 16, Birmingham Public Library Archives; New York *Times*, Nov. 17, 1935; Birmingham *Southern Labor Review*, May 17, 1939.

8. Horace Huntley, "Iron Ore Miners and Mine Mill in Alabama, 1933–1952," Ph.D. diss., Univ. of Pittsburgh, 1977, pp. 50–53; Birmingham *News*, May 9, 1934.

9. Bernstein, *Turbulent Years*, 322–42.

10. Galenson, *CIO Challenge to the AFL*, 20–75.

11. Neil Herring and Sue Thrasher, "UAW Sit-down Strike: Atlanta, 1936," in *Working Lives*, ed. Miller, 173–79; Atlanta *Constitution*, Feb. 7, 1937; Lucy Randolph Mason, *To Win These Rights: A Personal Story of the CIO in the South* (New York: Harper and Row, 1952), 34–36.

12. Mason, *To Win These Rights*, 62; F. Ray Marshall, *Labor in the South* (Cambridge, Mass.: Harvard Univ. Press, 1967), 186; George R. Leighton, "Birmingham, Alabama: The City of Perpetual Promise," *Harper's Magazine* 175 (Aug. 1937): 241; Rikard, "Experiment in Welfare Capitalism," 308–10; Alexander Kendrick, "Alabama Goes on Strike," *Nation*, Aug. 29, 1934, pp. 233–34.

13. New York *Times*, Aug. 2, 1937 (first quotation); Robert J. Norrell, "Labor at the Ballot Box: Birmingham's Big Mules Fight Back, 1938–1948," paper delivered at the annual meeting of the Southern Historical Association, Nov. 2, 1984; Billy Hall Wyche, "Southern Attitudes toward Industrial Unions, 1933–1941," Ph.D. diss., Univ. of Georgia, 1969, p. 61 (second quotation).

14. Tindall, *Emergence of the New South*, 515; Flint, "New Deal and Southern Labor," 85–88; David M. Tucker, *Memphis since Crump: Bossism, Blacks, and Civic Reformers, 1948–1968* (Knoxville: Univ. of Tennessee Press, 1980), 55 (Crump quotation).

15. Glenn Gilman, *Human Relations in the Industrial Southeast: A Study of the Textile Industry* (Chapel Hill: Univ. of North Carolina Press, 1956), 225–48; Mason, *To Win These Rights*, 19–20.

16. Ware, *Holding Their Own*, 45.

17. Myles Horton and Lawrence L. Bostian, "Highlander Folk School," in *Encyclopedia of Southern Culture*, ed. Wilson and Ferris, 1418; Mary Frederickson, "A Place to Speak Our Minds," in *Working Lives*, ed. Miller, 154–56.

18. Mary Frederickson, "Heroines and Girl Strikers: Gender Issues and Organized Labor in the Twentieth-Century South," in *Organized Labor in the Twentieth-Century South*, edited by Robert H. Zieger (Knoxville: Univ. of Tennessee Press, 1991), 93–101.

19. Tindall, *Emergence of the New South*, 524.

20. Goldfield, *Cotton Fields and Skyscrapers*, 187 (quotation); Tindall, *Emergence of the New South*, 526–27; Jerold S. Auerbach, *Labor and Liberty: The La Follette Committee and the New Deal* (Indianapolis: Bobbs-Merrill, 1966).

21. Gerald M. Capers, "Satrapy of a Benevolent Despot," in *Our Fair City*, ed. Allen, 226; Allan A. Michie and Frank Ryhlick, *Dixie Demagogues* (New York: Vanguard, 1939), 253; John C. Petrie, "Memphis Makes War on CIO," *Christian Century*, Oct. 13, 1937, p. 1273; George Lambert, "Memphis Is Safe for Ford," *Nation*, Jan. 22, 1938, p. 94; William D. Miller, *Mr. Crump of Memphis* (Baton Rouge: Louisiana State Univ. Press, 1964), 202; F. F. Doyle to Watkins Overton, Jan. 4, 1937, Mayors Correspondence Files, Drawer 3, Memphis-Shelby County Archives; Watkins Overton to E. H. Crump, Apr. 13, 1937, Mayors Correspondence Files, Drawer 2.

22. Memphis *Press-Scimitar*, Mar. 9–12 and Apr. 17, 1937; Memphis *Commercial Appeal*, Mar. 22–27 and Apr. 16–19, 1937; Roger Biles, "Ed Crump versus the Unions: The Labor Movement in Memphis during the 1930s," *Labor History* 25 (Fall 1984): 541–43.

23. "Statement," Sept. 18, 1937, Watkins Overton Papers, Box 10, Folder 11.

24. Memphis *Press-Scimitar*, Sept. 22 and 23, 1937; Miller, *Mr. Crump of Memphis*, 215; Mason, *To Win These Rights*, 105; E. H. Crump to Kenneth D. McKellar, Apr. 6, 1938, Kenneth D. McKellar Papers, McKellar-Crump Correspondence, Box 3, (quotation); Biles, "Ed Crump versus the Unions," 543–46.

25. Memphis *Commercial Appeal*, Aug. 25–30 and Dec. 24, 1940; A. B. Clapp to Walter Chandler, Dec. 4 and 7, 1940, Mayors Correspondence Files, Drawer 10, Memphis-Shelby County Archives.

26. George Morris to Norman Thomas, Mar. 8, 1934, H. L. Mitchell Papers, Reel 1, Brister Library, Memphis State University (quotation); Conrad, *Forgotten Farmers*, 89–98; "Southern Tenant Farmers' Union Calendar of Events, June–October 1936," William R. Amberson Papers, Box 1, Folder 7, Mississippi Valley Collection, Brister Library; William R. Amberson to Roger Baldwin, Dec. 30, 1935, William R. Amberson Papers, Box 1, Folder 6; Memphis *Press-Scimitar*, Sept. 25, 1937; Kate Born, "Memphis Negro Workingmen and the NAACP," *West Tennessee Historical Society Papers* 28 (1974): 105–6.

27. Dallas Chamber of Commerce, "The Dallas Market," 1941, Dallas Public Library, pp. 12, 13 (quotations); New York *Times*, Jan. 5, 1930; George Lambert, "Dallas Tries Terror," *Nation*, Oct. 9, 1937, p. 377.

28. Stanley Walker, "The Dallas Morning News," *American Mercury* 65 (Dec. 1947): 708–11.

29. WPA Writers' Project, *Dallas Guide and History*, 283–84; John J. Granberry, "Civil Liberties in Texas," *Christian Century*, Oct. 27, 1937, pp. 1326–27; Lambert, "Dallas Tries Terror," 376–78; Marshall, *Labor in the South*, 191 (quotation).

30. WPA Writers' Project, *Dallas Guide and History*, 284; Granberry, "Civil Liberties in Texas," 1327; George Green, "The ILGWU in Texas, 1930–1970," *Journal of Mexican-American History* 1 (Spring 1971): 154.

31. Glen R. Roberson, "City on the Plains: The History of Tulsa, Oklahoma," Ph.D. diss., Oklahoma State Univ., 1977, pp. 187–88.

32. Daniel Rosenberg, "Race, Labor, and Unionism: New Orleans Dockworkers, 1900–1910," Ph.D. diss., City University of New York, 1985, 303; Robert C. Francis, "Longshoremen in New Orleans," *Opportunity* 14 (Mar. 1936): 84; Carroll G. Miller, "A Study of the New Orleans Longshoremen's Unions From 1850 to 1962," M.A. thesis, Louisiana State University, 1962, 30–31.

33. Miller, "Study of the New Orleans Longshoremen's Unions," 36–37; Herbert R. Northrup, *Organized Labor and the Negro* (New York: Harper and Brothers, 1944), 149–50.

34. New Orleans *Times-Picayune*, July 2, 1938; Herbert R. Northrup, "The New Orleans Longshoremen," *Political Science Quarterly* 57 (Dec. 1942): 544; F. Ray Marshall, *Labor in the South*, 208–9.

35. Houston *Post-Dispatch*, Oct. 1, 13, 22, 1931; Houston *Post*, July 16, 1934, Jan. 4, 1937; James Martin SoRelle, "The Darker Side of 'Heaven': The Black Community in Houston, Texas, 1917–1945," Ph.D. diss., Kent State University, 1980, 163–65.

36. Robert H. Zieger, "Textile Workers and Historians," in Robert H. Zieger, ed., *Organized Labor in the Twentieth-Century South* (Knoxville: Univ. of Tennessee Press, 1991), 35–36; J. Wayne Flint, "The New Deal and Southern Labor," 80–83; James A. Hodges, *New Deal Labor Policy and the Southern Cotton Textile Industry*, 144–63; Jo Ann D. Carpenter, "Olin D. Johnston, the New Deal and the Politics of Class in South Carolina, 1934–1938," Ph.D. diss., Emory University, 1987, 258–60; Tindall, *Emergence of the New South*, 518.

37. Tindall, *Emergence of the New South*, 519 (quotation), 521; Hodges, *New Deal Labor Policy and the Southern Cotton Textile Industry*, 159, 197–98.

38. Hevener, *Which Side Are You On?*, 116; Tindall, *Emergence of the New South*, 528 (quotation).

39. Tindall, *Emergence of the New South*, 529.

40. Hevener, *Which Side Are You On?*, 153 (quotation), 158–70.

41. Mertz, *New Deal Policy and Southern Rural Poverty*, 227 (first quotation); Tindall, *Emergence of the New South*, 532 (second quotation).

42. Tindall, *Emergence of the New South*, 533 (quotation); Fickle, *The New South and the 'New Competition'*, 300–303.

43. Atlanta *Journal of Labor*, Mar. 1, 1940; Atlanta *Constitution*, Mar. 4, 1940 (quotation).

44. Marshall, *Labor in the South*, 221–22.

45. Ibid; Flynt, "The New Deal and Southern Labor," 71.

46. Marshall, *Labor in the South*, 222.

Chapter 6: THE NEW DEAL AND RACE RELATIONS

1. U.S. Bureau of the Census, *Negroes in the United States, 1920–1932* (Washington, D.C.: GPO, 1935), 277–81.

2. U.S. Bureau of the Census, *Fifteenth Census of the United States: 1930, Unemployment* (Washington, D.C.: GPO, 1933), 952–53; George W. Lee, *Beale Street: Where the Blues Began* (New York: Robert O. Ballou, 1934), 210 (Stuart quotation).

3. William J. Brophy, "Black Texans and the New Deal," in *Depression in the Southwest*, ed. Whisenhunt, 117; Alwyn Barr, *Black Texans: A History of Negroes in Texas, 1528–1971* (Austin, Tex.: Jenkins, 1973), 154–55; Biles, *Memphis in the Great Depression*, 92; Ralph J. Bunche, *The Political Status of the Negro in the Age of FDR* (Chicago: Univ. of Chicago Press, 1973), 1126 (quotation); Donald E. DeVore, "The Rise from the Nadir: Black New Orleans between the Wars, 1920–1940," M.A. thesis, Univ. of New Orleans, 1983, p. 56; Joseph A. Pierce, *The Atlanta Negro: A Collection of Data on the Negro Population of Atlanta, Georgia* (Washington, D.C.: American Youth Commission of the American Council on Education, 1940), 77; Paul Douglas Bolster, "Civil Rights Movement in Twentieth-Century Georgia," Ph.D. diss., Univ. of Georgia, 1972, p. 38; Robert J. Alexander, "Negro Business in Atlanta," *Southern Economic Journal* 17 (Apr. 1951): 456; Randy J. Sparks, " 'Heavanly Houston' or 'Hellish Houston'? Black Unemployment and Relief Efforts, 1929–1936," *Southern Studies* 25 (Winter 1986): 354.

4. Bolster, "Civil Rights Movement," 39.

5. Abrams, "North Carolina and the New Deal," 336; Charles S. Johnson, *Patterns of Negro Segregation* (New York: Harper and Row, 1943), 20, 50; T. J. Woofter, Jr., *Negro Problems in the Cities* (Garden City, N.Y.: Doubleday, Doran, and Co., 1928), 205–6; DeVore, "Rise from the Nadir," 118–19; Houston *Informer,* June 6, 1931; Thomas, *Study of the Social Welfare Status of the Negroes in Houston*, 61–62; Marcia E. Turner-Jones, "A Political Analysis of Black Educational History: Atlanta, 1865–1943," Ph.D. diss., Univ. of Chicago, 1982, p. 210; Pierce, *Atlanta Negro*, 24, 51.

6. Sternsher, ed., *The Negro in Depression and War*, 195; Thomas, *Study of the Social Welfare Status of the Negroes in Houston*, 93–94; Fleming, "Atlanta, the Depression, and the New Deal," 309; James Martin SoRelle, "The Darker Side of 'Heavan': The Black Community in Houston, Texas, 1917–1945," Ph.D. diss., Kent State Univ., 1980, p. 97; Johnson, *Patterns of Negro Segregation*, 49–50; "An Ordinance to Amend Section 6002 of the Code of the City of Birmingham of 1930," James M. Jones, Jr., Papers.

7. Nell Irvin Painter, *The Narrative of Hosea Hudson: His Life as a Negro Communist in the South* (Cambridge, Mass.: Harvard Univ. Press, 1979), 347n; "Ordinance to Amend Section 6002"; David McComb, *Hous-*

ton: The Bayou City (Austin: Univ. of Texas Press, 1969), 159; DeVore, "Rise from the Nadir," 48; Kesavan Sudheendran, "Community Power Structure in Atlanta: A Study in Decision Making, 1928–1939," Ph.D. diss., Georgia State Univ., 1982, pp. 280–82.

8. Dana F. White, "The Black Side of Atlanta: A Geography of Expansion and Containment, 1870–1970," *Atlanta Historical Journal* 26 (Summer–Fall 1982): 217–18; Biles, *Memphis in the Great Depression*, 90 (quotation).

9. Paul M. Pearson, "Federal Housing Projects for Negroes," *Southern Workman* 65 (Dec. 1936): 376–77; Pierce, *Atlanta Negro*, 82; Work Projects Administration of Georgia, "The Real Property, Land Use, and Low Income Housing Area Survey of Metropolitan Atlanta," 1940, p. 14, Houston Metropolitan Research Center, Houston Public Library; Thomas, *Study of the Social Welfare Status of the Negroes in Houston*, 30; Silver, *Twentieth-Century Richmond*, 125; W. D. Moore, "What Slum Clearance Means to Birmingham," Roberta Morgan Papers, Box 1, Folder 17, Birmingham Public Library Archives; Bunche, *Political Status of the Negro*, 567; WPA Writers' Project, *Dallas Guide and History*, 507; Sam R. Carter, *A Report on Survey of Metropolitan New Orleans Land Use, Real Property, and Low Income Housing Area* (New Orleans: Louisiana State Department of Public Welfare and Housing Authority of New Orleans, 1941), 54–57; DeVore, "Rise from the Nadir," 60.

10. Bunche, *Political Status of the Negro*, 28; Robert Haynes, "Black Houstonians and the White Democratic Primary, 1920–1945," in *Houston: A Twentieth-Century Urban Frontier*, edited by Francisco A. Rosales and Barry J. Kaplan (Port Washington, N.Y.: Associated Faculty Press, 1983), 123–27. Also see Darlene Clark Hine, *Black Victory: The Rise and Fall of the White Primary in Texas* (Millwood, N.Y.: KTO Press, 1979).

11. Clarence Albert Bacote, "The Negro in Atlanta Politics," *Phylon* 16 (Fourth Quarter 1955): 342–43; Augustus Alven Adair, "A Political History of the Negro in Atlanta, 1908–1953," M.A. thesis, Atlanta Univ., 1955, pp. 38–50; Turner-Jones, "Political Analysis of Black Educational History," 139–40; Nancy J. Weiss, *Farewell to the Party of Lincoln: Black Politics in the Age of FDR* (Princeton, N.J.: Princeton Univ. Press, 1983), 233.

12. Turner-Jones, "Political Analysis of Black Educational History," 189–95, 238; Bunche, *Political Status of the Negro*, 300, 485.

13. Bunche, *Political Status of the Negro*, 73–74; Roger Biles, "Robert R. Church, Jr., of Memphis: Black Republican Leader in the Age of Democratic Ascendancy, 1928–1940," *Tennessee Historical Quarterly* 42 (Winter 1983): 372–76.

14. Biles, "Robert R. Church," 372–76.

15. William R. Snell, "Masked Men in the Magic City: Activities of the Revised Klan in Birmingham, 1916–1940," *Alabama Historical Quarterly* 34 (Fall and Winter 1972): 225; Barr, *Black Texans*, 139; New York *Times*, Nov. 27, 1939; John Hammond Moore, "Communists and Fascists in a Southern City: Atlanta, 1930," *South Atlantic Quarterly* 67 (Summer

1968): 444–53; Edwin Tribble, "Black Shirts in Georgia," *New Republic*, Oct. 8, 1930, pp. 204–6; Charles H. Martin, "White Supremacy and Black Workers: Georgia's 'Black Shirts' Combat the Great Depression," *Labor History* 18 (Summer 1977): 366–81.

16. Walter Wilson, "Atlanta's Communists," *Nation*, June 25, 1930, pp. 703–31; Moore, "Communists and Fascists in a Southern City," 442–43; David Entin, "Angelo Herndon," M.A. thesis, Univ. of North Carolina, 1963, pp. 21–61; Charles H. Martin, *The Angelo Herndon Case and Southern Justice* (Baton Rouge: Louisiana State Univ. Press, 1976); Atlanta *Constitution*, Apr. 28, 1937.

17. See Dan T. Carter, *Scottsboro: A Tragedy of the American South* (Baton Rouge: Louisiana State Univ. Press, 1969).

18. Williams, "Struggles of the Thirties in the South," 173–74; Brownell, *Urban Ethos in the South*, 20; Bunche, *Political Status of the Negro*, 493–94; Walter White to Watkins Overton, telegram, Mar. 5, 1937, Watkins Overton Papers, Box 4, Folder 35.

19. Atlanta Urban League, "Annual Report, 1940," 3; Tempie Virginia Strange, "The Dallas Negro Chamber of Commerce: A Study of a Negro Institution," M.A. thesis, Southern Methodist Univ., 1945; Leedell W. Neyland, "The Negro in Louisiana since 1900: An Economic and Social Study," Ph.D. diss., New York Univ., 1958, p. 66.

20. Tindall, *Emergence of the New South*, 544–45; Raymond Wolters, *Negroes and the Great Depression: The Problem of Economic Recovery* (Westport, Conn.: Greenwood, 1970), 145 (quotation).

21. Weiss, *Farewell to the Party of Lincoln*, 56.

22. Wolters, *Negroes and the Great Depression*, 42–43; Allen F. Kifer, "The Negro under the New Deal, 1933–1941," Ph.D. diss., Univ. of Wisconsin, 1961, pp. 150–52.

23. Salmond, *Civilian Conservation Corps*, 91–92 (Fechner quotation); Kifer, "The Negro under the New Deal," 12–21; Bryant, "Oklahoma and the New Deal," 187; Weiss, *Farewell to the Party of Lincoln*, 53–54.

24. Salmond, *Civilian Conservation Corps*, 96–99; Kifer, "The Negro under the New Deal," 67–75.

25. Nancy L. Grant, *TVA and Black Americans: Planning for the Status Quo* (Philadelphia: Temple Univ. Press, 1990), 32–48, 83–92.

26. Ibid., 20–23, 61–62, 119–33.

27. Kenneth T. Jackson, *Crabgrass Frontier: The Suburbanization of the United States* (New York: Oxford Univ. Press, 1985), 213.

28. Tindall, *Emergence of the New South*, 546; Smith, *New Deal in the Urban South*, 165–85; Biles, *Memphis in the Great Depression*, 95.

29. Houston *Informer*, May 20, 1940; SoRelle, "Darker Side of 'Heavan,' " 247–49; Robert C. Weaver, "Racial Policy in Public Housing," *Phylon* 1 (Second Quarter 1940): 153–54; Smith, *New Deal in the Urban South*, 180 (quotation).

30. E. W. Taggart to J. C. De Hall, May 4, 1936, James M. Jones, Jr., Papers; Dorothy A. Autrey, "The National Association for the Advancement of Colored People in Alabama," Ph.D. diss., University of Notre Dame,

1985, 132–34; Memphis Housing Authority, "More than Housing," 1940, Memphis Public Library; L. M. Graves and Alfred H. Fletcher, "Some Trends in Public Housing," *American Journal of Public Health* 31 (Jan. 1941): 70. Lida and Kate Hewitt to Kenneth D. McKellar, Sept. 27, 1938; T. O. Fuller to Watkins Overton, Sept. 21, 1938; petition by J. H. Lynk et al. to Watkins Overton, Sept. 23, 1938; Mrs. S. W. Broome to Kenneth D. McKellar, Sept. 28, 1938, all in Mayor's Office Files, Drawer 2, "Complaints—Negro Slum Clearance, 1938," Memphis-Shelby County Archives; Memphis *Commercial Appeal* and *Press-Scimitar,* Sept. 26, 1938.

31. Howard, *WPA and Federal Relief Policy,* 292; Ruth Durant, "Home Rule in the WPA," *Survey Midmonthly* 75 (Sept. 1939): 274; Autrey, "National Association for the Advancement of Colored People in Alabama," 134; Tindall, *Emergence of the New South,* 547; Johnson, *Patterns of Negro Segregation,* 37; SoRelle, "Darker Side of 'Heavan,' " 138–39; Tate, "Easing the Burden," 123; Edward Lewis, "The Negro on Relief," *Journal of Negro Education* 5 (Jan. 1936): 73–78; Weiss, *Farewell to the Party of Lincoln,* 166–67, 177 (Bunche quotation).

32. Martha Swain, "The Forgotten Woman: Ellen S. Woodward and Women's Relief in the New Deal," *Prologue: Journal of the National Archives* 15 (Winter 1983): 210; Wolters, *Negroes and the Great Depression,* 208; Biles, *Memphis in the Great Depression,* 94.

33. Robert L. Zangrando, *The NAACP Crusade against Lynching, 1909–1950* (Philadelphia: Temple Univ. Press, 1980), 104, 111–19; Jacquelyn Dowd Hall, "A Truly Subversive Affair: Women against Lynching in the Twentieth-Century South," in *Women of America: A History,* edited by Carol Ruth Berkin and Mary Beth Norton (Boston: Houghton Mifflin, 1979), 360–88.

34. Weiss, *Farewell to the Party of Lincoln,* 169–70.

35. Zangrando, *NAACP Crusade against Lynching,* 123–49; Weiss, *Farewell to the Party of Lincoln,* 113–14 (White quotation).

36. Harvard Sitkoff, *A New Deal for Blacks: The Emergence of Civil Rights as a National Issue, the Depression Decade* (New York: Oxford Univ. Press, 1978), 61.

37. Weiss, *Farewell to the Party of Lincoln,* 134–35.

38. Harvard Sitkoff, "The Impact of the New Deal on Black Southerners," in *New Deal and the South,* ed. Cobb and Namorato, 126.

39. Wilma Dykeman and James Stokely, *Seeds of Southern Change: The Life of Will Alexander* (Chicago: Univ. of Chicago Press, 1962).

40. Salmond, *Southern Rebel.*

41. Howard, *WPA and Federal Relief Policy,* 285–90; Heinemann, *Depression and New Deal in Virginia,* 87; Tindall, *Emergence of the New South,* 478–79 (quotation).

42. Sitkoff, "Impact of the New Deal on Black Southerners," 129–30.

43. Tindall, *Emergence of the New South,* 543 (Vann quotation); Donald J. Lisio, *Hoover, Blacks, and Lily-Whites: A Study of Southern Strategies* (Chapel Hill: Univ. of North Carolina Press, 1985), 268–69.

44. Weiss, *Farewell to the Party of Lincoln,* 216, 233.

45. Ibid., 203–4, 288–89.

46. Sitkoff, "Impact of the New Deal on Black Southerners," 131.

47. Ibid., 133–34.

48. Harvard Sitkoff, "The New Deal and Race Relations," in *Fifty Years Later: The New Deal Evaluated*, edited by Harvard Sitkoff (New York: Knopf, 1985), 104–5.

Chapter 7: SOUTHERN POLITICS

1. Marian D. Irish, "The Southern One-Party System and National Politics," *Journal of Politics* 4 (Feb. 1942): 90.

2. Freidel, *F.D.R. and the South*, 3–13.

3. Ibid., 18–30.

4. Ibid., 30–31.

5. W. J. Cash, *The Mind of the South*, 365.

6. Tindall, *Emergence of the New South*, 389, 608–9.

7. Ibid., 608–10.

8. Freidel, *F.D.R. and the South*, 43–45; Grantham, *Life and Death of the Solid South*, 103–4.

9. Dorsett, *Franklin D. Roosevelt and the City Bosses*, 113.

10. Shields McIlwaine, *Memphis Down in Dixie* (New York: Dutton, 1948), 379–80; Miller, *Mr. Crump of Memphis*, 179–80.

11. Dorsett, *Franklin D. Roosevelt and the City Bosses*, 40; Roger Biles, "The Persistence of the Past: Memphis in the Great Depression," *Journal of Southern History* 52 (May 1986): 209–12.

12. E. H. Crump to Kenneth D. McKellar, Dec. 5, 1930, Kenneth D. McKellar Papers, McKellar-Crump Correspondence, Box 2, Folder "1930" (Crump quotation); McKellar to Crump, Nov. 26, 1930, telegram, Kenneth D. McKellar Papers, Mckellar-Crump Correspondence, Box 2, Folder "1930 July–Nov"; New York *Times*, Oct. 21, 1930. Also see Crump to McKellar, Dec. 2, 1930, Kenneth D. McKellar Papers, McKellar-Crump Correspondence, Box 2, Folder "1930 Dec."

13. New York *Times*, July 28 and Aug. 29, 1938; Watkins Overton affidavit, Aug. 27, 1938, Watkins Overton Papers, Box 1, Folder 52; U.S. Congress, Senate, *Report of the Special Committee to Investigate Senatorial Campaign Expenditures and Use of Government Funds in 1938*, 76th Cong., 1st sess., 1939, S. Rept. 1, pt. 1, p. 19, and pt. 2, p. 336.

14. T. Harry Williams, *Huey Long* (New York: Knopf, 1969), 425–27, 482, 483 (quotation).

15. Field, "Politics of the New Deal in Louisiana," 83–84, 109–12, 286–87; New York *Times*, Jan. 26, 1934; Work Projects Administration, "Administrations of the Mayors of New Orleans, 1803–1936," Mar. 1940, p. 238, Louisiana Division, New Orleans Public Library; T. Semmes Walmsley to Franklin D. Roosevelt, Aug. 25, 1933, copy of a letter provided to the author by Professor Arnold R. Hirsch, Univ. of New Orleans.

16. New York *Times*, July 21, 1935; C. H. Campbell, "Huey Long Chokes New Orleans," *Nation*, July 24, 1935, pp. 93–95; Arnold S. Fulton, "First Month of Dictator Long," *Nation*, Aug. 14, 1935, pp. 179–81; Williams, *Huey Long*, 849–53; New Orleans Bureau of Governmental Research, "City Problem Series," no. 43, July 6, 1936, Louisiana Collection, Howard-Tilton Memorial Library, Tulane University, New Orleans, Louisiana.

17. Hamilton Basso, "Can New Orleans Come Back?" *Forum* 103 (Mar. 1940): 126; Don Eddy, "Kingfish the Second," *American Magazine* 128 (Nov. 1939): 79 (quotation); Field, "Politics of the New Deal in Louisiana," 286–97; Edward F. Haas, "New Orleans on the Half-Shell: The Maestri Era, 1936–1946," *Louisiana History* 13 (Summer 1972): 284–88, 297.

18. New Orleans Bureau of Governmental Research, "City Problem Series," no. 45, Aug. 25, 1936, and no. 46, Sept. 28, 1936, Louisiana Collection, Howard-Tilton Memorial Library; Eddy, "Kingfish the Second," 79–80; Haas, "New Orleans on the Half-Shell," 289–90.

19. LaMonte, "Politics and Welfare in Birmingham," 135–37; Robert J. Norrell, "Labor at the Ballot Box: Alabama Politics from the New Deal to the Dixiecrat Movement," *Journal of Southern History* 57 (May 1991): 212–13.

20. "Miracle Man," *Alabama: The News Magazine of the Deep South*, May 17, 1937, p. 4; Birmingham *Post*, May 20, 1931; Birmingham *Times-Herald*, Feb. 8, 1940.

21. Birmingham *Age-Herald*, Sept. 13, 1933; LaMonte, "Politics and Welfare in Birmingham," 141.

22. Norrell, "Labor at the Ballot Box: Alabama Politics," 217–18; James M. Jones, Jr., to William B. Hartsfield, June 2, 1938, James M. Jones, Jr., Papers; Birmingham *Times-Herald*, Feb. 8, 1940.

23. Norrell, "Labor at the Ballot Box: Alabama Politics," 211–21; J. Barton Starr, "Birmingham and the 'Dixiecrat' Convention of 1948," *Alabama Historical Quarterly* 32 (Spring–Summer 1970): 23–50; Leah Rawls Atkins, "Senator James A. Simpson and Birmingham Politics of the 1930s: His Fight against the Spoilsmen and the Pie-Men," *Alabama Review* 41 (Jan. 1988): 15–19.

24. Dallas *Morning News*, Jan. 26, 1967; Ann P. Hollingsworth, "Reform Government in Dallas, 1927–1940," M.A. thesis, North Texas State Univ., 1971, pp. 10–16; New York *Times*, Oct. 19, 1930; Martin, "Dallas Makes the Manager Plan Work," 64; Louis P. Head, "Dallas Joins Ranks of Manager Cities," *National Municipal Review* 19 (Dec. 1930): 806–9; W. D. Jones, "Dallas Wins a Place in the Sun," *National Municipal Review* 24 (Jan. 1935): 11–14; WPA Writers' Project, *Dallas Guide and History*, 193–94, 202–3; New York *Times*, Apr. 12, 1931.

25. Dallas *Morning News*, Mar. 23 and 27, 1967; "'N.M.L.' Charged with Traitorous Propaganda to Install Imperialistic Government," *National Municipal Review* 21 (Mar. 1932): 140 (quotation); Fairbanks, "Good Government Machine," 5–12.

26. Michael C. D. MacDonald, *America's Cities: A Report on the Myth of Urban Renaissance* (New York: Simon and Schuster, 1984), 114; transcript of interview with R. L. Thornton, Jr., Nov. 8, 1980, Dallas Mayors Oral History Project, Dallas Public Library; Stanley Walker, *The Dallas Story* (Dallas: Dallas *Times-Herald*, 1956), 33–35.

27. Leslie, *Dallas*, 85, 64, 69. Dallas remains the largest city in the nation with a city manager form of government. Stephen L. Elkin, "State and Market in City Politics; or, The 'Real' Dallas," in *The Politics of Urban Development*, edited by Clarence N. Stone and Heywood T. Sanders (Lawrence: Univ. Press of Kansas, 1987), 50n.

28. Charles H. Trout, *Boston, the Great Depression, and the New Deal* (New York: Oxford Univ. Press, 1977), x (quotation).

29. Heinemann, *Depression and New Deal in Virginia*, 47 (Glass quotation); Tindall, *Emergence of the New South*, 612 (Roosevelt quotation).

30. Harry F. Byrd, "Return to Sound Principle," *Manufacturers' Record* 104 (Mar. 1935): 23; Heinemann, *Depression and New Deal in Virginia*, 101–2.

31. John Robert Moore, *Senator Josiah William Bailey of North Carolina: A Political Biography* (Durham, N.C.: Duke Univ. Press, 1968), 97, 105–9.

32. Williams, *Huey Long*, 619–706; Tindall, *Emergence of the New South*, 614 (Long quotation).

33. Rexford G. Tugwell, *The Democratic Roosevelt* (Garden City, N.Y.: Doubleday, 1957), 349; Alan Brinkley, "The New Deal and Southern Politics," in *New Deal and the South*, ed. Cobb and Namorato, 110–11.

34. Freidel, *F.D.R. and the South*, 56–66, 71–72; James T. Patterson, *Congressional Conservatism and the New Deal: The Growth of a Conservative Coalition in Congress, 1933–1939* (Lexington: Univ. Press of Kentucky, 1967), 243 (quotation).

35. Ibid., 91–92.

36. Sitkoff, *New Deal for Blacks*, 93–94.

37. William Anderson, *The Wild Man from Sugar Creek: The Political Career of Eugene Talmadge* (Baton Rouge: Louisiana State Univ. Press, 1975), 137; Glen Jeansonne, *Gerald L. K. Smith: Minister of Hate* (New Haven, Conn.: Yale Univ. Press, 1988), 47.

38. Anderson, *Wild Man from Sugar Creek*, 138–39; Jeansonne, *Gerald L. K. Smith*, 47 (quotation).

39. Patterson, *Congressional Conservatism and the New Deal*, 95.

40. Ibid., 85–91.

41. Tindall, *Emergence of the New South*, 620 (Bankhead quotation); James MacGregor Burns, *Roosevelt: The Lion and the Fox* (New York: Harcourt, Brace, and Co., 1956), 294 (Sumners quotation).

42. Patterson, *Congressional Conservatism and the New Deal*, 97 (Bailey quotation); Patenaude, *Texans, Politics and the New Deal*, 131–41.

43. Patterson, *Congressional Conservatism and the New Deal*, 127.

44. Martha Swain, *Pat Harrison: The New Deal Years* (Jackson: Univ. Press of Mississippi, 1978), 162–68.

45. Tindall, *Emergence of the New South*, 623.

46. Ibid.; Tony Freyer, *Hugo L. Black and the Dilemma of American Liberalism* (Glenview, Ill.: Scott, Foresman, 1990), 67–69.

47. John Robert Moore, "Senator Josiah W. Bailey and the 'Conservative Manifesto' of 1937," *Journal of Southern History* 31 (Feb. 1965): 21–39.

48. Patterson, *Congressional Conservatism and the New Deal*, 155, 214.

49. J. B. Shannon, "Presidential Politics in the South," *Journal of Politics* 1 (May 1939): 151–53.

50. J. B. Shannon, "Presidential Politics in the South: 1938," *Journal of Politics* 1 (Aug. 1939): 278; Charles M. Price and Joseph Boskin, "The Roosevelt 'Purge': A Reappraisal," *Journal of Politics* 28 (Aug. 1966): 665.

51. Samuel I. Rosenman, comp., *The Public Papers and Addresses of Franklin D. Roosevelt*, vol. 7 (New York: Macmillan, 1941), 65–69; Luther H. Ziegler, Jr., "Senator Walter George's 1938 Campaign," *Georgia Historical Quarterly* 43 (Dec. 1959): 343 (Roosevelt quotation); New York *Times*, Aug. 12, 1938.

52. Shannon, "Presidential Politics in the South: 1938," 296–97; Tindall, *Emergence of the New South*, 629 (Smith quotation).

53. Patterson, *Congressional Conservatism and the New Deal*, 284–87; Milton Plesur, "The Republican Comeback of 1938," *Review of Politics* 24 (Oct. 1962): 543–46.

54. Grantham, *Life and Death of the Solid South*, 114; V. O. Key, Jr., *Southern Politics in State and Nation* (New York: Knopf, 1949), 352–54.

55. Morton Sosna, *In Search of the Silent South: Southern Liberals and the Race Issue* (New York: Columbia Univ. Press, 1977); John T. Kneebone, *Southern Liberal Journalists and the Issue of Race, 1920–1944* (Chapel Hill: Univ. of North Carolina Press, 1985); and Anthony P. Dunbar, *Against the Grain: Southern Radicals and Prophets, 1929–1959* (Charlottesville: Univ. Press of Virginia, 1981).

56. Freidel, *F.D.R. and the South*, 97–98; Sosna, *In Search of the Silent South*, 90–98; Thomas A. Krueger, *And Promises to Keep: The Southern Conference for Human Welfare, 1938–1948* (Nashville: Vanderbilt Univ. Press, 1967), 25–30; Tindall, *Emergence of the New South*, 637 (Gee quotation).

57. Roy E. Fossett, "The Impact of the New Deal on Georgia Politics, 1933–1941," Ph.D. diss., Univ. of Florida, 1960, pp. 260–70; Bryant, "Oklahoma and the New Deal," 182–83; JoAnn D. Carpenter, "Olin D. Johnston, the New Deal, and the Politics of Class in South Carolina," pp. 97, 280, 404; Tindall, *Emergence of the New South*, 644; James William Dunn, "The New Deal and Florida Politics," Ph.D. diss., Florida State Univ., 1971, pp. 140–45.

58. Tindall, *Emergence of the New South*, 633; Brinkley, "New Deal and Southern Politics," 103–4.

59. Brinkley, "New Deal and Southern Politics," 104; Kneebone, *Southern Liberal Journalists and the Issue of Race*, 153; John Temple Graves II, "This is America: III. The South Still Loves Roosevelt," *Nation*, July 1, 1939, pp. 11–13.

60. Norrell, "Labor at the Ballot Box: Alabama Politics," 215 (Roosevelt quotation); Tindall, *Emergence of the New South*, 599 (Miller quotation); Steve Davis, "The South as 'the Nation's No. 1 Economic Problem': The NEC Report of 1938," *Georgia Historical Quarterly* 62 (Summer 1978): 128 (*Constitution* quotation), 129 (Graves quotation).

61. Richard B. Henderson, *Maury Maverick: A Political Biography* (Austin: Univ. of Texas Press, 1970), 145, 179–80; Chester M. Morgan, *Redneck Liberal: Theodore G. Bilbo and the New Deal* (Baton Rouge: Louisiana State Univ. Press, 1985), 165–85; Brinkley, "New Deal and Southern Politics," 106.

62. Key, *Southern Politics*, 645.

63. Brinkley, "New Deal and Southern Politics," 113; William E. Leuchtenburg, "Election of 1936," in *History of American Presidential Elections, 1789–1968*, edited by Arthur M. Schlesinger, Jr., vol. 3 (New York: Chelsea House, 1971), 2842; James T. Patterson, "The Failure of Party Realignment in the South, 1937–1939," *Journal of Politics* 27 (Aug. 1965): 603 (quotation).

64. Grantham, *Life and Death of the Solid South*, 207–8.

Chapter 8: CONCLUSION

1. Harold H. Martin, *William Berry Hartsfield: Mayor of Atlanta* (Athens: Univ. of Georgia Press, 1978), 28–31; MacDonald, *America's Cities*, 72.

2. MacDonald, *America's Cities*, 72; "Boom in Birmingham," *Time*, Nov. 25, 1940, pp. 88–89; WPA Writers' Project, *Houston: A History and Guide*, 123–25; Santerre, "Dallas' First Hundred Years"; Daniel, *Standing at the Crossroads*, 136.

3. See David R. Goldfield, *Promised Land: The South since 1945* (Arlington Heights, Ill.: Harlan Davidson, 1987); Charles P. Roland, *The Improbable Era: The South since World War II* (Lexington: Univ. Press of Kentucky, 1976); Carl Abbott, *The New Urban America: Growth and Politics in Sunbelt Cities* (Chapel Hill: Univ. of North Carolina Press, 1981); and Richard M. Bernard and Bradley R. Rice, eds., *Sunbelt Cities: Politics and Growth since World War II* (Austin: Univ. of Texas Press, 1983).

4. Cash, *Mind of the South*, 205; Numan V. Bartley, "The Era of the New Deal as a Turning Point in Southern History," in *New Deal and the South*, ed. Cobb and Namorato, 141.

5. James C. Cobb, *The Selling of the South: The Southern Crusade for Industrial Development, 1936–1980* (Baton Rouge: Louisiana State Univ. Press, 1982).

6. Bartley, *Creation of Modern Georgia*, 175 (Talmadge quotation); C. Vann Woodward, *The Burden of Southern History*, rev. ed. (Baton Rouge: Louisiana State Univ. Press, 1968), 7.

BIBLIOGRAPHICAL ESSAY

An understanding of the New Deal's impact on the South begins with knowledge of the region's history. A number of general studies are valuable, including C. Vann Woodward, *The Burden of Southern History*, rev. ed. (Baton Rouge: Louisiana State Univ. Press, 1968); Pete Daniel, *Standing at the Crossroads: Southern Life since 1900* (New York: Hill and Wang, 1986); Carl Degler, *Place over Time: The Continuity of Southern Distinctiveness* (Baton Rouge: Louisiana State Univ. Press, 1977); Frank E. Vandiver, ed., *The Idea of the South: Pursuit of a Central Theme* (Chicago: Univ. of Chicago Press, 1964); and W. J. Cash, *The Mind of the South* (New York: Knopf, 1941). The most detailed historiographic work on southern history is John B. Boles and Evelyn Thomas Nolen, eds., *Interpreting Southern History: Historiographical Essays in Honor of Sanford W. Higginbotham* (Baton Rouge: Louisiana State Univ. Press, 1987). All ten volumes of the Louisiana State University Press series History of the South are useful: see especially George B. Tindall, *The Emergence of the New South, 1913–1945* (Baton Rouge: Louisiana State Univ. Press, 1967).

A closer look at events of the 1920s may also be helpful in understanding the Depression decade. Begin with Arthur S. Link, "What Happened to the Progressive Movement in the 1920s?" *American Historical Review* 64 (July 1959): 833–51. On the Ku Klux Klan, see Kenneth T. Jackson, *The Ku Klux Klan in the City, 1915–1930* (New York: Oxford Univ. Press, 1967), and David Chalmers, *Hooded Americanism: The First Century of the Ku Klux Klan, 1865–1965* (Garden City, N.Y.: Doubleday, 1965). On the impact of fundamentalist religion, see Ray Ginger, *Six Days or Forever? Tennessee v. John Thomas Scopes* (Boston: Beacon, 1958); Suzanne Cameron Linder, *William Louis Poteat: Prophet of Progress* (Chapel Hill: Univ. of North Carolina Press, 1966); James J. Thompson, Jr., *Tried as by Fire: Southern Baptists and the Controversies of the 1920s* (Macon, Ga.: Mercer Univ. Press, 1982); and Kenneth K. Bailey, *Southern White Protestantism in the Twentieth Century* (New York: Harper and Row, 1964). Urban boosterism and economic growth are discussed in George B. Tindall, "Business

Progressivism: Southern Politics in the Twenties," *South Atlantic Quarterly* 62 (Winter 1963): 92–106; Charles Paul Garofalo, "The Sons of Henry Grady: Atlanta Boosters in the 1920s," *Journal of Southern History* 42 (May 1976): 187–204; idem, "The Atlanta Spirit: A Study in Urban Ideology," *South Atlantic Quarterly* 74 (Winter 1975): 34–44; Blaine A. Brownell, "A Symbol of Modernity: Attitudes toward the Automobile in Southern Cities in the 1920s," *American Quarterly* 24 (Mar. 1972): 20–44; idem, "The Commercial-Civic Elite and City Planning in Atlanta, Memphis, and New Orleans in the 1920s," *Journal of Southern History* 41 (Aug. 1975): 339–68; and George W. West, "How the 'Forward Atlanta' Fund Has Helped Atlanta," *American City* 43 (Oct. 1930): 139. The development of southern cities is covered in Blaine A. Brownell, *The Urban Ethos in the South, 1920–1930* (Baton Rouge: Louisiana State Univ. Press, 1975); one specific city is treated in Robert A. Lanier, *Memphis in the Twenties* (Memphis: Zenda Press, 1979). The fate of labor in the 1920s is discussed in Irving Bernstein, *The Lean Years: A History of the American Worker, 1920–1933* (Boston: Houghton Mifflin, 1960), and Liston Pope, *Millhands and Preachers: A Study of Gastonia* (New Haven, Conn.: Yale Univ. Press, 1942). On southern agriculture in the 1920s, see Patrick G. O'Brien, "A Reexamination of the Senate Farm Bloc, 1921–1933," *Agricultural History* 47 (July 1973): 248–63; and Philip A. Grant, Jr., "Southern Congressmen and Agriculture, 1921–1932," *Agricultural History* 53 (Jan. 1979): 338–51. The views of the Nashville Agrarians are presented in Twelve Southerners, *I'll Take My Stand: The South and the Agrarian Tradition* (New York: Harper and Brothers, 1930).

Helpful works on conditions in the Great Depression are Broadus Mitchell, *Depression Decade: From New Era through New Deal* (New York: Rinehart, 1947); Michael A. Bernstein, *The Great Depression: Delayed Recovery and Economic Change in America* (Cambridge: Cambridge Univ. Press, 1987); John L. Robinson, ed., *Living Hard: Southern Americans in the Great Depression* (Lanham, Md.: Univ. Press of America, 1981); Donald W. Whisenhunt, *The Depression in Texas: The Hoover Years* (New York: Garland, 1983); Julia Kirk Blackwelder, "Quiet Suffering: Atlanta Women in the 1930s," *Georgia Historical Quarterly* 61 (Summer 1977): 112–24; and John L. Robinson, "Great Depression," in *Encyclopedia of Southern Culture,* edited by Charles Reagan Wilson and William Ferris (Chapel Hill: Univ. of North Carolina Press, 1989). Useful oral histories of the era include Studs Terkel, *Hard Times: An Oral History of the Great Depression* (New York: Pantheon, 1970); Ann Banks, *First-Person America* (New York: Knopf, 1980); Robert S. McElvaine, *Down and Out in the Great Depression: Letters from the Forgotten Man* (Chapel Hill: Univ. of North Carolina Press, 1983); and Tom Terrill and Jerrold Hirsch, eds., *Such as Us: Southern Voices of the Thirties* (Chapel Hill: Univ. of North Carolina Press, 1978). Contemporary accounts are included in Richard Lowitt and Maurine Beasley, eds., *One Third of a Nation: Lorena Hickok Reports on the Great Depression* (Urbana: Univ. of Illinois Press, 1981); Cliff Kuhn, "Reminiscences:

Interviews with Atlanta New Deal Social Workers," *Atlanta Historical Journal* 30 (Spring 1986): 107–16; and John F. Bauman and Thomas H. Coode, *In the Eye of the Great Depression: New Deal Reporters and the Agony of the American People* (DeKalb: Northern Illinois Univ. Press, 1988). Also see the WPA state and local guides for more detailed information about the Depression's impact on the American people.

Among the general studies of the New Deal, the most detailed is Arthur M. Schlesinger, Jr., *The Age of Roosevelt* (Boston: Houghton Mifflin, 1957–60). Its three volumes are *The Crisis of the Old Order, 1919–1933* (1957), *The Coming of the New Deal* (1959), and *The Politics of Upheaval* (1960). The best one-volume work remains William E. Leuchtenburg, *Franklin D. Roosevelt and the New Deal* (New York: Harper and Row, 1963). Also see Paul K. Conkin, *The New Deal* (Arlington Heights, Ill.: Harlan Davidson, 1975); John Braeman, Robert H. Bremner, and David Brody, eds., *The New Deal: The National Level* (Columbus: Ohio State Univ. Press, 1975); Barry D. Karl, *The Uneasy State: The United States from 1915 to 1945* (Chicago: Univ. of Chicago Press, 1983); Robert S. McElvaine, *The Great Depression: America, 1929–1941* (New York: Times Books, 1984); Anthony J. Badger, *The New Deal: The Depression Years, 1933–1940* (New York: Farrar, Straus, and Giroux, 1989); Harvard Sitkoff, ed., *Fifty Years Later: The New Deal Evaluated* (New York: Knopf, 1985); Alonzo L. Hamby, ed., *The New Deal: Analysis and Interpretation* (New York: Longman, 1981); Stephen W. Baskerville and Ralph Willett, eds., *Nothing Else to Fear: New Perspectives on America in the Thirties* (Manchester: Manchester Univ. Press, 1978); Steve Fraser and Gary Gerstle, eds., *The Rise and Fall of the New Deal Order, 1930–1980* (Princeton, N.J.: Princeton Univ. Press, 1989); and Roger Biles, *A New Deal for the American People* (DeKalb: Northern Illinois Univ. Press, 1991). The best historiographic essays are Jerold S. Auerbach, "New Deal, Old Deal, or Raw Deal: Some Thoughts on New Left Historiography," *Journal of Southern History* 35 (Feb. 1969): 18–30; and Richard S. Kirkendall, "The New Deal as Watershed: The Recent Literature," *Journal of American History* 54 (Mar. 1968): 839–52.

Franklin D. Roosevelt has been the subject of many biographies. Of particular interest is Frank Freidel, *F.D.R. and the South* (Baton Rouge: Louisiana State Univ. Press, 1965). More comprehensive biographical treatments are Frank Freidel, *Franklin D. Roosevelt: A Rendezvous with Destiny* (Boston: Little, Brown, 1990); James MacGregor Burns, *Roosevelt: The Lion and the Fox* (New York: Harcourt, Brace, and Co., 1956); idem, *Roosevelt: The Soldier of Freedom* (New York: Harcourt, Brace, Jovanovich, 1970); and William E. Leuchtenburg, ed., *Franklin D. Roosevelt: A Profile* (New York: Hill and Wang, 1967). The most detailed treatments are the first four volumes of Frank Freidel's incomplete multivolume epic, published by Little, Brown: *The Apprenticeship* (1952), *The Ordeal* (1954), *The Triumph* (1956), and *Launching the New Deal* (1973).

Biographies of key southerners in the New Deal era include John A. Salmond, *A Southern Rebel: The Life and Times of Aubrey Willis Williams,*

1890–1965 (Chapel Hill: Univ. of North Carolina Press, 1983); Martha Swain, *Pat Harrison: The New Deal Years* (Jackson: Univ. Press of Mississippi, 1978); Chester M. Morgan, *Redneck Liberal: Theodore G. Bilbo and the New Deal* (Baton Rouge: Louisiana State Univ. Press, 1985); Polly Ann Davis, *Alben Barkley: Senate Majority Leader and Vice President* (New York: Garland, 1979); John Robert Moore, *Senator Josiah William Bailey of North Carolina: A Political Biography* (Durham, N.C.: Duke Univ. Press, 1968); Richard B. Henderson, *Maury Maverick: A Political Biography* (Austin: Univ. of Texas Press, 1970); Robert D. Pope, "Senatorial Baron: The Long Political Career of Kenneth D. McKellar," Ph.D. diss., Yale Univ., 1976; William D. Miller, *Mr. Crump of Memphis* (Baton Rouge: Louisiana State Univ. Press, 1964); Irwin M. May, Jr., *Marvin Jones: The Public Life of an Agrarian Advocate* (College Station: Texas A&M Univ. Press, 1980); Anthony Champagne, *Congressman Sam Rayburn* (New Brunswick, N.J.: Rutgers Univ. Press, 1984); Robert A. Caro, *The Years of Lyndon Johnson: The Path to Power* (New York: Knopf, 1982); William Anderson, *The Wild Man from Sugar Creek: The Political Career of Eugene Talmadge* (Baton Rouge: Louisiana State Univ. Press, 1975); Winfred B. Moore, Jr., "New South Statesman: The Political Career of James Francis Byrnes, 1911–1941," Ph.D. diss., Duke Univ., 1975; JoAnn D. Carpenter, "Olin D. Johnston, the New Deal, and the Politics of Class in South Carolina, 1934–1938," Ph.D. diss., Emory Univ., 1987; Tony Freyer, *Hugo L. Black and the Dilemma of American Liberalism* (Glenview, Ill.: Scott, Foresman, 1990); John D. Stark, *Damned Upcountryman: William Watts Ball, A Study in American Conservatism* (Durham, N.C.: Duke Univ. Press, 1973); Monroe Lee Billington, *Thomas P. Gore: The Blind Senator from Oklahoma* (Lawrence: Univ. Press of Kansas, 1967); Keith L. Bryant, *Alfalfa Bill Murray* (Norman: Univ. of Oklahoma Press, 1968); Glen Jeansonne, *Gerald L. K. Smith: Minister of Hate* (New Haven, Conn.: Yale Univ. Press, 1988); T. Harry Williams, *Huey Long* (New York: Knopf, 1969); and Alan Brinkley, *Voices of Protest: Huey Long, Father Coughlin, and the Great Depression* (New York: Knopf, 1982).

The New Deal in the South is the subject of James C. Cobb and Michael V. Namorato, eds., *The New Deal and the South* (Jackson: Univ. Press of Mississippi, 1984). Specific state studies include Ronald L. Heinemann, *Depression and New Deal in Virginia: The Enduring Dominion* (Charlottesville: Univ. Press of Virginia, 1983); John Dean Minton, *The New Deal in Tennessee, 1932–1938* (New York: Garland, 1979); George T. Blakey, *Hard Times and New Deal in Kentucky, 1929–1939* (Lexington: Univ. Press of Kentucky, 1986); Michael S. Holmes, *The New Deal in Georgia: An Administrative History* (Westport, Conn.: Greenwood, 1975); Anthony J. Badger, *North Carolina and the New Deal* (Raleigh: North Carolina Department of Cultural Resources, Division of Archives and History, 1981); Lionel V. Patenaude, *Texans, Politics and the New Deal* (New York: Garland, 1983); Kenneth E. Hendrickson, Jr., ed., *Hard Times in Oklahoma: The Depression Years* (Oklahoma City: Oklahoma Historical Society, 1983); Roger D. Tate, Jr., "Easing the Burden: The Era of Depression and New Deal in Mississippi," Ph.D. diss., Univ. of Tennessee, 1978; Stephen F. Strausberg, "The Effectiveness of the New Deal in Arkansas," in *The Depression in the Southwest*, edited by Donald W. Whisenhunt (Port Washington, N.Y.: Kennikat, 1980); and John Braeman, Robert H. Bremner, and David Brody, eds., *The New Deal: The State and Local Levels* (Columbus: Ohio State Univ. Press, 1975), which contains chapters on Louisiana, Oklahoma, and Virginia. Also see James T. Patterson, *The New Deal and the States: Federalism in Transition* (Princeton, N.J.: Princeton Univ. Press, 1969).

General studies of agriculture during the period are Theodore Saloutos, *The American Farmer and the New Deal* (Ames: Iowa State Univ. Press, 1982); idem, "New Deal Agricultural Policy: An Evaluation," *Journal of American History* 61 (Sept. 1974): 394–416; Richard S. Kirkendall, *Social Scientists and Farm Politics in the Age of Roosevelt* (Columbia: Univ. of Missouri Press, 1966); Van Perkins, *Crisis in Agriculture: The Agricultural Adjustment Administration and the New Deal, 1933* (Berkeley: Univ. of California Press, 1969); Christiana McFadyen Campbell, *The Farm Bureau and the New Deal: A Study of the Making of National Farm Policy, 1933–40* (Urbana: Univ. of Illinois Press, 1962); Sidney Baldwin, *Poverty and Politics: The Rise and Decline of the Farm Security Administration* (Chapel Hill: Univ. of North Carolina Press, 1968); and the relevant chapters in Gilbert C. Fite, *American Farmers: The New Minority* (Bloomington: Indiana Univ. Press, 1981). Biographies of New Deal agriculturalists are Gilbert C. Fite, *George N. Peek and the Fight for Farm Parity* (Norman: Univ. of Oklahoma Press, 1954); Edward L. Schapsmeier and Frederick A. Schapsmeier, *Henry A. Wallace of Iowa: The Agrarian Years, 1910–1940* (Ames: Iowa State Univ. Press, 1968); William D. Rowley, *M. L. Wilson and the Campaign for the Domestic Allotment* (Lincoln: Univ. of Nebraska Press, 1970); Roy V. Scott and J. G. Shoalmire, *The Public Career of Cully A. Cobb: A Study in Agricultural Leadership* (Jackson: Univ. Press of Mississippi, 1973); and Wilma Dykeman and James Stokely, *Seeds of Southern Change: The Life of Will Alexander* (Chicago: Univ. of Chicago Press, 1962).

On the New Deal and southern agriculture, see Gilbert C. Fite, *Cotton Fields No More: Southern Agriculture, 1865–1980* (Lexington: Univ. Press of Kentucky, 1984); Pete Daniel, *Breaking the Land: The Transformation of Cotton, Tobacco, and Rice Cultures since 1880* (Urbana: Univ. of Illinois Press, 1985); Jack Temple Kirby, *Rural Worlds Lost: The American South, 1920–1960* (Baton Rouge: Louisiana State Univ. Press, 1987); Nan Elizabeth Woodruff, *As Rare as Rain: Federal Relief in the Great Southern Drought of 1930–31* (Urbana: Univ. of Illinois Press, 1985); Robert E. Snyder, *Cotton Crisis* (Chapel Hill: Univ. of North Carolina Press, 1984); Anthony J. Badger, *Prosperity Road: The New Deal, Tobacco, and North Carolina* (Chapel Hill: Univ. of North Carolina Press, 1980); Donald S. Holley, *Uncle Sam's Farmers: The New Deal Communities in the Lower Mississippi Valley* (Urbana: Univ. of Illinois Press, 1975); David E. Conrad, *The Forgotten Farmers: The Story of the Sharecroppers in the New Deal* (Urbana: Univ. of Illinois Press, 1965); Donald H. Grubbs, *Cry from the Cotton: The Southern*

Tenant Farmers' Union and the New Deal (Chapel Hill: Univ. of North Carolina Press, 1971); Paul E. Mertz, *New Deal Policy and Southern Rural Poverty* (Baton Rouge: Louisiana State Univ. Press, 1978); M. S. Venkataramoni, "Norman Thomas, Arkansas Sharecroppers, and the Roosevelt Agricultural Policies, 1933–1937," *Mississippi Valley Historical Review* 47 (Sept. 1960): 225–46; Jerold Auerbach, "Southern Tenant Farmers: Socialist Critics of the New Deal," *Labor History* 7 (Winter 1966): 3–18; Charles S. Johnson, Edwin R. Embree, and W. W. Alexander, *The Collapse of Cotton Tenancy* (Chapel Hill: Univ. of North Carolina Press, 1935); H. L. Mitchell, *Mean Things Happening in This Land: The Life and Times of H. L. Mitchell, Co-Founder of the Southern Tenant Farmers' Union* (Montclair, N.J.: Allanheld, Osman, 1979); Henry I. Richards, *Cotton and the AAA* (Washington, D.C.: Brookings Institution, 1936); Donald Worster, *Dust Bowl: The Southern Plains in the 1930s* (New York: Oxford Univ. Press, 1979); and Paul Bonnifield, *The Dust Bowl: Men, Dirt, and Depression* (Albuquerque: Univ. of New Mexico Press, 1979).

On TVA and public power, see Thomas K. McCraw, *TVA and the Power Fight, 1933–1939* (Philadelphia: Lippincott, 1971); Erwin C. Hargrove and Paul K. Conkin, eds., *TVA: Fifty Years of Grass-Roots Bureaucracy* (Urbana: Univ. of Illinois Press, 1983); Michael J. McDonald and John Muldowny, *TVA and the Dispossessed: The Resettlement of Population in the Norris Dam Area* (Knoxville: Univ. of Tennessee Press, 1982); Preston J. Hubbard, *Origins of the TVA: The Muscle Shoals Controversy, 1920–1932* (Nashville: Vanderbilt Univ. Press, 1961); and Philip J. Funigiello, *Toward a National Power Policy: The New Deal and the Electric Utility Industry, 1933–1941* (Pittsburgh: Univ. of Pittsburgh Press, 1973). On rural electrification, see D. Clayton Brown, *Electricity for Rural America: The Fight for the REA* (Westport, Conn.: Greenwood, 1980); and H. S. Person, "The Rural Electrification Administration in Perspective," *Agricultural History* 24 (Apr. 1950): 70–89.

The best studies of the NRA are Bernard Bellush, *The Failure of the NRA* (New York: Norton, 1975); Ellis W. Hawley, *The New Deal and the Problem of Monopoly* (Princeton, N.J.: Princeton Univ. Press, 1966); and John Kennedy Ohl, *Hugh S. Johnson and the New Deal* (DeKalb: Northern Illinois Univ. Press, 1985). More specific examinations of the textile industry in the South include James A. Hodges, *New Deal Labor Policy and the Southern Cotton Textile Industry, 1933–1941* (Knoxville: Univ. of Tennessee Press, 1986), and Louis Galombos, *Competition and Cooperation: The Emergence of a National Trade Association* (Baltimore: Johns Hopkins Univ. Press, 1966). On petroleum, see Linda J. Lear, "Harold L. Ickes and the Oil Crisis of the First Hundred Days," *Mid-America* 63 (Jan. 1981): 3–17. On coal, see James P. Johnson, "Drafting the NRA Code of Fair Competition for the Bituminous Coal Industry," *Journal of American History* 53 (Dec. 1966): 521–41, and John W. Hevener, *Which Side Are You On? The Harlan County Coal Miners, 1931–1939* (Urbana: Univ. of Illinois Press, 1978). On lumber, see James E. Fickle, *The New South and the 'New Competition':*

Trade Association Development in the Southern Pine Industry (Urbana: Univ. of Illinois Press, 1980).

Comprehensive treatments of New Deal social welfare policy are William R. Brock, *Welfare, Democracy, and the New Deal* (Cambridge: Cambridge Univ. Press, 1988); William W. Bremer, "Along the 'American Way': The New Deal's Work Relief Program for the Unemployed," *Journal of American History* 62 (Dec. 1975): 636–52; Charles H. Trout, "Welfare in the New Deal Era," *Current History* 65 (July 1973): 11–14, 39; and Frances Fox Piven and Richard A. Cloward, "The New Deal and Relief" in *Poverty and Public Policy in Modern America*, edited by Donald T. Critchlow and Ellis W. Hawley (Chicago: Dorsey Press, 1989). Also see Anthony J. Badger, "The New Deal and the Localities," in *The Growth of Federal Power in American History*, edited by Rhodri Jeffreys-Jones and Bruce Collins (De-Kalb: Northern Illinois Univ. Press, 1983); Martha Swain, "The Forgotten Woman: Ellen S. Woodward and Women's Relief in the New Deal," *Prologue: Journal of the National Archives* 15 (Winter 1983): 201–13; James T. Patterson, *The New Deal and the States: Federalism in Transition* (Princeton, N.J.: Princeton Univ. Press, 1969); idem, *America's Struggle against Poverty, 1900–1980* (Cambridge, Mass.: Harvard Univ. Press, 1981); and Daniel J. Leab, " 'United We Eat': The Creation and Organization of the Unemployed Councils in the 1930s," *Labor History* 8 (Fall 1967): 300–315.

Studies of New Deal agencies merit attention. See John A. Salmond, *The Civilian Conservation Corps, 1933–1942: A New Deal Case Study* (Durham, N.C.: Duke Univ. Press, 1967); Donald S. Howard, *The WPA and Federal Relief Policy* (New York: Russell Sage Foundation, 1943); and Bonnie Fox Schwartz, *The Civil Works Administration, 1933–1934: The Business of Emergency Employment in the New Deal* (Princeton, N.J.: Princeton Univ. Press, 1984). Also see Janet Poppendieck, *Breadlines Knee-Deep in Wheat: Food Assistance in the Great Depression* (New Brunswick, N.J.: Rutgers Univ. Press, 1986). On social security, see Roy Lubove, *The Struggle for Social Security, 1900–1935* (Pittsburgh: Univ. of Pittsburgh Press, 1986), and W. Andrew Achenbaum, *Social Security: Visions and Revisions* (Cambridge: Cambridge Univ. Press, 1986). On the WPA's Project One, see Jane DeHart Matthews, *The Federal Theatre, 1935–1939: Plays, Relief, and Politics* (Princeton, N.J.: Princeton Univ. Press, 1967); Monty Noam Penkower, *The Federal Writers' Project: A Study in Government Patronage of the Arts* (Urbana: Univ. of Illinois Press, 1977); Richard McKenzie, *The New Deal for Artists* (Princeton, N.J.: Princeton Univ. Press, 1973); William F. McDonald, *Federal Relief Administration and the Arts* (Columbus: Ohio State Univ. Press, 1969); and Joanne Bentley, *Hallie Flanagan: A Life in the American Theatre* (New York: Knopf, 1988).

Southern case studies of New Deal programs are limited. Consult Larry Whatley, "The Works Progress Administration in Mississippi," *Journal of Mississippi History* 30 (Feb. 1968): 35–50; James Ware, "The Sooner NRA: New Deal Recovery in Oklahoma," *Chronicles of Oklahoma* 54 (Fall 1976): 339–51; Gail S. Murray, "Forty Years Ago: The Great Depression Comes to

Arkansas," *Arkansas Historical Quarterly* 29 (Winter 1970): 291–312; Robert J. Leupold, "The Kentucky WPA: Relief and Politics, May–November 1935," *Filson Club Historical Quarterly* 69 (Apr. 1975): 152–68; "PWA and Georgia: The State's No-Debt Policy Raises the President's Ire," *Newsweek*, Dec. 5, 1938, p. 12; Robert E. Moran, Jr., "Public Relief in Louisiana from 1928 to 1960," *Louisiana History* 14 (Fall 1973): 369–85; Jane Walker Herndon, "Ed Rivers and Georgia's 'Little New Deal,' " *Atlanta Historical Journal* 30 (Spring 1986): 97–105; Martha Swain, "A New Deal for Mississippi Women, 1933–1943," *Journal of Mississippi History* 46 (Aug. 1984): 191–212; Ronald L. Heinemann, "Blue Eagle or Black Buzzard? The National Recovery Administration in Virginia," *Virginia Magazine of History and Biography* 89 (Jan. 1981): 90–100; and James A. Burran, "The WPA in Nashville," *Tennessee Historical Quarterly* 34 (Fall 1975): 293–306.

On labor, see Irving Bernstein, *Turbulent Years: A History of the American Worker, 1933–1941* (Boston: Houghton Mifflin, 1971); idem, *A Caring Society: The New Deal, the Worker, and the Great Depression* (Boston: Houghton Mifflin, 1985); Christopher L. Tomlins, *The State and the Unions: Labor Relations, Law, and the Organized Labor Movement in America, 1880–1960* (Cambridge: Cambridge Univ. Press, 1985); idem, "AFL Unions in the 1930s: Their Performance in Historical Perspective," *Journal of American History* 65 (Mar. 1979): 1021–42; Stanley Vittoz, *New Deal Labor Policy and the American Industrial Economy* (Chapel Hill: Univ. of North Carolina Press, 1987); and David Brody, *Workers in Industrial America: Essays on the Twentieth Century Struggle* (New York: Oxford Univ. Press, 1980).

On labor in the South, begin with F. Ray Marshall, *Labor in the South* (Cambridge, Mass.: Harvard Univ. Press, 1967); Robert H. Zieger, ed., *Organized Labor in the Twentieth-Century South* (Knoxville: Univ. of Tennessee Press, 1991); Billy Hall Wyche, "Southern Industrialists View Organized Labor in the New Deal Years, 1933–1941," *Southern Studies* 19 (Summer 1980): 157–71; Philip Taft, *Organizing Dixie: Alabama Workers in the Industrial Era* (Westport, Conn.: Greenwood, 1981); Gary M. Fink and Merl E. Reed, eds., *Essays in Southern Labor History* (Westport, Conn.: Greenwood, 1977); Lucy Randolph Mason, *To Win These Rights: A Personal Story of the CIO in the South* (New York: Harper and Row, 1952); and John A. Salmond, *Miss Lucy of the CIO: The Life and Times of Lucy Randolph Mason, 1882–1959* (Athens: Univ. of Georgia Press, 1988).

Also see such specific studies as Daniel Nelson, "The Rubber Workers' Southern Strategy: Labor Organizing in the New Deal South, 1933–1943," *Historian* 46 (May 1984): 319–38; Charles H. Martin, "Southern Labor Relations in Transition: Gadsden, Alabama, 1930–1943," *Journal of Southern History* 47 (Nov. 1981): 545–68; John Wesley Kennedy, "The General Strike in the Textile Industry, September, 1934," M.A. thesis, Duke Univ., 1947; John E. Allen, "The Governor and the Strike: Eugene Talmadge and the General Strike, 1934," M.A. thesis, Georgia State Univ., 1977; Jacquelyn Dowd Hall, James Leloudis, Robert Korstad, Mary Murphy, Lu Ann Jones, and Christopher B. Daly, *Like a Family: The Making of a Southern Cotton Mill World* (Chapel Hill: Univ. of North Carolina Press, 1987); Jacquelyn Dowd Hall, "Disorderly Women: Gender and Labor Militancy in the Appalachian South," *Journal of American History* 73 (Sept. 1986): 354–82; Horace Huntley, "Iron Ore Miners and Mine Mill in Alabama, 1933–1952," Ph.D. diss., Univ. of Pittsburgh, 1977; Alexander Kendrick, "Alabama Goes on Strike," *Nation*, Aug. 29, 1934, pp. 233–34; Neil Herring and Sue Thrasher, "UAW Sit-down Strike: Atlanta, 1936," in *Working Lives: The Southern Exposure History of Labor in the South*, edited by Marc S. Miller (New York: Pantheon, 1980); John C. Petrie, "Memphis Makes War on CIO," *Christian Century*, Oct. 13, 1937, pp. 1273–74; George Lambert, "Memphis Is Safe for Ford," *Nation*, Jan. 22, 1938, pp. 93–94; George Lambert, "Dallas Tries Terror," *Nation*, Oct. 9, 1937, pp. 376–78; Roger Biles, "Ed Crump versus the Unions: The Labor Movement in Memphis during the 1930s," *Labor History* 25 (Fall 1984): 533–52; George Green, "The ILGWU in Texas, 1930–1970," *Journal of Mexican-American History* 1 (Spring 1971): 144–69; Robert C. Francis, "Longshoremen in New Orleans," *Opportunity* 14 (Mar. 1936): 82–85, 93; Herbert R. Northrup, "The New Orleans Longshoremen," *Political Science Quarterly* 57 (Dec. 1942): 526–44; Virginia Holmes Brown, *The Development of Labor Legislation in Tennessee* (Knoxville: Univ. of Tennessee for the Div. of Univ. Extension, 1945); Frank DeVyver, "The Present Status of Labor Unions in the South," *Southern Economic Journal* 5 (Apr. 1939): 485–98; and Jean Carol Trepp, "Union-Management Cooperation and the Southern Organizing Campaign," *Journal of Political Economy* 41 (Oct. 1933): 602–24. On the later Operation Dixie, see Barbara S. Griffith, *The Crisis of American Labor: Operation Dixie and the Defeat of the CIO* (Philadelphia: Temple Univ. Press, 1987).

The literature on blacks in the New Deal is substantial. Comprehensive studies are Harvard Sitkoff, *A New Deal for Blacks: The Emergence of Civil Rights as a National Issue, the Depression Decade* (New York: Oxford Univ. Press, 1978); John B. Kirby, *Black Americans in the Roosevelt Era: Liberalism and Race* (Knoxville: Univ. of Tennessee Press, 1980); Raymond Wolters, *Negroes and the Great Depression: The Problem of Economic Recovery* (Westport, Conn.: Greenwood, 1970); Nancy J. Weiss, *Farewell to the Party of Lincoln: Black Politics in the Age of FDR* (Princeton, N.J.: Princeton Univ. Press, 1983); Ralph J. Bunche, *The Political Status of the Negro in the Age of FDR* (Chicago: Univ. of Chicago Press, 1973); Leslie H. Fishel, Jr., "The Negro in the New Deal Era," *Wisconsin Magazine of History* 48 (1964–65): 111–26; Allen F. Kifer, "The Negro under the New Deal," Ph.D. diss., Univ. of Wisconsin, 1961; Robert L. Zangrando, *The NAACP Crusade against Lynching, 1909–1950* (Philadelphia: Temple Univ. Press, 1980); Bernard Sternsher, ed., *The Negro in Depression and War: Prelude to Revolution, 1930–1945* (Chicago: Quadrangle, 1969); B. Joyce Ross, "Mary McLeod Bethune and the NYA," *Journal of Negro History* 60 (Jan. 1975): 1–28; Mark W. Kruman, "Quotas for Blacks: The PWA and the Black Construction Worker," *Labor History* 16 (Winter 1975): 37–51;

John A. Salmond, "The CCC and the Negro," *Journal of American History* 52 (June 1965): 75–88; Nancy L. Grant, *TVA and Black Americans: Planning for the Status Quo* (Philadelphia: Temple Univ. Press, 1990); and Dona Cooper Hamilton, "The National Urban League and New Deal Programs," *Social Service Review* 58 (June 1984): 227–43.

    Race relations in the South during the New Deal years are covered in Dan T. Carter, *Scottsboro: A Tragedy of the American South* (Baton Rouge: Louisiana State Univ. Press, 1969); Horace R. Cayton and George S. Mitchell, *Black Workers and the New Unions* (Chapel Hill: Univ. of North Carolina Press, 1939); Darlene Clark Hine, *Black Victory: The Rise and Fall of the White Primary in Texas* (Millwood, N.Y.: KTO Press, 1979); Charles H. Martin, *The Angelo Herndon Case and Southern Justice* (Baton Rouge: Louisiana State Univ. Press, 1976); Herbert R. Northrup, *Organized Labor and the Negro* (New York: Harper and Brothers, 1944); Nell Irvin Painter, *The Narrative of Hosea Hudson: His Life as a Negro Communist in the South* (Cambridge, Mass.: Harvard Univ. Press, 1979); Mingo Scott, Jr., *The Negro in Tennessee Politics* (Nashville: Rich Print Co., 1964); David M. Tucker, *Lieutenant Lee of Beale Street* (Nashville: Vanderbilt Univ. Press, 1971); Robert J. Alexander, "Negro Business in Atlanta," *Southern Economic Journal* 17 (Apr. 1951): 451–64; Clarence Albert Bacote, "The Negro in Atlanta Politics," *Phylon* 16 (Fourth Quarter 1955): 333–50; Joseph M. Brittain, "The Return of the Negro to Alabama Politics, 1930–1954," *Negro History Bulletin* 22 (May 1959): 196–98; Robert Haynes, "Black Houstonians and the White Democratic Primary, 1920–1945," in *Houston: A Twentieth-Century Urban Frontier*, edited by Francisco A. Rosales and Barry J. Kaplan (Port Washington, N.Y.: Associated Faculty Press, 1983); Michael S. Holmes, "The Blue Eagle as 'Jim Crow Bird': The NRA and Georgia's Black Workers," *Journal of Negro History* 57 (July 1972): 276–83; Edward Lewis, "The Negro on Relief," *Journal of Negro Education* 5 (Jan. 1936): 73–78; Charles H. Martin, "White Supremacy and Black Workers: Georgia's 'Black Shirts' Combat the Great Depression," *Labor History* 18 (Summer 1977): 366–81; John Hammond Moore, "The Angelo Herndon Case," *Phylon* 32 (Spring 1971): 60–71; Robert J. Norrell, "Caste in Steel: Jim Crow Careers in Birmingham, Alabama," *Journal of American History* 73 (Dec. 1986): 669–94; Herbert R. Northrup, "The Negro and Unionism in the Birmingham, Ala., Iron and Steel Industry," *Southern Economic Journal* 10 (1943–44): 27–40; John C. Petrie, "Demand Justice for Negroes," *Christian Century*, July 4, 1934, p. 910; Louie Davis Shivery, "The Neighborhood Union," *Phylon* 3 (Second Quarter 1942): 149–62; William R. Snell, "Masked Men in the Magic City: Activities of the Revised Klan in Birmingham, 1916–1940," *Alabama Historical Quarterly* 34 (Fall and Winter 1972): 206–27; Randy J. Sparks, " 'Heavenly Houston' or 'Hellish Houston'? Black Unemployment and Relief Efforts, 1929–1936," *Southern Studies* 25 (Winter 1986): 353–66; Lawrence Sullivan, "The Negro Vote," *Atlantic Monthly* 166 (Oct. 1940): 477–84; Edwin Tribble, "Black Shirts in Georgia," *New Republic*, Oct. 8, 1930, pp. 204–6; "White Man's Country," *Time*, Dec. 9,

1940, p. 17; Larry W. Dunn, "Knoxville Negro Voting and the Roosevelt Revolution, 1928–1936," *East Tennessee Historical Society Publications* 43 (1971): 71–93; Donald E. DeVore, "The Rise from the Nadir: Black New Orleans between the Wars, 1920–1940," M.A. thesis, Univ. of New Orleans, 1983; Laroy Howard Milton Haynes, "The Ecological Distribution of Negro Population in Atlanta in 1939," M.A. thesis, Atlanta Univ., 1940; Gloria Brown Melton, "Blacks in Memphis, Tennessee, 1920–1955: A Historical Study," Ph.D. diss., Washington State Univ., 1982; James Martin SoRelle, "The Darker Side of 'Heaven': The Black Community in Houston, Texas, 1917–1945," Ph.D. diss., Kent State Univ., 1980; Tempie Virginia Strange, "The Dallas Negro Chamber of Commerce: A Study of a Negro Institution," M.A. thesis, Southern Methodist Univ., 1945; Marcia E. Turner-Jones, "A Political Analysis of Black Educational History: Atlanta, 1865–1943," Ph.D. diss., Univ. of Chicago, 1982; Alwyn Barr, *Black Texans: A History of Negroes in Texas, 1528–1971* (Austin, Tex.: Jenkins, 1973); Joseph A. Pierce, *The Atlanta Negro: A Collection of Data on the Negro Population of Atlanta, Georgia* (Washington, D.C.: American Youth Commission of the American Council on Education, 1940); Paul M. Pearson, "Federal Housing Projects for Negroes," *Southern Workman* 65 (Dec. 1936): 371–79; Dana F. White, "The Black Side of Atlanta: A Geography of Expansion and Containment, 1870–1970," *Atlanta Historical Journal* 26 (Summer–Fall 1982): 199–225; Roger Biles, "Robert R. Church, Jr., of Memphis: Black Republican Leader in the Age of Democratic Ascendancy, 1928–1940," *Tennessee Historical Quarterly* 42 (Winter 1983): 362–82; Roderick N. Ryon, "An Ambiguous Legacy: Baltimore Blacks and the CIO, 1936–1941," *Journal of Negro History* 65 (Winter 1980): 18–33; and William Jefferson Harrison, "The New Deal in Black St. Louis: 1932–1940," Ph.D. diss., St. Louis Univ., 1976.

In addition to the aforementioned biographies of southern politicians, several studies add to our understanding of southern politics in the New Deal era. Begin with James T. Patterson, *Congressional Conservatism and the New Deal: The Growth of a Conservative Coalition in Congress, 1933–1939* (Lexington: Univ. Press of Kentucky, 1967); V. O. Key, Jr., *Southern Politics in State and Nation* (New York: Knopf, 1949); Dewey W. Grantham, *The Life and Death of the Solid South: A Political History* (Lexington: Univ. Press of Kentucky, 1988); and George E. Mowry, *Another Look at the Twentieth-Century South* (Baton Rouge: Louisiana State Univ. Press, 1973). Also see James T. Patterson, "The Failure of Party Realignment in the South, 1937–1939," *Journal of Politics* 27 (Aug. 1965): 602–17; David L. Porter, *Congress and the Waning of the New Deal* (Port Washington, N.Y.: Kennikat, 1980); W. Wayne Shannon, "Revolt in Washington: The South in Congress," in *The Changing Politics of the South*, edited by William C. Havard (Baton Rouge: Louisiana State Univ. Press, 1972); Lionel V. Patenaude, "Garner, Sumners, and Connally: The Defeat of the Roosevelt Court Bill in 1937," *Southwestern Historical Quarterly* 74 (July 1970): 36–51; Thomas H. Coode, "Tennessee Congressmen and the New Deal,

1933–1938," *West Tennessee Historical Society Papers* 31 (1977): 132–58; idem, "Georgia Congressmen and the First Hundred Days of the New Deal," *Georgia Historical Quarterly* 53 (June 1969): 129–46; A. Cash Koeniger, "The New Deal and the States: Roosevelt versus the Byrd Organization in Virginia," *Journal of American History* 68 (Mar. 1982): 876–96; Robert J. Norrell, "Labor at the Ballot Box: Alabama Politics from the New Deal to the Dixiecrat Movement," *Journal of Southern History* 57 (May 1991): 201–34; J. B. Shannon, "Presidential Politics in the South," *Journal of Politics* 1 (May 1939): 146–70; J. B. Shannon, "Presidential Politics in the South: 1938," *Journal of Politics* 1 (Aug. 1939): 278–300; Charles M. Price and Joseph Boskin, "The Roosevelt 'Purge': A Reappraisal," *Journal of Politics* 28 (Aug. 1966): 660–70; Luther H. Ziegler, Jr., "Senator Walter George's 1938 Campaign," *Georgia Historical Quarterly* 43 (Dec. 1959): 333–52; James William Dunn, "The New Deal and Florida Politics," Ph.D. diss., Florida State Univ., 1971; John Robert Moore, "Senator Josiah W. Bailey and the 'Conservative Manifesto' of 1937," *Journal of Southern History* 31 (Feb. 1965): 21–39; Roy E. Fossett, "The Impact of the New Deal on Georgia Politics, 1933–1941," Ph.D. diss., Univ. of Florida, 1960; Betty M. Field, "The Politics of the New Deal in Louisiana, 1933–1939," Ph.D. diss., Tulane Univ., 1973; William R. Majors, *End of Arcadia: Gordon Browning and Tennessee Politics* (Memphis: Memphis State Univ. Press, 1982); Allen A. Michie and Frank Ryhlick, *Dixie Demagogues* (New York: Viking, 1939); Jennings Perry, *Democracy Begins at Home: The Tennessee Fight on the Poll Tax* (Philadelphia: Lippincott, 1944); George B. Tindall, *The Persistent Tradition in New South Politics* (Baton Rouge: Louisiana State Univ. Press, 1975); Lee Coller, "The Solid South Cracks," *New Republic*, Mar. 23, 1938, pp. 185–86; and Alexander Kendrick, "Huey Long's Revolution," *Nation*, Aug. 22, 1934, pp. 233–34.

Several studies examine the South's liberals in the 1930s. See Thomas A. Krueger, *And Promises to Keep: The Southern Conference for Human Welfare, 1938–1948* (Nashville: Vanderbilt Univ. Press, 1967); Morton Sosna, *In Search of the Silent South: Southern Liberals and the Race Issue* (New York: Columbia Univ. Press, 1977); John T. Kneebone, *Southern Liberal Journalists and the Issue of Race, 1920–1944* (Chapel Hill: Univ. of North Carolina Press, 1985); Anthony P. Dunbar, *Against the Grain: Southern Radicals and Prophets, 1929–1959* (Charlottesville: Univ. Press of Virginia, 1981); Warren Ashby, *Frank Porter Graham, a Southern Liberal* (Winston-Salem, N.C.: J. F. Blair, 1980); Charles W. Eagles, *Jonathan Daniels and Race Relations: The Evolution of a Southern Liberal* (Knoxville: Univ. of Tennessee Press, 1982); Margaret E. Armbrester, "John Temple Graves, II: A Southern Liberal Views the New Deal," *Alabama Review* 32 (July 1979): 203–13; James A. Hodges, "George Fort Milton and the New Deal," *Tennessee Historical Quarterly* 36 (Fall 1977): 383–409; Hollinger F. Barnard, ed., *Outside the Magic Circle: The Autobiography of Virginia Foster Durr* (University: Univ. of Alabama Press, 1985); H. Glyn Thomas, "The Highlander Folk School: The Depression Years," *Tennessee Historical*

Quarterly 23 (Dec. 1964): 358–71; and Ann Wells Ellis, "Uncle Sam Is My Shepherd: The Commission on Interracial Cooperation and the New Deal in Georgia," *Atlanta Historical Journal* 30 (Spring 1986): 47–63.

The impact of the New Deal on cities is detailed in Mark I. Gelfand, *A Nation of Cities: The Federal Government and Urban America, 1933–1965* (New York: Oxford Univ. Press, 1975), and Lyle W. Dorsett, *Franklin D. Roosevelt and the City Bosses* (Port Washington, N.Y.: Kennikat, 1977). For the New Deal's impact on southern cities, see Douglas L. Smith, *The New Deal in the Urban South* (Baton Rouge: Louisiana State Univ. Press, 1988); David R. Goldfield, "The New Deal as a Big Deal for Southern Cities," *Newsletter of the North Carolina Institute of Applied History* 3 (Mar. 1984): 10–13; Roger Biles, "The Urban South in the Great Depression," *Journal of Southern History* 56 (Feb. 1990): 71–100; idem, *Memphis in the Great Depression* (Knoxville: Univ. of Tennessee Press, 1986); Jo Ann E. Argersinger, *Toward a New Deal in Baltimore: People and Government in the Great Depression* (Chapel Hill: Univ. of North Carolina Press, 1988); Robert C. Cotner, ed., *Texas Cities and the Great Depression* (Austin: Texas Memorial Museum, 1973); Paul S. Lofton, "A Social and Economic History of Columbia, South Carolina, during the Great Depression, 1929–1940," Ph.D. diss., Univ. of Texas at Austin, 1977; Barbara C. Bailey, "The Trying Years: A History of Bessemer, Alabama, 1929–1939," M.A. thesis, Samford Univ., 1977; Douglas L. Fleming, "Atlanta, the Depression, and the New Deal," Ph.D. diss., Emory Univ., 1984; E. Thomas Lovell, "Houston's Reaction to the New Deal, 1932–1936," M.A. thesis, Univ. of Houston, 1964; and Kesavan Sudheendran, "Community Power Structure in Atlanta: A Study in Decision Making, 1928–1939," Ph.D. diss., Georgia State Univ., 1982. Also see the relevant chapters in Don H. Doyle, *Nashville since the 1920s* (Knoxville: Univ. of Tennessee Press, 1985); David McComb, *Galveston: A History* (Austin: Univ. of Texas Press, 1986); Christopher Silver, *Twentieth-Century Richmond: Planning, Politics, and Race* (Knoxville: Univ. of Tennessee Press, 1984); Walter J. Fraser, Jr., *Charleston! Charleston! The History of a Southern City* (Columbia: Univ. of South Carolina Press, 1989); Edward Shannon LaMonte, "Politics and Welfare in Birmingham, Alabama: 1900–1975," Ph.D. diss., Univ. of Chicago, 1976; and Glen R. Roberson, "City on the Plains: The History of Tulsa, Oklahoma," Ph.D. diss., Oklahoma State Univ., 1977.

More narrowly focused studies of the New Deal's effect on southern cities are Charles F. Palmer, *Adventures of a Slum Fighter* (Atlanta: Tupper and Love, 1955); C. H. Campbell, "Huey Long Chokes New Orleans," *Nation*, July 24, 1935, pp. 93–95; "Dallas Decides that Excessive 'Economy' Is Extravagance," *American City* 49 (Aug. 1934): 61; Don Eddy, "Kingfish the Second," *American Magazine* 128 (Nov. 1939): 77–82; Douglas L. Fleming, "The New Deal in Atlanta: A Review of the Major Programs," *Atlanta Historical Journal* 30 (Spring 1986): 223–45; Edward Haas, "New Orleans on the Half-Shell: The Maestri Era, 1936–1946," *Louisiana History* 13 (Summer 1972): 283–310; L. M. Graves and Alfred H. Fletcher, "Developing a

Housing Program in a Southern City," *American Journal of Public Health* 27 (July 1937): 645–54; L. M. Graves and Alfred H. Fletcher, "Problems of a Housing Enforcement Program," *American Journal of Public Health* 28 (June 1938): 695–705; L. M. Graves, Alfred H. Fletcher, and Charles Gilman Hyde, "Housing Problem in a Southern City," *American Journal of Public Health* 25 (Jan. 1935): 21–30; "Housing Authorities Describe Local Conditions Demonstrating Need for Slum Reclamation," *American City* 53 (Nov. 1938): 58; "Housing Projects Approved for Cities," *American City* 53 (Apr. 1938): 93; Robert P. Ingalls, "Antiradical Violence in Birmingham during the 1930s," *Journal of Southern History* 47 (Nov. 1981): 521–44; W. D. Jones, "Dallas Wins a Place in the Sun," *National Municipal Review* 24 (Jan. 1935): 11–14; Mark B. Lapping, "The Emergence of Federal Public Housing: Atlanta's Techwood Project," *American Journal of Economics and Sociology* 32 (Oct. 1973): 379–85; John C. Petrie, "Survey Shows Housing Scandals," *Christian Century*, Feb. 21, 1934, p. 265; Ralph Picard, "Centralizing Welfare Work in Memphis," *American City* 51 (June 1936): 105; Lewey Robinson, "Unpaved Streets Surfaced by Relief Labor," *American City* 50 (Nov. 1935): 53–54; "Slum Clearance in Birmingham, Alabama," *American City* 50 (Nov. 1935): 43; "Techwood Homes, Atlanta, Is a Working Reality," *American City* 51 (Oct. 1936): 58–59; Franklin O. Thomson, "Houston Makes Giant Strides," *Houston* 7 (Jan. 1937): 9; Ed Weathers, "Carnival Knowledge," *City of Memphis* 2 (Apr. 1977): 31–37; and "WPA Aids Deserving: $4,245,000 Spent in Houston Area," *Houston* 7 (Oct. 1936): 8–9.

On the question of the New Deal's impact on southern urban distinctiveness, see David R. Goldfield, *Cotton Fields and Skyscrapers: Southern City and Region, 1607–1980* (Baton Rouge: Louisiana State Univ. Press, 1982); idem, "The Urban South: A Regional Framework," *American Historical Review* 68 (Dec. 1981): 1009–34; Carl Abbott, *The New Urban America: Growth and Politics in Sunbelt Cities* (Chapel Hill: Univ. of North Carolina Press, 1981); Blaine A. Brownell and David R. Goldfield, eds., *The City in Southern History: The Growth of Urban Civilization in the South* (Port Washington, N.Y.: Kennikat, 1977); Rupert B. Vance and Nicholas J. Demerath, eds., *The Urban South* (Chapel Hill: Univ. of North Carolina Press, 1954); Gerald M. Capers, "The Rural Lag on Southern Cities," *Mississippi Quarterly* 21 (Fall 1968): 253–61; James C. Cobb, "Urbanization and the Changing South: A Review of Literature," *South Atlantic Urban Studies* 1 (1977): 253–66; and Richard M. Bernard and Bradley R. Rice, eds., *Sunbelt Cities: Politics and Growth since World War II* (Austin: Univ. of Texas Press, 1983).

INDEX